REMARKABLE
WOMEN
—— IN ——
New York State
HISTORY

Edited by HELEN ENGEL & MARILYNN SMILEY

THE
History
PRESS

Published by The History Press
Charleston, SC 29403
www.historypress.net

Copyright © 2013 by the American Association of University Women—New York State Inc.

All rights reserved

First published 2013

ISBN 978.1.5402.3315.8

Library of Congress CIP data applied for.

Contents

CONTENTS

CONTENTS

Acknowledgements

Many thanks to all the authors who identified women in their communities and took the time to research and write about them; to all participating branches; to the Syracuse Branch for its monetary donation to help fund this project; and to the American Association of University Women of New York State (AAUW NYS) Board members for their continued support throughout this project.

Special thanks to Eleanor Filburn, Emily Oaks, Ronald Engel, Carlie Marie Engel, Mary Lou Davis and Edwina Martin for their efforts in helping us complete this book.

INTRODUCTION

Many women of New York State have truly made a difference in their professions, their communities, the state and the nation. Realizing that some have received little or no recognition for their accomplishments outside their own locality, while others have enjoyed national reputations, the members of the American Association of University Women of New York State (AAUW NYS) have written about women who have made a difference in their own communities and beyond. Members sent biographies of some well-known women, and many who are not recognized outside their own communities. Other members sent their autobiographies. Each of these women is important in her own way.

Biographies include women from the past and present, AAUW members and nonmembers, professional women in many fields, community leaders and activists. The time span is from the 1700s to today. It would be impossible to chronicle all the contributions of women in New York State in one volume, but this book is representative of what women have done and are still doing. It is unique since it features women from many walks of life over a long period of time. Members of AAUW NYS hope you enjoy learning more about these outstanding women.

REMARKABLE WOMEN IN NEW YORK STATE HISTORY

DORIS ALLEN

1921–
EDUCATOR/POLITICIAN

Doris Caroline Brown was born on September 30, 1921, on her parents' farm in Redfield, New York. She was the youngest of three children of David and Agnes Brown. She had a sister, Agnes (Aggie), and a brother, David (Buck).

In her memoir, *Yesterdays*, she described life on the farm—the hard work and the isolation, especially in winter, when snowstorms shut them off from the outside world. There were no snow ploughs yet. The snow was tamped down by horses pulling a roller. Families needed to entertain themselves. Sometimes neighbors would get together to socialize and maybe hold a dance in someone's home. During the summers, there would be swimming, picnics, family reunions and trips to Redfield. As a small child, Doris went to see a traveling group perform *Uncle Tom's Cabin*. That was when she fell in love with the theater. For weeks afterward, she would act out all the roles in the privacy of the barn. She loved little Eva most of all and fashioned blond curls by splitting dandelion stems and attaching them to her own Dutch boy haircut.

Grade school ran from first through eighth grades and started at age seven. Doris and Buck walked one mile to the one-room schoolhouse. One teacher taught all the grades. Doris knew how to read before she entered first grade. Her teacher realized that the school "library" of one bookshelf, where the books were the same from year to year, did not meet Doris's needs. She brought books from a local library for her. Fridays were set aside for recitations and sometimes for plays. The teacher had the students memorize poems and recite them in front of the class, teaching them to speak clearly. Doris liked to hold her fellow students' attention, a skill she put to use later in life as she entered politics. In grade seven, the teacher brought books on Greek and Roman civilization, preparing Doris for the eighth-grade history regents, which students had to pass to enter high school. Doris got a perfect score.

Doris entered the Redfield Union High School in the fall of 1934, the first in her family to get a secondary education. She excelled in all areas. Her favorite subjects were English and history. Her father was a highly intelligent, self-taught man who also had a keen interest in history. He read the newspaper every day, and with the advent of rural electrification, the family got a radio. They listened to Lowell Thomas every evening. Politics and current events were discussed around the dinner table. This was during the Depression. Doris admired President Roosevelt and became a lifelong Democrat.

In high school, Doris was active in 4-H and performed in operettas. She went on an overnight trip to Cornell with 4-H. This event marked the beginning of her love of travel. At graduation in 1938, Doris was valedictorian of her class. She had skipped two grades in elementary school and was only sixteen years old.

She entered Oswego Normal School in the fall of the same year. Hers was the first group to graduate after the school became a four-year college (Oswego State Teachers College). She threw herself into her studies and loved every minute of it. She also tried many activities outside the classroom. She settled for the Debate Society, was a soloist with the choir, was on the Women's Athletic Council and worked all four years on the school newspaper, the *Oswegonian*, becoming its first female editor in chief in her senior year, 1941–42. She was on the dean's list every semester. As a member of the newspaper staff, Doris went on a trip to Columbia University for a conference. She decided then that Columbia was the place where she would get her master's degree. Doris graduated from Oswego State Teachers College in 1942. She was salutatorian of her class.

Her first job was in Whitesboro, New York, as a kindergarten teacher. While she was there, she encouraged her fellow teachers to start a union. After two years at Whitesboro, Doris did go to Columbia University, receiving her MA in education in 1946. While she was at Columbia, she wrote a booklet on the *History of Redfield*. It was chosen by five hundred students for reading. The book was republished by the Halfshire Historical Society in Redfield in the 1980s and is still in print.

Doris returned to Oswego in 1946 and became an associate professor, master teacher and demonstrator for the kindergarten class at the Campus School of the Oswego State Teachers College. The same year, she had a textbook published: *Bardeen's Stories and Studies for Children in Reading*.

The following year, Doris married Edwin (Jiggs) Allen. He had returned from the war and was advertising manager for the *Palladium-Times*, Oswego's daily newspaper. She "stayed home" for ten years, from 1947 to 1957, to raise their three children: Elizabeth, John and Phyllis.

She was not idle during this period. In 1952, she became the first woman elected to the Oswego Common Council, serving one term. During that period, Hamilton Homes, a housing project for low-income families, became a reality, providing affordable, comfortable housing for hundreds of families over the years. Doris also became secretary of the first Planning Commission, which brought about the first zoning ordinance in Oswego. She went to Montreal to attend a city planning conference to prepare for this work. She helped create the first industrial park in Oswego and worked on the revision of the city charter. During this time, Doris also did publicity for the Red Cross.

From 1957 to 1976, Doris taught in the Oswego City School System. She was K-3 principal of School 2 and taught in two additional elementary schools. She was director of Head Start in the late '60s and early '70s. During her tenure, she was twice nominated by her fellow teachers for the Empire State Award.

In 1963, Doris published a second textbook, L.W. Singer's *4th, 5th, and 6th Grade Social Studies*, a book in which students do research on given topics. In the 1960s, she also wrote an article on handwriting for the *Book of Knowledge*. In 1976, she became contributing editor of the magazine *Day Care and Early Education, Human Behavior Plus*. In 1976, Doris was elected Oswego County's delegate to the Democratic National Convention in New York City, representing the Thirty-third Congressional District, supporting Jimmy Carter.

Later that year, Doris and her husband retired to North Carolina. There she returned to one of her early loves, performing in professional theater for six years. She also worked on the political campaign of Governor Hunt. She gave presentations on the history, geography and industry of North Carolina. When Jehan Sadat, wife of President Sadat of Egypt, came to North Carolina with a group of four professional women, Doris was asked to escort and entertain them.

After her husband's death in 1981, Doris moved to Syracuse, New York. She continued to be active in the theater. In 1983, the year when "Britain Salutes New York," an event was organized to promote British goods. Doris was invited to be in charge of information and volunteer services. She was given an office in Columbus Circle. While doing this work in New York City, she met Edwina Sandys, granddaughter of Winston Churchill. Miss Sandys promoted more than goods; she brought one hundred cultural activities to New York City. When four hundred invitations to a reception and dinner at the United Nations were lost on the way from England, Doris was given the guest list and asked to straighten it out. And she did. While living in Syracuse, Doris helped with the planning for the fiftieth anniversary of D-Day in 1995. She was present in Normandy during the commemoration.

Doris moved back to Oswego in 1997. She was active in local theater until 2004 and served for a number of years as president of the Oswego Players. In 2003, she published *Yesterdays*, a memoir of her years growing up in Redfield and her four years at Oswego State Teachers College. She continues to be active with book reviews, and in 2007, she created a mini-play in which women at tea, in costumes from the Civil War period, act out scenes from Doris Kearns Goodwin's book *A Team of Rivals*.

Doris now resides at Seneca Hill. In spite of failing eyesight, she gives bridge lessons to residents and has given two presentations on the history of Oswego, all done from memory, as she can no longer read her notes.

Author's note: Since this was written, Doris has had eye surgery. Her eyesight has been restored.

Allen, Doris. Telephone conversations/interviews by Inger Stern, March 2007 and January and March 2008.

Allen, Doris Caroline Brown. *Yesterdays.* Oswego, NY: Oswego Micro Publishing Company, 2003.

Syracuse Post-Standard. Article in *Neighbors* supplement, March 2007.

Researcher and author: Inger Stern, Oswego Branch

MURIEL JODST ALLERTON

1919–
MAYOR/JOURNALIST/VOLUNTEER/HUMANITARIAN/ACTIVIST

Muriel Allerton is best known to the residents of central New York as the first female mayor of Fulton, New York, but her life is full of many other achievements as well.

Born on November 23, 1919, in a hospital in West New York, New Jersey, Muriel Jodst grew up in nearby Guttenberg, New Jersey. Her father ran a butcher store, and the family lived above it. Muriel's mother and grandmother kept the household running smoothly. An only child, she spent a lot of time with her many friends, joined the Girl Scouts and did what she could in the community. During World War II, there was great fear of an invasion on the East Coast, and she followed her father when he served as a patrol for the area.

After graduating from high school in West New York, she attended and graduated from a secretarial school in New York City and got a job at Cooper Union for the Advancement of Science and Art. While working, she attended New York University's evening division and earned a BA degree in journalism. She also took graduate courses at Sarah Lawrence College. While at New York University, she was editor of the school's newspaper. That experience helped her develop contacts and friendships with many people in New York City.

During World War II, through her job as secretary in the engineering department at Cooper Union, she met her future husband, Joe Allerton, who was teaching there. Everyone worked to protect the institution in case of an enemy invasion, and she was a member of the "suicide squad," which was prepared to race to the roof of the building to put out any fires. Joe Allerton was also working on a project in downtown New York City and could not reveal what he was doing. He found out later, to his horror, that his research was part of the Manhattan Project in the development of the atomic bomb.

In 1945, Joe went to the University of Michigan to pursue a PhD in chemical engineering. Muriel refused to accompany him until she completed her journalism degree in 1947. The minute she finished, she headed for Michigan; she did not even wait to attend her own graduation. The two of them enjoyed living in Ann Arbor, Michigan, but left soon after Joe's graduation in 1948.

During the next years, from 1948 to 1963, Joe worked for jobs with various food companies in the New York City area, and they lived in Hartsdale and White Plains, New York. Four children (Peter, Steve, Paul and Martha) were born.

The family lived in neighborhoods that had young couples with small children, and the mothers started a nursery school and took turns teaching. Muriel also did substitute teaching in the public schools. She said that she had no real career then, but at that time, most women did not work outside the home. While living in White Plains, she became involved in the League of Women Voters.

They moved to Fulton, New York, in 1963 when her husband got a job as manager of technical service at Nestlé Company. (He conducted experimental work on developing new candy bars and provided technical assistance to plant operations.) Muriel immediately became actively involved (as board member or officer) in many community organizations: Fulton Historical Society, Fulton Art Association, Oswego Opera Theater, Fulton Soup Kitchen (at the State Street United Methodist Church), Fulton American Field Service Committee (as president), Oswego County Council on the Arts, Oswego County Press Club, Professional Journalists & Communicators of Oswego County, Fulton Music Association (as charter member), State University of New York–Oswego College Council, Fulton Salvation Army Advisory Board, Retired Senior Volunteer Program (RSVP), Fulton Red Cross and Fulton Friends of History.

As a freelance journalist, she held jobs as writer, publicist and reporter for local newspapers the *Oswego Valley News* and the *Oswego Palladium-Times*. In 1981, she joined striking reporters to form a new newspaper, the *Daily Messenger*, to give the community another voice; that paper lasted four years. Muriel also contributed to a monthly column and a radio show for WZZZ and handled publicity for many community groups, including the Red Cross, the Fulton Hospital Auxiliary and the Cracker Barrel Fair.

While living in Fulton, she realized that the city did not have a League of Women Voters. When she contacted the national office, she learned that Norma Bartle and Sally Soluri from Oswego had also contacted that office, and the three of them founded a chapter in Oswego County. A member of the league informed Muriel that the secretary of the mayor of Fulton was ill and asked her if she would fill in for three days a week. Muriel kept this job for more than nine years during the late 1970s and early 1980s. Part of the job was working on the campaign of Mayor Ron Woodward. Nine years later, when he became ill, a committee asked Muriel if she would run for that office. Encouraged by her husband and friends, she ran, won the election and held the office for two two-year terms (1987 to 1991). She has referred to this as a good experience and continues to have many friends at city hall.

She had numerous accomplishments as mayor. She established a recycling program, assisted in plans for a co-generation plant at the Nestlé Company, computerized the chamberlain's office and acquired computers for city offices, updated water lines and sewers, streamlined the city charter, established a personnel office and encouraged better working relations, worked with the school administration, started the West First Street Center to assist the needy of the community, revived the city tree lighting ceremony, initiated the Fulton River Festival and served as a member of the governor's Upstate Elected Officials Council.

After her terms as mayor, Muriel continued to be involved in her community, serving on Fulton's Neighborhood Based Alliance Advisory Council (1992–), the AIDS Advisory Council Board (1993–), the Board of Church and Community Workers (1992–), the United Way of Greater Fulton (as secretary, 1992–93), the Fulton Community Revitalization Corporation, Neighborhood Watch and the Fulton Empire Zone Board, as well as many of the organizations listed previously.

Some of her well-deserved honors include Oswego's Woman of Achievement Award by Zonta, the Woman of the Year by the Business and Professional Women, the Paul Harris Award from Rotary (1992), State University of New York–Oswego's Community Recognition Award (presented on May 3, 1993, by college president Stephen Weber), the Muriel Allerton Scholarship (presented each year at the Muriel Allerton Scholarship Award Dinner by the Professional Journalists and Communicators organization to a graduating senior from an Oswego County high school who plans to major in a communications-related field in college) and the Lifetime Achievement Award and Concert dedicated to Muriel and Joe Allerton and Mary and Ernie Hamer by the Fulton Music Association (held on May 2009). On May 25, 2010, she was named the New York State Senate Woman of Distinction for exemplary service to her community. At that time, State Senator Darrel J. Aubertine stated, "Muriel came to Central New York close to fifty years ago and over that time has certainly made her presence known. She truly is a woman of distinction and a pioneer in this community as the first woman mayor of Fulton. She stands out in the ways she has given of herself to so many in the Fulton area as a volunteer, as an advocate, and as a friend. Anyone who knows Muriel knows well how deep her compassion, loyalty, and commitment run."

Allerton, Murial. Interview recorded by Marilynn J. Smiley, February 15, 2009.

Oswegonian. "Muriel Allerton to Receive Community Recognition Award." April 27, 1995.

Palladium-Times. "Former Fulton Mayor Honored by State Senate and Senator." June 7, 2010.

———. "Fulton Music Association Concert Dedicated to Allertons, Hamers." May 1, 2009.

Researcher and author: Marilynn J. Smiley, Oswego Branch

SUSAN BROWNELL ANTHONY

1820–1906
WOMEN'S RIGHTS ACTIVIST

Susan Brownell Anthony was born in Adams, Massachusetts, on February 15, 1820. She was the second child born to Lucy Read, a Baptist, and Daniel Anthony, a Quaker. The Anthonys believed firmly in equality of the sexes and so educated their daughters and sons, as well as Mr. Anthony's male and female factory workers. Susan worked early on as a schoolteacher and became aware of the vastly different wages offered to men and women.

Her father brought the family to Rochester, New York, via the Erie Canal in 1845. Miss Anthony became active in the temperance and antislavery movements early in her life. A prohibition against women speaking at antislavery meetings again raised her consciousness of women's inferior status, and this eventually led her to the suffrage movement. She met Elizabeth Cady Stanton not long after the first women's rights convention in Seneca Falls in 1848. Although retaining her interest in temperance and abolition, Susan Anthony dedicated the rest of her adult life to writing, speaking, recruiting and fundraising for the suffrage movement. She traveled the entire United States, its territories and in Europe in the suffrage cause.

Miss Anthony and thirteen other Rochester women voted in the presidential election of 1872. Her arrest in her parlor by a United States marshal for voting eventually brought her to trial in federal court in Canandaigua, New York, on June 17, 1873. A directed guilty verdict resulted in a $100 fine, which Miss Anthony refused to pay.

In 1900, Miss Anthony was asked to help raise the remainder of the $50,000 required by the University of Rochester in order to admit women to its student body. Her life insurance policy provided the last $1,000 needed.

She died on March 17, 1906, at her home at 17 Madison Street in Rochester, now a National Historic Landmark. Ten thousand mourners paid homage to her at her funeral. One of her last public utterances came in a speech before a United States Congressional hearing in which she said, "Failure is impossible." The United States Constitution was finally amended to concede the vote to women in 1920.

American Women of Achievement. "Susan B. Anthony, Woman Suffragist." Philadelphia, PA: Chelsea House Publishers, 1988.

Photograph from the Library of Congress.
Researcher and author: Lynne M. Mitchell, Greater Rochester Area Branch

LUCILLE DESIREE BALL

1911–1989
ACTRESS

Lucille Desiree Ball was born August 6, 1911, in Jamestown, New York, to Henry Durrell and Desiree Ball. Her father was an electrician, and soon after her birth, he moved the family to Montana and then to Michigan, where he worked as a telephone lineman. In February 1915, he contracted typhoid fever and died. Her mother, pregnant with her brother Fred, returned to Jamestown, where she found work in a factory and married again.

Lucille's stepfather soon moved her mother to Detroit, leaving Fred with Desiree's parents and Lucille with her impoverished step-grandparents. Finally, at age eleven, Lucille was reunited with her mother and stepfather. She had displayed an interest in theater and drama even as a child, and at age fifteen, she convinced her mother to let her enroll in a drama school in New York City. It was not a successful venture, and the school wrote to her mother that Lucille had no future in the theater. Lucille stayed in New York City and by 1927 had found work as a model, first for fashion designer Hattie Carnegie and then with Chesterfield cigarettes.

In the early 1930s, Lucille dyed her hair blonde and moved to Hollywood. She soon secured bit parts in a string of films, appearing ultimately in a total of seventy-two, including a string of second-tier films that earned her the title of "Queen of B Movies." She met Desi Arnaz in one of the earliest of these, and they married within a year. Lucille dyed her hair its famous red in 1942, but her stage and film career stagnated. At Desi's urging, she turned to radio and soon landed a lead role in the very successful *My Favorite Husband*. CBS wanted her to recreate a similar program for the small screen (television), but Lucille insisted that it include Desi. The network was not interested, so the couple put together an *I Love Lucy*-type act and took it on the road. Its success prompted CBS to offer a contract. During negotiations with the network, the couple formed their own company, Desilu Productions, and retained full ownership rights to the program.

I Love Lucy made its debut October 15, 1951, its success unmatched during its six-year run. In one of the most memorable television episodes ever, Lucy gave birth to Little Ricky the same day Lucille delivered Desi Jr. by C-section, January 19, 1953. Lucille was a perfectionist and spent many hours rehearsing her antics and facial expressions. She paved the way for future female stars in television comedy. The show ended in 1957, but Desilu Productions continued producing hit television shows, both comedy and drama. Lucille and Desi divorced in 1960. Two years later, now married to Gary Morton, she bought out Desi and took over the company, becoming the first woman to run a major television production studio. She sold the company in 1967 for $17 million. She continued acting, including two sitcoms, *The Lucy Show* (1962) and *Here's Lucy* (1968), and a made-for-TV movie, *Stone Pillow*, in 1985.

Lucille's contributions to the theatrical world have been recognized and honored many times. She was the first woman to receive the International Radio and Television Society's Gold medal, and she received four Emmys, was inducted into the Television Hall of Fame and was honored at the Kennedy Center for the Performing Arts.

Lucille died on April 26, 1989. Her hometown celebrates her life through the Lucille Ball–Desi Arnaz Center, which houses a museum featuring *I Love Lucy* sets and a store of Lucy-Desi memorabilia. The center hosts two events yearly, one in May celebrating comedy and the other in August celebrating her birthday. In addition, the local amateur little theater group, which owns its own building, was renamed the Lucille Ball Little Theater of Jamestown Inc. on May 24, 1991.

Biography.com. "Lucille Ball Biography," 2010. www.biography.com/
    people/lucille-ball-9196958.

Researcher and author: B. Dolores Thompson, Jamestown Branch

ANNETTE BARBER

1859–1945
PHYSICIAN

When Warren County, New York, was formed in 1813, all of the doctors listed for the county's medical society were men. A woman might take on the role of herbalist, drying and harvesting medicinal herbs in her home to be used to soothe a variety of common ailments, or she might serve as a midwife assisting in the birth of a child at home. At the time of the Civil War, women began to nurse sick and wounded soldiers as they persistently clamored for more responsibility for care of the sick. Their roles as nurses, especially on the battlefield, were not well accepted.

It was the end of the nineteenth century before Glens Falls considered a hospital for the care of the sick. The idea was promoted by Dr. R. Jerome Eddy in the wake of new knowledge about aseptic surgery and anesthesia, methods that would permit healing and disease prevention. The Parks Hospital in Glens Falls was opened in 1900 as a charity hospital. A trained nurse served as the superintendent, handling administrative matters and supervising the staff of nurses, women rigidly trained for their work. They served long hours for small wages and lived in accommodations at the hospital. Jennie S. Downs, Lucy Wooster, Mrs. Gertrude Peck, Ida Palmer, Miss Vedder, Leta Card, Florence Wetmore, Blanche Thayer, Mrs. Lutts, Maude D. Burke and Rose Q. Strait served as the hospital superintendents from the formation of the facility until 1941. During these early years, a nursing school was opened that trained RNs to staff the hospital, to go to other hospital facilities or to serve in the Red Cross. The school operated until 1932, with the nurses serving as valuable assets to the hospital operations.

In 1853, Dr. Elizabeth Blackwell became the first female doctor in the United States. Women's Medical College, St. Luke's and Presbyterian Hospital in New York City began the training of female doctors, and it was through Blackwell's efforts that the first women entered the field of medicine as doctors.

Dr. Annette Barber became the first female doctor in Warren County. She was born in Chazy, New York, on March 16, 1859. She attended Plattsburgh High School and later graduated from Women's Medical College in Manhattan in 1898 as a medical doctor at the age of forty. For many years, she taught school while saving for her medical education. Her decision to come to Glens Falls is noted in a letter she wrote to a family member: "I have agitated the subject of Glens Falls since I got as far as Saratoga and everyone says that's the place. It's a very progressive town and I am afraid I shall make a mistake if I don't consider it." She set up an office at 11 Birch Avenue in 1899. By September 1900, she was writing about her financial success: "Hold your breath! I've taken in $52 this month, so far, and there are six days more. I'll get $100 a month yet."

Dr. Barber eventually moved her office to 261 Glen Street, where she ran her private hospital/home. She later relocated to 8 Notre Dame Street, where she served maternity or critical care patients before the advent of the hospital. A tiny woman, she was often seen pedaling her bicycle with her medicine bag dangling from the handlebars as she made her rounds of house calls. In 1904, she was a member of the Humane Society in Glens Falls, Sandy Hill, Fort Edward and South Glens Falls, an organization that worked with needy and abused children and adults, as well as animals. Dr. Barber had the job of seeing that young children who were in the care of the society attended Sunday school. Dr. Barber purchased a convertible coupe, which she drove slowly to Chazy for family visits, taking two days to arrive with a stopover in Elizabethtown. Her niece, Mary Barber Gray, described her as a very independent woman with a keen sense of humor. Her practice continued for forty years, until she was in her eighties. She resided at the Glens Falls home on Warren Street, later moving to live with her niece, Lucy Pease, and her husband in west Chazy. An illness sent her to Ogdensburg, where she died on April 26, 1945, in her eighty-sixth year. She is buried at Riverview Cemetery in Chazy.

Van Dyke, Marilyn. "Women and Medicine in Warren County." *Pastimes* (Summer 2005): 4, 5. Chapman Historical Museum, 348 Glen Street, Glens Falls, New York.

Researcher and author: Kathleen Hoeltzel, Adirondack Branch

HELEN E. BARKER

1825–1880
HUMANITARIAN/ACTIVIST

Helen E. Pettit was born in Onondaga County in Pompey, New York, the only daughter of Dr. Ebert M. Pettit, an "optical surgeon and dealer in patent medicines," and Euretta Sweet Pettit. In about 1835, the Pettits moved to Fredonia, New York, in Chautauqua County. In 1837, the family, which included Helen and her two siblings, relocated within the county to Versailles, where Helen lived for twenty-five years. Versailles is located at the edge of the Cattaraugus Territory.

The Pettit family was actively involved in humanitarian efforts on behalf of their Native American neighbors, and as an adult, Helen, a firm believer in the need for education, supported education for Native American children. For nearly twenty-five years, Helen's family was also actively involved in the Underground Railroad. Her paternal grandparents owned a salve factory in Cordova, about twenty miles from Versailles. Besides providing a substantial income for the family, the factory was used as a cover for the Underground Railroad. Both of her grandparents were actively involved, with her grandfather being a conductor.

Dr. and Mrs. Pettit, with Helen and eventually Helen's husband, Darwin R. Barker, ran an herb farm in Versailles. The herbs were grown for the salve factory, but the farm, too, was a cover. Taking his lead from his father,

Dr. Pettit was an abolitionist and became a conductor. While records were not kept of persons transported and such, for obvious reasons, the fact that Helen's whole family was involved (Helen and her mother by supplying food and clothing for runaways) is confirmed in the memoir her father wrote, *Sketches in the History of the Underground Railroad.*

In 1846, Darwin R. Barker of Fredonia became a partner in the eye salve business. That same year, he and Helen were married. They lived in Versailles until 1863, when they moved to Fredonia. Helen's husband bought and donated to the village of Fredonia the land and building for the Darwin R. Barker (Association) Library. That building is now the Darwin R. Barker Museum and is attached to a newer building that houses the library.

Because of their activism and the high profiles maintained by her father and husband—and also because during the era in which she lived, a man's candle often burned brighter than a woman's—Helen E. Barker's name is not as easily recognizable as the names of the men in her family. She was, however, an activist in her own right.

Her work with Native Americans was mentioned earlier, but we also know that she and her mother were abolitionists who helped meet the needs of runaway slaves working their way to Canada. When she moved to Fredonia as an adult, Helen continued her work to promote education and literacy. When the Civil War ended, Helen collected clothing and monetary donations, which she then sent to the South to help support former slaves going to school for the first time. She was influential in the formation of Sunday schools and was one of the first female Sunday school superintendents of the First Baptist Church in Fredonia. She gained national recognition as one of the founding constituents of the Woman's Christian Temperance Union.

Helen E. Barker was a woman to be reckoned with. She made a difference.

Fredonia Censor. Obituary of Helen Pettit Barker, May 28, 1980. Ancestry.com, March 5, 2009. www.rootsweb.ancestry.com.

Pettit, Eber M. *Sketches in the History of the Underground Railroad.* Westfield, NY: Chautauqua Region Press, 1999.

Woodbury Straight, Wendy J. "Helen Pettit Barker." Ancestry.com, December 2, 2009. www.rootsweb.ancestry.com.

Researcher and author: Susan Pepe, Dunkirk Fredonia Branch

MARY DOWNING SHELDON BARNES

1850–1898
EDUCATOR/WRITER

Mary Sheldon Barnes, the oldest daughter of Mr. and Mrs. Edward Austin Sheldon, was born in the sky parlor of the United States Hotel in Oswego, New York, afterward known as the "Old Normal," on September 15, 1850. Her father was an educator who founded the Oswego Normal School in 1861 and served as its president almost until the end of the century.

Mary was taught to read by her father, was educated in the Oswego public schools and entered the Classical Course at the Normal School at age sixteen. That same year, she began teaching gymnastics. After graduating from the Normal School, she entered Michigan University in September 1871 as a sophomore in the Classical Course. In order to specialize in physics, she took as many science courses as possible and graduated in 1874. She was one of just seven girls in a class of eighty. In fact, she was one of the first women to attend a coeducational institution of higher learning.

In 1874, she returned to Oswego to teach Latin, Greek and history (instead of the sciences, which she had wanted to teach) and applied the scientific method to the field of history.

During 1876, she was invited to become chair of the chemistry department at Wellesley College (then in its infancy), but she refused and was then invited to become a professor of history. She worked so hard—teaching, lecturing and studying—that after two and a half years she exhausted herself and had to remain a year at home for rest.

Four years later, in 1880, she went to Europe with her friend, Dr. Mary V. Lee, who taught at the Normal School in Oswego. Mary Sheldon felt that she needed to broaden her experience and knowledge. For a year, they toured England, France, Italy, Egypt, Germany and Switzerland. Then, in 1881, she returned to England and entered Cambridge University as a special "out-student" of Newnham College. There she studied modern history and was especially influenced by one of the professors, J.R. Seeley.

Returning to America in 1882, she taught English and history at the Oswego Normal School. She completed her method of teaching history. In 1884, she married Mr. Earl Barnes, also an Oswego graduate. She continued writing and published *Studies in American History* in 1891. This volume, along with her earlier *Studies in General History* (1885), were the first textbooks in America to apply the scientific or inductive method to historical study below college work. The books had a wide sale and were a great influence on changing historical studies in high schools. Before, history had been a deadening, cramming memorization of dry facts. She made it into an intelligent study of original facts.

While Mary and her husband were studying at Cornell University in 1888, they went abroad with Professor George Burr and spent a year in European libraries gathering material for Andrew White's *Warfare of Science*. Afterward, Mr. Barnes chaired the Department of European History at Indiana University, and both worked there.

When Leland Stanford Jr. University opened in 1891, Mr. Barnes joined the faculty as a full professor of education, and shortly after, Mary was appointed assistant professor of history. She was the first woman to be hired at that school. While there, she developed courses in the history of the Pacific Coast, made excavations and gathered collections of artifacts for the library and museum.

In 1897, both Mary and her husband went abroad for travel and study. While doing research at the British Museum, she was stricken with a fatal illness and died in surgery on August 27, 1898. Following her desire, her body was cremated, and her ashes were buried at the Protestant Cemetery in Rome.

Mary was one of the first to have her pupils use historical sources and study them critically. Her ideas are embodied in the several books she wrote. She was known to have been a brilliant teacher. In appearance, she was small and delicate but agile and graceful, with beautiful flashing blue eyes. Her manner was gay and informal. If her success as a teacher was due in part to the inspiration of her father or to her training, travel, study and experiences, it was also due to her buoyant personality.

Rogers, Dorothy. *Oswego: Fountainhead of Teacher Education*. New York: Appleton-Century-Crofts, 1961.

Scott, Jonathan French. "Barnes, Mary Downing Sheldon." *Dictionary of American Biography*. Vol. 1. New York: Charles Scribner's Sons, 1957.

State Normal and Training School. *First Half Century, 1861–1911: Historical and Biographical.* Oswego, NY, 1911.

Photograph courtesy of the State University of New York–Oswego, Penfield Library Archives.
Researcher: Nancy Johnson
Author: Marilynn J. Smiley, Oswego Branch

CLARA HARLOWE BARTON

1821–1912
FOUNDER, AMERICAN BRANCH OF THE INTERNATIONAL RED CROSS

Upstate New Yorkers are proud of Clara Barton, who founded the first local society of the American Branch of the International Committee of the Red Cross (ICRC) on August 22, 1881, at the small town of Dansville, New York. She had held the first national meeting on May 21, 1881, but faced much skepticism and criticism. She often returned to Dansville, where she had her country residence from 1876 to 1886. Before the United States Congress could ratify the articles of the Red Cross, her neighbors in Dansville decided to honor her by establishing the first local society of the American Red Cross. Fifty-seven members signed the charter.

Clarissa Harlowe Barton was born December 25, 1821, at Oxford, Massachusetts. Her father and mother were abolitionists and helped to establish the first Universalist church in the village of Oxford. Clara developed an interest in nursing and became famous for her work as a nurse in the Civil War. In 1862, she traveled behind the lines, reaching some of the grimmest battlefields of the war. In 1864, she was appointed by General Benjamin Butler as "Lady in Charge" of the hospitals at the front of the Union Army of the James.

In 1865, President Lincoln placed her in charge of the search for missing soldiers of the Union army. This led her to a nationwide project to try to find all missing soldiers of the war. After the war, she lectured about her experiences, both in the war and in her efforts to find missing soldiers. She met Susan B. Anthony and worked in the women's suffrage movement. She worked with Frederick Douglass as an abolitionist and worked for black civil rights.

In 1870, she took a trip through Europe, where she worked with the ICRC during the Franco-Prussian War. The ICRC had been created to give help to all victims of war and was committed to neutrality. When Barton returned to the United States in 1873, she worked to have our government recognize the ICRC. She won her argument by arguing that the Red Cross could serve not only victims of war but also those of any great national disaster.

Barton became president of the new American branch of the ICRC, organized at Dansville, New York, in 1881. After the birth of the American Red Cross, she continued to travel to disasters all over the world. In 1893, the ICRC helped with the Sea Islands hurricane disaster. Clara aided refugees and prisoners of war during the Spanish-American War. In 1896, she sailed to Constantinople after the Hamidian Massacres and negotiated with Abdul Hamid II to open the first American Red Cross headquarters in Asia Minor. She worked in hospitals in Cuba in 1898 at the age of seventy-seven.

Not until 1904, at eighty-three years of age, did she retire as president of the American Red Cross. She died at her home outside Washington, D.C., in Glen Echo, Maryland, on April 12, 1912.

Red Cross. "Clara Barton." www.redcross.org/about-us/history/clara-barton.

Wikipedia. "Clara Barton." http://en.wikipedia.org/wiki/Clara-Barton.

Photograph from the Library of Congress.
Researcher and author: Martha Treicher, Bath Branch

STANIS MARUSAK BECK

1944–
VOLUNTEER

Stanis Marusak Beck is distinguished for having founded the Babylon Village Arts Council. She served as its first president and instituted the Bay Fest at the Babylon Village Pool.

For many years, Stanis wrote a column on environmental issues for the *Babylon Beacon*. In 1990, she spearheaded a twentieth-anniversary celebration of Earth Day in collaboration with the Pilot Club. With a grant from New York senator Owen Johnson, she enabled Babylon High School to refurbish its dishwasher and buy melmac dishes to replace paper plates in the cafeteria.

When her two daughters were in school, Stanis saw a need for more social opportunities for Babylon youth. The result was Friday Night Live, a program featuring an open gym, movies and snacks for teens at Babylon High School.

As a member of the Babylon Rotary Club, Stanis has compiled a booklet of social services for senior citizens available in the Babylon area. Stanis taught English for five weeks to students in central Mexico, and in collaboration with the Babylon Rotary Club, she was instrumental in providing playground equipment for a number of disadvantaged schools in Mexico.

In Babylon, Stanis led a successful petition drive to save a historic house from bulldozers, she organized the first of many career days at North Babylon High School and she and her husband, Michael, have sponsored several foreign exchange students from various countries.

For her many community service projects, Stanis has been honored with awards from the Pilot Club, the Village of Babylon, the Suffolk County legislature, the Babylon Village Arts Council and Kappa Delta Pi (the international honor society in education, Columbia University Chapter).

Stanis was born on July 12, 1944, in Jersey City, New Jersey. She attended St. Dominic's Academy; earned a BA in English literature from Notre Dame College, Staten Island; and then earned an MSW from Fordham University. More recently, she earned an MA degree from Columbia University in organizational psychology. She is a social worker in private practice in Babylon, New York.

She is currently very happy in her brand-new role as a grandparent.

Information obtained from Stanis Marusak Beck by Eleanor Burns, 2011.

Researcher and author: Eleanor Burns, Islip Area Branch

GRACE VAN TUYL BENTLEY

1919–
COMMUNITY SERVICE

Grace Van Tuyl Bentley was born in Yonkers, New York, on October 24, 1919, one of three daughters of Hiram and Mary Van Tuyl. In 1928, they moved to Lansdowne, Pennsylvania, a Philadelphia suburb, where her father had taken a new job that ended during the Great Depression when the company folded. Her father's skills as an auditor and statistical specialist helped him find a job in New York City when few jobs were to be found anywhere. The family moved to White Plains, New York, soon after Grace's eighth-grade graduation.

High school years were spent in White Plains, and Grace excelled, graduating in 1937 as class salutatorian. She was president of the French Club and, based on her test performance, received a medal for language proficiency from the French government. She was involved in Girl Scouts and received its highest honor, the Golden Eaglet badge.

A visit from the Oberlin College admissions director to her high school attracted Grace. The college offered a substantial scholarship based on her high school performance, and she decided to attend. At that time, going to college at some distance meant taking the train and accumulating a collection of appropriate clothing akin to a trousseau. Arrival on campus was exciting. All members of the freshmen class were pictured in a "face book" that served to introduce them to one another. It was an exciting time for Grace, with many opportunities for cultural and social events and many dates with a variety of interesting young men.

Grace majored in sociology. Young women at the time did not usually anticipate a career in that area of study. The plan most often was to get the college degree and then attend secretarial college to prepare for a job.

Soon after her arrival at college, her mother sent a newspaper clipping describing the city's new YMCA director. He had a son, Russ Bentley, slightly older than Grace, who was attending Oberlin College. Grace did not meet him on campus, but they met when both were back in White Plains for Christmas vacation.

College graduation came in 1941, and two weeks later, Grace and Russ Bentley were married in White Plains. They lived in New Rochelle in a small third-floor apartment in a private home. The little apartment had no refrigerator, and she made use of the owner's on the first floor. Dishes were washed in the bathroom sink. It was their first home and they loved it.

Russ worked at Sears-Roebuck in White Plains. Grace, after taking some secretarial courses, became secretary to one of the officers at National City Bank on Broadway in New York City and took the train each day into the city.

In December of that year, Russ was sent to Brooklyn to buy Lionel trains for his Sears store. While there, he heard the news of the Japanese attack on Pearl Harbor. Grace remembered their conversation that night. Shortly thereafter, she returned home from work one night to find a note from Russ. It said that a good friend had encouraged him to join the army's Quartermasters Corp, and the two of them had gone off to enlist.

Russ was sent to Fort Dix, New Jersey, in early 1942. Grace continued with her bank job, and then, when Russ was relocated to Fort Lee, Virginia, she quit her job and joined him. He had to live on base but could visit her in the room that she rented in a private home. She found employment on post, taking dictation from an officer.

They spent their first anniversary in Virginia. Russ completed Officer Candidate School and was sent overseas, his destination unknown. Five days after the Allied landings in North Africa, Russ arrived in Casablanca. He later went on to Italy, following and supplying the troops. Grace worked at the Office of Price Administration in Washington, D.C., and shared an apartment with her sister. She had an "A" gasoline ration card and was able to drive three others to work each day.

Russ was sent back to the States in 1944. Upon arrival, the army gave him R&R time in Lake Placid. Grace joined him, and then the two of them went back to Virginia and Fort Lee. Again, he had to live on base, and she found a room in Hopewell, Virginia. This time, there was no job for her, but their first child, Alan, was born in 1945.

The war ended, and so did the army enlistment. They returned to New Rochelle, where the Sears job was waiting for Russ. Finding an apartment was difficult after the war, but they eventually found a fourth-floor walk-up. The rental deal was sealed when Russ provided the owner with a new Sears vacuum cleaner.

In the late 1950s, the Bentleys went to a friend's wedding and met some people from Cortland, New York. Russ had spent some time in Cortland and had always hoped to return. At the wedding, he learned that a hardware store was for sale. He visited, made an offer and purchased the store, as well as a house for his family. Russ moved to Cortland, and Grace stayed behind to sell their home. The family now included two additional children: Priscilla, born in 1950, and Douglas, born in 1951. The house was sold and the move was made—complete, as Grace remembered, with three children, a cat and a parakeet. There was some apprehension about the house in Cortland, since she'd not been involved in its purchase, but the fit was excellent, and they remain in that same house fifty years later.

The move to the small town was a major change for Grace, but she was soon involved in the store and in the life of her family, the city and the schools. She worked daily in the hardware store and was a true partner, with involvement in all aspects of the business. She helped with the buying and enjoyed the trips with her husband to Chicago to see new wares and make selections. A visit to Bentley's True Value Hardware Store was a pleasant experience. If they did not have what you wanted, Grace or Russ would order it. They might help you see that something else could work as well or better, or they might send you to another store that had what you wanted. When the "big stores" (like Walmart) came to town, Bentley's Hardware responded by adding to its specialty: a sterling reputation, excellent service, delivery, repair and special need items. The Bentleys owned and operated the hardware store for a total of thirty-eight years until they closed it in 1997.

Soon after the move to Cortland, Grace joined the Young Women's Christian Association (YWCA) and became an active member of the Progress Club for Newcomers. She served multiple terms on the YWCA's board of directors and on many committees. She is a life member and remains active with participation in the water exercise program, as well as others.

Grace was a charter member of the Cortland Branch of the American Association of University Women (AAUW) when it was begun there in 1965. She initially served as publicity chairperson and, over the years, has served in every possible capacity and has been active in district level work as well. In 1982, when the branch seemed to be faltering, she was asked to serve as president, and she led the branch back to health. She led the group again, serving as co-president from 2001 to 2003. She speaks of AAUW and its work with such enthusiasm and respect that she has been a good recruiter of new members. She was the eager fundraising chair for the annual AAUW Christmas fruitcake sale for many years and recalled with fondness the year she was responsible for selling eight hundred fruitcakes. She has opened her home to the parents of college students many times as a part of the branch bed-and-breakfast fundraising, and when the branch was hosting Congressman Sherwood Boehlert as a member of a panel discussing the Vietnam War, she invited him and his assistant to her home for dinner. That's Grace, always ready and willing to do what needs to be done.

She was asked to join the Cortland Free Library Board in 1972. When she retired from the board in 2005, she was fêted as the "quintessential library board member." She served many years as secretary and was board president for a four-year term when the state imposed new regulations on local libraries and extra fundraising was required because of budget cuts. She worked on the Personnel Committee for most of her board tenure and was instrumental in the careful handling of personnel matters. She helped create the "Friends of the Library" group, which provides volunteer and financial support. On the library board, she demonstrated, as she has elsewhere, her ability to ask the "right" question, the pertinent question, that gets to the heart of the matter and gets everyone thinking on the topic at hand and on the bigger picture.

Her commitment to the Cortland community and to her family can be illustrated by many examples in addition to the library board. She was co-owner/operator of a very successful hardware store. She co-managed a host of rental properties that she and her husband bought over the years. Their goal was affordable, attractive property for rent in the downtown area.

She was and remains an active member of AAUW, the YWCA, the Ladies Literary Club (where each year she researches and presents a paper), the Presbyterian church (where she has been a member for more than forty-five years, including longtime service as a choir member, committee member and sometime pianist, as well as elder, deacon and Sunday school teacher) and the Cortland Country Club (where she has been a member for more than fifty years and remains an intrepid golfer).

When the city decided to hire a financial director, the mayor appointed her to the search committee. She served on the citizens' committee for recycling and played a role in determining the system now in use. Grace spent much of her own time and effort researching systems in place in many other cities.

When she was diagnosed with celiac disease, she learned all she could about the disorder, shared the information, joined a support group and continues to prepare and share recipes with those newly diagnosed. She made the disease known to others so menu planners for groups would be aware of the special food restrictions of some and could cook or plan accordingly. She continues to provide support and advice to grandchildren and great-grandchildren and has been known to provide housing, furniture, meals-on-wheels and solid advice to them.

A daughter-in-law's diagnosis of multiple sclerosis made necessary Grace's greater involvement in providing care for three of her grandchildren. She stepped in and for many years gave the children the help and support they needed on an almost daily basis. Their grandmother was and remains a major force in their lives.

Based on her extensive research on drugs, Grace made a presentation to the Cortland Police Commission in an effort to make citywide changes in availability and sales of drugs. When a local tobacco shop made products available to people too young to make such purchases, she joined in harassing the shop until it closed.

More recently, a change in her husband's health required some modifications at home. Grace sought and found the necessary home healthcare, and she learned to perform many of the required services. When it became difficult for Russ to enter and exit their car, Grace accomplished a trade for a van. She is a caregiver but is careful to care for herself too.

She is a reader, a writer, a correspondent to friends and to the newspaper, an avid finder and sender of clippings that friends will enjoy, a wonderful cook, a supportive and kind friend and a wife, mother, grandmother and great-grandmother of the highest order. Grace described their three adult children as a lawyer, a community activist and an engineer and takes pride in their accomplishments. Grace and Russ enjoyed traveling, especially at the seventeen Elderhostels they attended. Her love of the French language led to trips to France, where they rented places in the countryside and where they were able to reconnect with some of the French people Russ had met in Morocco during World War II.

She maintains friendships with many people. Upon leaving college in 1941, she and four classmates began the writing of a round-robin letter that makes the cycle of members twice yearly. That has continued until now. All letters are collected and saved by one member. One wonders what a remarkable book could be written using the collection of history and life events accumulated in those letters. The five have met at college reunions and other times as well. The seventieth anniversary of their college graduation was in 2011.

Grace Bentley is indeed a woman of distinction and service. Several years ago, her twin granddaughters wrote of their grandmother, "Grace Bentley's character could only be described as warm and gentle, learned and wise, sincere and sensitive, and purely good in the deepest sense of the word." Grace Bentley is a woman who has made a difference, and now in her ninetieth year, she continues to do so.

Bentley, Grace. Interview recorded by C. Jane Snell, 2009.

Researcher and author: C. Jane Snell, Cortland Branch

DAYRA BERNAL-LEDERER

1960–
PROFESSIONAL COUNSELOR

Dayra was born in the Republic of Panama, where she lived the first twenty years of her life. She is the youngest of three children and the only female. Growing up in a small country with a caring family, remarkable female role models and the same classmates (some remain lifetime friends) during twelve years of school, she learned to value what is positive in the context of the human experience. However, after those first two decades, she yearned to study abroad, and this inspired her to attend higher education in the United States.

Dayra earned a double Master of Science degree in rehabilitation administration and services and in counseling from Southern Illinois University–Carbondale and a Bachelor of Arts in psychology, with a minor in biology from the College of St. Benedict in Minnesota. She's a Rotary International scholar and a member, by invitation, of the Chi Sigma Iota international honor society for counselors.

Dayra is a licensed mental health counselor in the state of New York and is nationally certified in her profession. She is also a certified holistic stress management instructor. Currently, she is an independent professional counselor, consultant and instructor in New York City. Her practice focuses on helping people with disabilities and other individuals, including other professionals in health and human services, with career decisions. In addition, she provides support to people experiencing job loss, job maintenance or other career transition issues. Dayra's unique approach includes holistic stress management, particularly recognizing and managing workplace burnout and achieving a balanced lifestyle. She offers counseling services and work- and wellness-related workshops and conducts conferences/training in partnership with a healthcare practitioner and certified yoga therapist.

Before entering private practice, Dayra spent more than two decades working in the fields of rehabilitation, healthcare and human services as an administrator, clinician and counselor. She worked closely with both the nonprofit and for-profit sectors. Dayra helped pioneer the first Project with Industry (PWI) in Panama with the technical support of Goodwill International and a grant from the U.S. Agency for International Development. She has worked extensively outside New York City, including in Chicago, Minneapolis/St. Paul and her native country, Panama.

She is an active member of numerous women's and professional organizations, including the National Council of Jewish Women (NCJW); the American Association of University Women (AAUW), a former New York City branch member and now a member at large and was nominated as emerging leader of her branch at the 2009 AAUW New York State Convention; the American Counseling Association–National Career Development Association; and the National Rehabilitation Counseling Association–New York Rehabilitation Counseling Association State Chapter, among a long list of others.

Dayra lives in New York City on the Upper West Side of Manhattan. Downtime is for long walks, finding green or blue oases such as parks, rivers or ocean harbors. She also enjoys hiking, reading and discovering new places with her husband, Michael. When traveling throughout Europe, North America or Panama and while visiting family, she especially enjoys listening to personal stories and observing various lifestyles. She treasures these opportunities to foster well-being, to grow and to be of service to others.

Dayra Bernal-Lederer's 2010 autobiography, AAUW member at large.

PREAWPHAN BHITIYAKUL

19??–
VOLUNTEER

Preawphan Bhitiyakul was born in Bangkok, Thailand, where her father worked for the government at the National Mint. Their home was only one block from the King's Palace, so her childhood play activities were restricted. However, her grandmother nicknamed her "Nuise" because she always had a bump on her head. This became the name by which she is still known today.

Nuise finished nursing school in Thailand and within two weeks of graduation married Somsak Bhitiyakul. They moved in 1967 to

Milwaukee, Wisconsin, for his medical training. In Milwaukee, their first child, a daughter, was born, and Nuise learned to keep house and cook. She became an American homemaker while her husband finished his degree in internal medicine. The decision was made that he should continue his education, so they moved again to Providence, Rhode Island. Here, in 1971, a son was born, and Dr. Bhitiyakul completed his training in the field of nephrology. They remained in Providence, where he became a teaching fellow at Brown University.

By 1975, Dr. Bhitiyakul was yearning to open his own practice and was advised to search out the Hudson Valley area in New York State. They visited Kingston, where he dropped in at the Kingston Hospital emergency room and was quickly requested to "come to work tomorrow." At the time, there was no kidney specialist in Kingston. In 1977, Dr. Bhitiyakul founded and became director of a kidney dialysis center in Kingston and remains director today. Subsequently, he was given an award by the local Rotary Club. Nuise accompanied him to the award dinner, and there she was invited to become the first female member of the local Rotary (it being the first year women were accepted into the national organization).

Thus began the career of Nuise Bhitiyakul, which has continued for more than twenty years and has grown exponentially. She had already become a member of the board of directors of both the Kingston Hospital and the Benedictine Hospital Auxiliaries. Now she became the first woman on the board of directors of the Kingston Rotary Club; she still serves on all of them.

In 1988, the Kingston Rotarians began a project to restore the park on the Hudson River where the day-liner boats landed in the nineteenth century to connect with the trains taking tourists to the Catskill Mountain Hotels. The Rotary volunteers worked all day clearing brush and establishing walking paths at the park. Nuise was asked to furnish lunch for the workers. It is still remembered how she sent a truck with tables, chairs and food the first time. The park is now a popular walking and picnic area, and there are plans for more growth in the future.

In 2005, Nuise became a member of the board of directors of the International Medical Relief Foundation. This took her back to Thailand, where the HIV population was becoming a national problem. The rural temple near Bangkok had become home to families of the infected, but the temple's drinking water was not safe. In 2007, Nuise helped to get a grant of $135,000 that enabled the start of a purification system that now satisfies the needs of the temple inhabitants.

Many times, Nuise and Dr. Bhitiyakul have traveled to Thailand to spend two to three weeks at a clinic under the program Healing the Children. In New York State, she was instrumental in organizing some one thousand Thai nurses and was the first president in 1995 of the Thai Nurses Association of North Eastern America.

In 1996–97, Nuise was co-chair of the American Medical Association Education and Research Foundation in alliance with the Medical Society of the State of New York. From 2005 to 2009, she chaired this group, in 2009, she was president and in 2013 is again chairing this group. From 2000 to 2008, Nuise was chairperson of the World Community Service for Rotary International District 7210 in New York, and she was named Rotarian of the Year for this group in 2007.

Nuise has also worked as board member of the local Girl Scouts, the area Red Cross and the American Cancer Society of Ulster County. She was given an honorary award from the Thai Red Cross College in 2006 (first alumna in the United States).

Family values and the American ideals of women's rights and individual freedom are very important to Nuise Bhitiyakul. Her father taught her that time is short and we must today do all we can. She says, "I can do it…we *must* do it." Of course, she has already done much.

Bhitiyakul, Preawphan. Interview recorded by Virginia Kohli, 2010.
———. Telephone conversation with Helen Engel, January 11, 2013.

Researcher and author: Virginia Kohli, Kingston Branch

KATHERINE BURR BLODGETT

1898–1979
SCIENTIST/INDUSTRIAL CHEMIST

Katherine Blodgett was born in Schenectady, New York, the second child of Katherine Burr and George Blodgett. Just before she was born, her father was shot and killed at home by a burglar. Afterward, the family moved to France, where she spent her early childhood. They later moved to New York City, where Katherine attended a private school. She won a scholarship to Bryn Mawr, later graduating with a degree in physics at age nineteen.

Returning to Schenectady, Katherine applied for a job at the General Electric Company (GE) where her father had worked and became the first female scientist hired by the GE Research Laboratory. The following year, she received her master's degree from the University of Chicago. In 1926, she became the first woman to earn a PhD from Cambridge University in England. Her dissertation concerned the "Behavior of Electrons in Ionized Mercury Vapor."

Returning to GE, Katherine discovered a method for applying layers of very thin coatings of glass and metal. She was able to reduce glare by eliminating reflection from the lower surface of glass. This was important for many uses, including in eyeglasses, microscopes, telescopes, camera lenses and automobile windshields. She received three patents for her work. Katherine also invented a color gauge to measure film thickness and a method for de-icing airplane wings. During wartime, she developed poison gas absorbents for use in gas masks and worked on producing smokescreens.

In addition to her work as a scientist, Katherine did volunteer work, wrote humorous poems and acted in community theater. She was fluent in French.

She received many honors, including the United States Chamber of Commerce "Woman Achievement" Award for scientific and civic contributions and the Garvin Medal of the American Chemical Society, and she was the first woman to receive the Photographic Society of America Award. The mayor of Schenectady proclaimed June 13, 1951, as Katherine Blodgett Day. She received honorary doctorates from Elmira and Russell Sage Colleges.

About.com. Inventors. "Katherine Blodgett." http://inventors.about.com/library/inventors/bl_Katherine_Blodgett.htm.

Biography Center. "Katherine Blodgett." www.biography-center.com/biographies/6997/Blodgett_Katherine.htm.

Wikipedia. "Katherine Burr Blodgett." en.wikipedia.org/wiki/Katherine_Burr_Blodgett.

Researcher and author: Julie Burgess, Schenectady Branch

AMELIA JENKS BLOOMER

1818–1894
NEWSPAPER EDITOR/WOMEN'S RIGHTS ADVOCATE

American advocate of women's rights in the early days of the feminist movement, Amelia Jenks Bloomer spent most of her life working for the cause. She was also a reformer of women's clothing and helped promote "bloomers."

Amelia Jenks was born into a family of modest means in the village of Homer, Cortland County, New York, on May 27, 1818. Her formal education consisted of only a few years in grammar school at the Cortland Academy in Homer, New York.

Amelia Bloomer was a small, slight, dark-haired woman with good features and a pleasant expression, but she appeared shy and retiring. Many colleagues thought of her as a sternly serious person, lacking in any sense of humor.

At the age of twenty-two, she married Dexter Bloomer and moved to Seneca Falls, where he was a lawyer and part owner of the *Seneca Falls County Courier*. A man of Quaker background, he influenced his young wife with progressive social principles and encouraged her to write articles on temperance and other social issues for his newspaper and for other periodicals.

Amelia Bloomer taught school and was driven to work against social injustice and inequity. Her interests led her to join several temperance groups and women's rights organizations in the Seneca Falls area. Her convictions inspired countless other women to similar efforts.

In 1848, Bloomer attended the Woman's Rights Convention at Seneca Falls. Encouraged by women's rights leaders such as Elizabeth Cady Stanton and Susan B. Anthony, Bloomer began publishing her views on temperance and social issues in *The Lily* in 1849. Initially, the publication focused on temperance, but under the guidance of Elizabeth Cady Stanton, who contributed to the paper under the pseudonym "Sunflower," the focus soon became the broader issues of women's rights. Contents of *The Lily* ranged from recipes to moralist tracts, including topics such as marriage law reform and higher education for women, which slowly educated women about the truth of women's inequities and the possibilities of major social reform.

In publication through 1853, *The Lily* eventually had a circulation of more than four thousand. This newspaper is believed to have been a model for later periodicals focused on women's suffrage. Bloomer described her feelings as the first woman to write a news vehicle for women, saying, "It was a needed instrument to spread abroad the truth of a new gospel to women, and I could not withhold my hand to stay the work I had begun. I saw not the end from the beginning and dreamed where to my propositions to society would lead me."

In 1851, *The Lily* supported a reform in women's fashion that came to bear Bloomer's name. In her publication, Bloomer promoted a change in dress standards for women that would be less restrictive in regular activities. "The costume of women should be suited to her wants and necessities. It should conduce at once to her health, comfort, and usefulness; and, while it should not fail also to conduce to her personal adornment, it should make that end of secondary importance." Female fashion in the 1850s consisted of unhealthy, tightly laced corsets, layers of petticoats that could weigh well over ten pounds and floor-length dresses that had to be dragged through filth during the era of unpaved streets that were not swept clean. The bloomer costume dispensed with corsets in favor of loose bodices; substituted baggy, ankle-length pantaloons for petticoats; and cut the gowns to above the knee.

Mrs. Bloomer was by no means the originator of this fashion innovation in 1851. The reformed dress of short skirt and full trousers was actually introduced by Bloomer's cousin, Elizabeth Smith Miller. However, because Bloomer advertised this reformed clothing style in *The Lily* and wore it in her lecture work, it became universally known as the "Bloomer Costume," or "bloomers."

Women's rights advocates such as Elizabeth Cady Stanton and Susan B. Anthony wore the reform dress for a year or so but abandoned it when they concluded that the ridicule it frequently elicited was preventing a fair hearing of their views. Mrs. Bloomer continued to wear the dress until the late 1850s, but being conservative by nature (she never shared the liberal religious views or abolitionist sentiments of her sisters in the movement), even she eventually opposed bloomers as inexpedient.

Even as support for *The Lily* waned, Bloomer continued to publish while at the same time holding the position of deputy postmistress in Seneca Falls. She and her husband moved to Mount Vernon, Ohio, in 1854. She kept her paper and aided him with publication of his, the *Western Home Visitor*. Amelia Bloomer was an exception to the nineteenth-century rule for women. She and her husband had moved from progressive Seneca Falls, New York, to the newly established Mount Vernon, Ohio. The ideas that she expressed in the *Western Home Visitor* were met with not only skepticism but also outright criticism of her, her womanhood and even her husband, for "allowing" her to write such things. After a few months in Mount Vernon, Dexter Bloomer decided to sell his paper and move westward. In spite of her support for equal rights for women, Amelia Bloomer followed the wishes of her husband and sold *The Lily* to move with him to Council Bluffs, Iowa.

To the modern observer, Amelia's ability to reconcile her role as women's rights advocate and her role as a dutiful wife seems contradictory. Bloomer, however, considered her leaving *The Lily* an act of love and not obedience. In her farewell letter, she wrote, "But the Lily, being as we conceive of secondary importance, must not stand in the way of what we believe our interest. Home and husband being dearer to us than all beside, we cannot hesitate to sacrifice all for them."

Amelia Bloomer remained a suffrage pioneer and writer throughout her life, writing for a wide array of periodicals. She led suffrage campaigns in Nebraska and Iowa, served as president of the Iowa Woman Suffrage Association from 1871 until 1873 and corresponded with and arranged lectures for Lucy Stone, Susan B. Anthony and Elizabeth Cady Stanton in Iowa. She retired into private life in the 1870s, troubled by poor health. She died at Council Bluffs on the last day of 1894.

Although Bloomer's work was far less renowned than that of her contemporaries, she made many significant contributions to the women's movement, including dress reform and work in the temperance movement. Moreover, *The Lily* was a voice for many reformers such as Elizabeth Cady Stanton and Susan B. Anthony, speaking on the need for enfranchisement for women. Amelia Bloomer's work never matched the incessant and selfless activity of some of her contemporaries, but she contributed to the suffrage movement far more profoundly than the generally facetious use of her name would indicate.

Amelia Bloomer's memory lives on today. Her home at Seneca Falls, New York, known as the Amelia Bloomer House, was listed on the National Register of Historic Places in 1980. In addition, her spirit has been commemorated in the Amelia Bloomer Project List of Recommended Feminist Books for Youth, which was started in 2002 by the Feminist Task Force of the Social Responsibilities Round Table of the American Library Association. Each year, a bibliography of appealing feminist books that have been published in the United States is selected for young readers, from early age to eighteen. Criteria include significant feminist content, excellence in writing, appealing format and age appropriateness for young readers.

A few years ago, a book by Shana Carey introduced nineteenth-century feminist activist Amelia Bloomer to the picture-book crowd. Published in

2000, *You Forgot Your Skirt, Amelia Bloomer!* uses humor and history to bring the life and work of this pioneering newspaper editor, feminist thinker, public speaker and suffragist to a new generation.

Amelia Bloomer Project, 2010. http://ameliabloomer.wordpress.com.

Answers.com. Used for verifying general information.

Bloomer, Dexter C. *Life and Writings of Amelia Bloomer.* Boston: Arena Publishing, 1895. Reprint, New York: Schocken Books, 1975. Includes bibliographical references.

Britannica Concise Encyclopedia. N.p.: Encyclopedia Britannica, 2010.

Coon, Anne C. *Hear Me Patiently: The Reform Speeches of Amelia Jenks Bloomer.* Vol. 138. Westport, CT: Greenwood Publishing Group, 1994.

Kerley, Jessica Paige. "Domesticating the Frontier," 2001. www2.kenyon. edu/Khistory/frontier/ameliabloomer.htm.

The Lily: A Ladies' Journal. Devoted to temperance and literature. Seneca Falls, NY, 1849.

Wikipedia. "National Register of Historic Places." http://en.wikipedia.org/wiki/National_Register_of_Historic_Places.

Researchers and authors: Kathleen Beardsley, Cortland Branch, and Elizabeth Russo, Amsterdam, Gloversville, Johnstown Branch

JANE MATILDA BOLIN

1908–2007
ATTORNEY/JUDGE/ACTIVIST

"Mr. President, today I honor the life and legacy of Ms. Jane Bolin." In her tribute to Jane Matilda Bolin, then senator Hillary Clinton went on to call Ms. Bolin a trailblazer. "Her lifelong dedication to social justice, civil rights, and to the betterment of our American society serves as an inspiration to us all." Indeed, Clinton was right. Ms. Bolin experienced many firsts in her life, even though she was faced with pervasive discrimination and prejudice.

Jane Bolin was born in Poughkeepsie, New York, on April 11, 1908. She was one of four children of Gaius Bolin and Matilda Emery. Her father was the first African American graduate of Williams College and practiced law in Poughkeepsie. Her mother died when Jane was eight years old. Jane graduated from Poughkeepsie High School at fifteen and from Wellesley College in 1928. She was one of two black students in her class in the latter. She was named a Wellesley Scholar, a distinction that only the top twenty of the class earned. Bolin was also the first African American woman to graduate from Yale University School of Law, which she did in 1931; she was one of three women in her class.

Bolin shared honestly about the discrimination that she experienced at both schools. In an essay on the matter, she wrote, "There were but few friendships developed...on the whole I was ignored outside the classroom... [those] days for the most part evoke sad and lonely personal memories." In an interview with the *New York Times* in 1993, Bolin recalled that there were southerners at the law school who took pleasure in letting swinging classroom doors hit her in the face. Her childhood was also significantly affected by news and pictures of lynchings in the South. Bolin credited all those experiences for her lifetime interest in issues of racial discrimination, the effects of poverty and other social problems in this country.

Bolin returned to Poughkeepsie and began her career as a clerk in her father's law office. After passing the bar exam in 1932, Bolin joined the New York City Bar Association, the first black woman to do so. Bolin married attorney Ralph E. Mizelle, and they opened a practice in New York City. In 1937, she was named an assistant corporation counsel for New York City and served on the Domestic Relations Court. In 1939, Mayor Fiorello LaGuardia appointed her a judge of the Domestic Relations Court, now renamed the Family Court of New York. This made her the first African American woman in the United States to become a judge, and she was just thirty-one years old. The ceremony where she was sworn in as judge made news around the world. She served with distinction and was reappointed to ten-year terms by Mayors William O'Dwyer, Robert F. Wagner Jr. and John V. Lindsay. Bolin achieved major changes, which included the assignment of probation officers to cases without regard for race or religion and a requirement that publicly funded child-care agencies had to accept children regardless of ethnic background.

When her son, Yorke Bolin Mizelle, was born in 1941, Bolin took a leave of absence from the court. Her husband died in 1943, and she balanced being a mother and having a career. Bolin once shared, "I don't think I short-changed anybody but myself. I didn't get all the sleep I needed, and I didn't get to travel as much as I would have liked, because I felt my first obligation was to my child." In 1950, Bolin married Reverend Walter P. Offutt Jr. He died later in 1974.

In 1979, Judge Bolin retired after forty years as a judge, having reached her mandatory retirement age of seventy. In a letter at her retirement, she wrote, "It is easy to imagine how a young, protected child who sees portrayals of brutality is forever scarred and becomes determined to contribute in her own small way to social justice." Indeed, she had. However, she did not stop there. Bolin continued as an activist for children's rights and education. After retirement, she volunteered as a math and reading tutor in the New York City public schools and was appointed to the Regents Review Committee of the New York State Board of Regents.

Bolin also served on the board of the Child Welfare League of America and the Neighborhood Children's Center and took an active role in the National Association for the Advancement of Colored People, locally and nationally. She was also involved with the Committee on Children of New York City, the Scholarship and Service Fund for Negro Students, the Committee Against Discrimination in Housing and the Urban League of Greater New York.

Bolin died on January 8, 2007, at ninety-eight years old in Queens, New York. She is survived by her son, granddaughter and great-granddaughter. In her remarks to honor Judge Bolin, Hillary Clinton quoted her: "We have to fight every inch of the way and in the face of sometimes insufferable humiliations." Jane Matilda Bolin never stopped fighting and left a remarkable example for others to follow.

Hine, Darlene Clark, ed. *Black Women in America: An Historical Encyclopedia.* Brooklyn, NY: Carlson Publishers, 1993.

Martin, Douglas. "Jane Bolin, the Country's First Black Woman to Become a Judge, Is Dead at 98." *New York Times,* January 10, 2007. www.nytimes.com/2007/01/10/obituaries/10bolin.html.

Thompson, Kathleen, and Hilary Mac Austin, eds. *The Face of Our Past: Images of Black Women from Colonial America to the Present.* Bloomington: Indiana University Press, 1999.

Wikipedia. "Jane Bolin." http://en.wikipedia.org/wiki/Jane Bolin.

Photograph from the Library of Congress.
Researcher and author: Wendy Maragh Taylor, Poughkeepsie Branch

JOAN BOZER

19??–
COMMUNITY LEADER

Joan Bozer modestly said when sending information for this piece that her long list of accomplishments came from living an active adult life for more than fifty years. Her accomplishments are far more numerous than most who have lived that long, and she hasn't stopped. The *Buffalo News* carried an article on the Buffalo Tour of Solar Homes on October 1, 2011. The Bozer home was listed as one of the homes on the tour. The article went on to explain that the Bozers use passive energy panels to help heat their home and have installed solar energy panels to produce electricity. One of Joan's favorite causes is cleaning up the environment. She is cofounder and co-chair of the Western New York Sustainable Energy Association.

Joan Bozer served nine terms on the Erie County legislature representing several different districts in the city of Buffalo. During her time, the boundaries of her district were changed, and recently she has given presentations on issues relating to redistricting. As a county legislator, she was universally recognized for creative, inclusive and out-of-the-box thinking. Her favorite project from that time was saving the architecturally significant Old Buffalo Post Office Building, which then became home to Erie Community College.

A native of Westchester County, Joan grew up in Pelham Manor, New York. She attended Dean Junior College in Massachusetts and has a BA from State University of New York, Empire State College. Joan married John M. Bozer when he was a senior at Columbia University Medical School. They moved to Buffalo, where he practiced medicine as a prominent cardiologist for fifty-two years. They have four children, two of whom live in Buffalo, and seven grandchildren.

Before entering politics, Joan served as president of the Junior League of Buffalo and the Buffalo League of Women Voters. Joan helped found Women for Downtown (now Working for Downtown) and Buffalo Friends of Olmstead Parks (now Buffalo Olmstead Parks Conservancy) and is now a trustee of the conservancy. She was a cofounder of the Women's Pavilion of the Pan American Centennial in 2001. She has served on the National Board of the Friends of the Women's Right's National Park and is the cofounder of the Buffalo Niagara Chapter of the Friends of the Women's Rights National Park.

In 2008, she co-chaired the First Biennial Seneca Falls Dialogues on the 160th anniversary of the "Seneca Falls Declaration of Sentiments."

As a board member of the New York State League of Women Voters, Joan chaired "Briefings on the Status of Women Around the World" at the United Nations. She is a founder of the International Trade Council (now Buffalo Niagara World Trade Center) and is a part of the Western New York Sustainable Energy Association Trust. Joan is on the board of the Association for a Buffalo Presidential Center, exploring the legacies of Presidents Millard Fillmore and Grover Cleveland. She is also a member of the American Association of University Women, Buffalo Branch.

Joan Bozer's awards include the Zonta Club Marian de Forest Community Service Award, the Buffalo News Citizen of the Year Award, the Landmarker Award from the Landmark Society and the Red Jacket Award from the Buffalo Historical Society, and she was inducted into the Western New York Women's Hall of Fame.

All of this speaks to the influence of Joan on her community and beyond. It is more than fifty years of community service very well spent.

Information obtained from Joan Bozer by Julia (Judy) C. Weidemann, fall of 2011.

Researcher and author: Julia (Judy) C. Weidemann, Buffalo Branch

CATHARYNA BRETT

1687–1763
DUTCHESS COUNTY'S FIRST REAL ESTATE DEALER

Madam Brett, as she was called by succeeding generations, first arrived at what was later to be called Dutchess County in the fall of 1708. Born in 1687 to a well-to-do Walloon family in New York City, Catharyna Rombout found herself without a fiduciary inheritance and land-poor upon the death of her mother, Helena, in 1707. She married Roger Brett in 1703. He had arrived in the New World with Lord Cornbury, governor of New York. Brett was a well-respected captain in the Royal Navy.

It was not long before Captain Brett met his future wife, as the Rombout family was active in the social life of the royal circle. After their marriage, the Bretts moved into the Rombout family home on Broadway. As the family had great wealth, there was no reason for Roger Brett to be gainfully employed apart from attending to the business needs of the family.

A drastic change in lifestyle came about for the Bretts in 1707. Upon the death of her mother, Catharyna received only nine pence and the house on Broadway, which she could no longer afford, as well as twenty-eight thousand acres of wilderness in the Hudson Valley, one-third of the Rombout Patent that had been negotiated by her father, Francis Rombout, with the Wappinger Indians in 1683.

Knowing that their future and livelihood lay in the Hudson Valley, Roger Brett mortgaged the Broadway house and headed to the wilderness to build a home and gristmill for his family near the junction of the Fishkill Creek and the Hudson River. Catharyna, in her third pregnancy, arrived with her two young sons, Thomas and Francis, in the fall of 1708. Although there was the King's Highway, a very narrow dirt road running from New York City to Albany (present-day Route 9), the major means of travel was by sloop on the Hudson River.

The Bretts began developing their inheritance by leasing lands to tenants for farming; selling tracts of land would come later. The settlers relied on water commerce (in sloops) to take their produce to the city and return with supplies. Returning on his sloop from New York in June 1718, Roger Brett encountered a fierce squall near the Fishkill Landing. The sail quickly filled with wind, and the boom snapped across the deck, striking Brett on the head and sweeping him into the water to drown.

With the death of her husband, Madam Brett became the partner of George Clarke, secretary of the province, who had been the partner of Roger Brett. He held the mortgage to the most southern portion of the Rombout Patent, as the Bretts had needed capital to establish themselves in Dutchess. As her partner, he guided her to several important land sales and clients. The most outstanding ones were Dirck Brinkerhoff, Cornelius Van Wyck and Theodorus Van Wyck. Theodorus and Cornelius were known to have been surveyors for Madam Brett. With these sales, Catharyna was able to pay off the mortgage and became the sole proprietor of her land.

Madam Brett never remarried, but she had the support of her sons and the other colonists. She had to provide food, clothing and shelter for family and servants. One of her greatest responsibilities was maintaining and running the gristmill at the mouth of the Fishkill Creek.

The Wiccopee Indians played an important role in Catharyna's life. They often camped on land in front of her house, and her children played with Sachem Ninham's children. The Bretts became familiar visitors to the Indian village. This friendship was to prove beneficial when a land dispute arose between Madam Brett and the English and Scotch settlers in Poughkeepsie. When the dispute could not be settled, Lewis, an Englishman, sent some Indians to attack the Bretts. Daniel Ninham, son of Sachem Ninham, warned Madam Brett, and she was able to escape. An official survey resolved the dispute in favor of Madam Brett, and the Wiccopee Indians were given a gift of money as a gesture of goodwill by the Van Cortlandts, Verplancks and Madam Brett, holders of the Rombout Patent.

As with many of the colonists, religion played an important role in the lives of the Bretts, especially Catharyna. They donated land for a church in Fishkill, as it was the center of the farms along the Fishkill Creek. The church building was begun in 1716, two years before Roger's death. In all, it took seven years to complete the building. "Madam Brett's Road" (now Route 52) ran from Beacon (known as Fishkill Landing) to Fishkill.

During her life, from 1687 to 1763, Catharyna accomplished many things, but she is known for establishing commerce and selling lands to create farms in southern Dutchess. She is buried under the pulpit of the First Reformed Church of Fishkill, which she helped to found.

Cassidy, Henry. *Cathryna Brett, Portrait of a Colonial Businesswoman.* Vol. 13. Poughkeepsie, NY: Dutchess County Historical Society, 1992.

Researcher and author: Barbara Wilman, Poughkeepsie Branch

JOAN BRILL

1930–
PIANIST/HARPSICHORDIST/AUTHOR

Joan Rothman Brill was born in Greenport, Long Island, New York, and grew up in Southold, New York, on the north shore of Long Island. She graduated as valedictorian from Southold High School in 1948 with the highest average in the history of the school. She made her piano debut at Carnegie Hall in 1958, following her scholarship studies at the Juilliard School. Ms. Brill has appeared as piano soloist at Long Island University, State University of New York (SUNY) at Stony Brook, the Parrish Art Museum and the John Drew Theater in East Hampton. She was also piano soloist with the Oceanside Symphony, the South Fork Chamber Orchestra, the Clearwater (Florida) Symphony Orchestra and the Tampa Bay Symphony Orchestra. Many audiences have heard her as pianist-harpsichordist with the Brill-Gaffney Trio, which appeared all over Long Island (before the deaths of Judie and Bill Gaffney, the other members of the group).

A summa cum laude graduate of Long Island University in 1970, she holds a Master of Music degree in piano (1971) from SUNY at Stony Brook. Ms. Brill continued to polish her technique with the distinguished artist and Bach specialist Rosalyn Tureck. She has also studied with Josef Raieff, Leonid Hambro, Alexander Lipsky and Martin Canin. Joan Brill is included in *The World's Who's Who of Musicians* and *Who's Who of American Women*. She was the collaborator with the Keys Chorale in Key West, Florida, for nine years and appears often with the Keys Chamber Orchestra and Keys Chamber Ensemble.

Joan Brill has produced two CDs of piano music: *Piano Encores* by Joan Brill and *More Piano Encores* by Joan Brill. More than 1,500 copies of the CDs have been sold and/or distributed.

In 2008, her book, *My Father and Albert Einstein*, was published by iUniverse. It describes the summer of 1939, when David Rothman, a local hardware store owner, and Albert Einstein spent a great deal of time together in Southold, playing the violin and discussing the great works of science and philosophy. Ms. Brill was interviewed about her book by Dick Gordon of North Carolina for broadcast on National Public Radio. The interview may be heard by going to thestory.org online. You may click on "Archive" and then "March 18, 2011" to listen to the second half of that day's interview.

Joan Brill's 2010 autobiography, East Hampton Branch.

FRANCES MARION BROWN

1915–2000
THEATER DIRECTOR/EDUCATOR

Frances Marion Brown enriched the educational and cultural life in Oswego, New York, through her contributions to the school district and to the Oswego Players, a local theatrical group.

Born in 1915 in Oswego, she was educated at St. Mary's School and Oswego High School. As an undergraduate at Syracuse University, she majored in speech and drama. There were few career choices for women at that time, and she had decided while in grade school that she wanted to become a teacher. When she graduated from college in 1937, there was a job opening at Kingsford Park School (K-9) in Oswego, and she started her career as an educator. A few years later, she began teaching English and drama at Oswego High School, retiring in 1979 after devoting forty-three years to the Oswego School District. Occasionally, she taught children's theater as a summer or night class at the State University of New York–Oswego. Although she had originally planned to go into college teaching, she decided to stay in her hometown—her father had died four years after she graduated from college, she liked public school teaching and she stated that she would rather be a "big frog in a little pond than a little frog in a big pond." She also taught adult classes in English as a Second Language to Holocaust refugees who lived at Fort Ontario in Oswego from 1944 to 1946.

In 1938, she became a charter member of the newly organized Oswego Players and directed its first production, which was *The Late Christopher Bean*. Brown became a driving force in this organization, serving as president for at least seven years and holding offices as vice-president, secretary and liaison officer. She also participated as actress, director, prompter and backstage worker. During the first fifty years of the Oswego Players, she directed at least seventeen plays, celebrating the fiftieth anniversary by again directing *The Late Christopher Bean*, the group's first production.

At first, the Oswego Players presented plays in the Oswego High School auditorium and other schools, with rehearsals held at the YMCA or any available space. In 1961, the Oswego Common Council allowed the Players and the Oswego Art Guild to use the old Quartermaster Building at Fort Ontario as a community arts center if they would renovate, repair and maintain the interior of the building. Both groups worked hard to make this brick building, which was built by the United States Army in 1903, habitable. The formal opening was held in June 1964. Many exceptional dramatic performances have been staged there over the years, and these continue to provide cultural enrichment for the community. Due to Fran Brown's vision, talent, energy, effort and many contributions, the Oswego Players named its part of that building the Frances Marion Brown Theater.

She was a board member of the New York State Theatre Association and Theatre Festival Association and was president of the Theatre Association of New York State. In 1962, she was given the New York State Community Theatre's coveted Mary Eva Duthie Award when the Oswego Players was named as New York State's most outstanding community theater.

Active in the community, she was a member of the Civic Resources Committee of the Oswego County legislature, the American Association of University Women, the United Service Organization Committee during World War II and countless others in which she took leadership roles. In 1978, she was honored as Oswego's Woman of the Year.

Brown, Frances Marion. Interview by Deborah K. Engelke and Judith Wellman, April 6, 1988. Oral History Program at the State University of New York College at Oswego, New York.

McCann, Donald, and Nona Turano. *50ᵗʰ Anniversary Oswego Players, Inc., 1938–1988*. Oswego, NY: Oswego Printing Company Inc., 1988.

Researcher and author: Marilynn Smiley, Oswego Branch

MARTHA SMITH BREWER BROWN

1821–1911
ADVENTURER

Martha Smith Brewer Brown was born on September 24, 1821, in Southwick, Massachusetts, the ninth of twelve children. At the age of six, she went to live with her Aunt Ashley, with whom she endured a hard life. At age eleven, her father moved the family to Springfield, where he became a farmer. In 1839, when her father died, the family moved to Chicopee, and her mother took in factory boarders to support herself. Martha had a decent education for a girl of her time, studying until the age of fifteen, having also studied a little French.

Relocating to her brother Harvey's house in Brooklyn, she met Edwin Brown. At first, she refused him and returned to her mother in Chicopee, where she put in fourteen-hour days at dressmaking. In 1843, Captain Brown returned to Chicopee determined to marry her, which he did on May 23, 1843. She had been working so many years by now that she asserted her independence by retaining her Smith and Brewer identities.

In July, Captain Brown left on a two-year cruise around the world, leaving Martha at Orient Point, New York, to visit with relatives. Returning after only a year, having purchased a ship, the *Lucy Ann*, he also bought a house for his growing family. On May 2, 1845, a daughter, Ella Oriana, was born. Two and a half years later, Ella was left with relatives, while Captain Brown and Martha (who could no longer stand the separations from her husband) set sail in the *Lucy Ann* on August 31, 1847, for whaling grounds of the Pacific Ocean.

Life aboard the ship was hard, with dangerous storms, seasickness and little to pass the time but reading, walking the deck, sewing and occasionally caring for a sick crew member. Martha, Captain Brown and the crew jumped rope for exercise. Martha soon found herself homesick and missed her daughter terribly. She began a journal on October 18, 1847.

Once, a young crew member was dying of consumption. Captain and Mrs. Brown were very solicitous of his well-being, as well as that of his relationship with God. Martha's own life was built on an unshakable faith in God. Despite their prayers and ministrations, the lad succumbed and was buried at sea.

Martha also cited in her journal several instances of her husband as a caring, softhearted individual. He once turned the *Lucy Ann* around to rescue a kitten that had fallen overboard. Furthermore, as captain, he did not show a harsh temper, swear or believe in flogging—which he did only once for a three-time offender—but instead meted out very unpleasant duties as punishment.

As the *Lucy Ann* reached the Pacific Ocean, there were many sightings of whales, though it was a disappointment to discover that they were impossible to spear. The first sighting of thirty to forty whales—enough to fill the ship with oil, blubber and whale bone—came five months into the voyage on January 12, 1848, off the coast of Australia. They captured their first whale, as well as a few porpoises for fresh meat. As they neared Tasmania, Martha found herself longing to be on land. On February 11, 1848, they lost a small boat and crew transporting provisions from New Zealand. Martha longed for something to eat besides hardtack and salted meat.

By February 23, 1848, the ship was nearing Hawaii. Martha was pregnant and suffering morning sickness and so remained in Hawaii when the *Lucy Ann* finally docked there in April. She was not sorry to have made the trip even after seven and a half months at sea. Alone and without her husband or any friends, she was not happy on the island.

On May 7, 1848, Martha wrote to her husband about the church and social activities she participated in with the missionary families but was still constantly missing her daughter, who had just turned four. She spent much time sewing and reflecting on her relationship with God, as well as sharing the fears of her female contemporaries that she was "never good enough." As a wife, she often lamented her penurious circumstances, most especially her poor mode of dress and the need to do her own laundry.

Though she played her role as an adoring and submissive wife, it was not without protest. She appealed to his pride as a husband when she informed him that being properly dressed was most important to those with whom she was staying in Hawaii. Besides wishing to be with him to avoid spending so much money, she very much missed his companionship.

As her confinement drew near, she was concerned about finding assistance, even if it were to come from a native. Fortunately, her friend Mrs. Gray offered to help. On August 26, 1848, Martha gave birth to a son named William Henry.

The next weeks were spent socializing and anxiously awaiting the arrival of her husband. To further disturb her, she dreamed one night that her husband was lost at sea. To add to her distress, her friends the Grays were homeward bound. A measles outbreak killed many of the natives and some residents. She had heard from the captains of earlier arriving ships that her husband missed her as much as she missed him.

During the voyage, Captain Brown wrote a letter to his brother, Christopher, explaining what happened on the trip from the time he left Martha in Hawaii until his return there. He missed a prime opportunity for filling his ship in June and July off Okhotsk Sea. However, beginning in August, he had great luck farther south, although his ship almost sank during a gale. Whale-chasing boats were lost but no men. Despite heavy seas, he had expected to continue for several years. He returned to Oahu, where he repaired his ship and saw his son, William Henry. All three left again on December 21, 1848, to finish the remainder of their expedition, having spent six weeks resting in Oahu.

In February 1849, Martha made her last entry into her journal: "We have had problems with bugs and roaches. Captain Brown suffered serious burns trying to blow up the roaches."

After rest stops at Samoa and Upolie, the *Lucy Ann* resumed the journey in heavy seas. Martha, having spent eight months on land, suffered seasickness, so Captain Brown assumed the role of caretaker for his son. Enduring more storms and capturing more whales, the *Lucy Ann* finally dropped anchor in Gardiner's Bay on July 7, 1849, reaching Greenport, its point of departure, after twenty-two months at sea. On the final leg of their journey, Martha wrote in her husband's log: "Dear, allow me to inform you that this is the last time you are to leave or visit these waters which have become familiar to you."

Martha eventually gave birth to ten children, six of whom survived to adulthood. She died in 1911 at age ninety.

Brown, Martha Smith Brewer. *She Went A-Whaling: The Journal of Martha Smith Brewer Brown from Orient, Long Island, New York, Around the World on the Whaling Ship* Lucy Ann, *1847–1849.* Edited by Anne MacKay. Long Island, NY: Oysterponds Historical Society, 1993.

Researcher and author: Marlene Gilliam, Islip Area Branch

ANNA ODOR BUCHHOLZ

1921–2007
POLITICIAN/EDUCATOR

Anna Buchholz was a woman of grace who earned everyone's respect for her strong personal ethic, her integrity, her intelligence and her perseverance to achieve what she believed. She left her indelible mark on Dutchess County, the town of Poughkeepsie politics and on our state. She had a deep commitment to grass-roots public service, once stating, "It's our rent in life for living on earth."

Anna was a trailblazer. After three unsuccessful campaigns for county legislature, she persevered to win her fourth in 1971. In 1975, she campaigned for "honest and open" government to become supervisor of the town of Poughkeepsie. This was a time when few women were considered electable by the major political parties. Buchholz, who was dubbed "No Ordinary Woman," won the election and served for seven terms until her retirement in 1989.

Anna was born in Williamstown, Kentucky. As a child, she worked along with the laborers on the family farm, milking cows, feeding chickens and helping to can and cook in the kitchen. Reflecting on the feminist movement at one time, she stated, "I didn't have to be liberated; I was never occupied; I was like everyone else."

She was imbued early with a work ethic—as a child tackling farm chores, as a student in a one-room schoolhouse under the scrutiny of the teacher who was her mother and as a teen who graduated high school at fifteen, only to be told six years later after she had earned a master's degree, "Child, you are too young to get your PhD; you will have to wait a year."

In 1944, at the University of Illinois, she received her degree in German literature and language. Her dissertation on the religious renaissance of the German novel and her interest in religion attracted her to Quakerism. She taught at the university for a few years and then, in 1949, volunteered with the American Friends Service Committee and helped restore stability to the people of Ludwigshafen, Germany, a bombed-out industrial city. She learned to drive a dump truck to lead a work group to clear rubble; directed a neighborhood center housing a daycare facility, a library and a shoe repair shop; and conducted group sessions on the topic of reconciliation. She returned to the States in 1950 to become a German instructor at Vassar College in Poughkeepsie.

She also met Werner Buchholz (an IBM pioneer in early computer science credited with having coined the word "byte"). They married in 1952. The '50s found Anna a wife and mother of two sons, a teacher of folk dance to inner-city children, a Friend, a board member of the League of Women Voters (and then president) and a board member of the New York State League (and then president). She regularly attended Town of Poughkeepsie board meetings, joined the Grinnell Library Board and Brandeis, became director of Women in Community Service and was a member of the county's Economic Opportunity Committee to help the homeless.

By the late '60s, Anna had become a county Democratic committeeperson. She ran unsuccessfully three times for county legislature at a time when Dutchess County was heavily Republican; Democrats didn't get elected, and women didn't run for office. But Anna's persistence on a fourth try landed her a seat as a county legislator in 1971. She is credited with having paved the way for other Democratic women to seek office. Although she was subsequently defeated in the following election because her sense of what was right led her to champion a popular redistricting in which her opponent unseated her, she persevered to "serve the public" and turned her sights to local government.

In 1975, soon after she had kicked off her campaign to run for supervisor of the town of Poughkeepsie, the eldest Buchholz son was killed in a tragic accident. Anna found the inner strength to continue her campaign. And she won, again and again, seven times in fact. She had restored the people's faith in "open and honest" government. Her leadership was nonpartisan, fortified by consensus and peaceful resolution and based on the soundness of her personal ethic and integrity.

In 1976, Governor Mario Cuomo appointed her to his Community Affairs Advisory Board; to its successor, his Task Force on Mandates; and to the Greenway Council. Additionally, she was a member of the Mid-Hudson Regional Economic Development Council, the American Association of University Women (and its past president), the Business & Professional Women's Club and the Dutchess County Girl Scouts, and she was on the board of directors of the Mid-Hudson Civic Center.

In 2002, Anna received two honors: the Town Democratic Committee's first Citizen of the Year Award and AAUW's Woman of the Year Award. In 2008, Anna was posthumously honored when the Town Democratic Committee renamed its now-annual award the Anna Buchholz Citizen of the Year Award.

Throughout her retirement until she suffered a stroke and died in November 2007, "Ann" (as she was known to many), a woman with an unwillingness to give up in politics and in life, continued in Democratic politics, avidly attending town board meetings and working on committee issues and on candidates' campaigns.

She is survived by her husband, Werner, and Dr. Sham Rang Singh Khalsa, their son.

Information obtained by Barbara Mindel (Anna's administrative assistant during her years as supervisor). Biography approved by Anna's husband, Werner Buchholz.

Researcher and author: Barbara Mindel, Poughkeepsie Branch

MARY AGNES BURCHARD

1901–1996
MEDICAL MISSIONARY

Dr. Mary Agnes Burchard devoted thirty years of her life, based on her deep Christian faith, to serving the poor in Brindaban, India. She served as a medical missionary during the final years that India was a colony of Great Britain.

Mary Agnes was born in Jamestown, New York, on June 8, 1901. She graduated from Jamestown High School and from Mount Holyoke College four years later. She worked briefly for the Cattaraugus County Health Department Laboratory and then accepted the post of Girl Reserve Secretary with the Jamestown YWCA. In the fall of 1929, she enrolled in the medical school of the University of Michigan and, upon graduation, interned at the Women's and Children's Hospital of Chicago. A number of circumstances led her to accept a position with the Women's Foreign Missionary Society of the Methodist Episcopal Church in October 1934. She then went on her way to Brindaban, which lies about one hundred miles south of Delhi.

Brindaban is an important Hindu pilgrimage site and teems year-round with pilgrims attending the 6,500 sacred shrines and temples. Thousands of these pilgrims are widows, held responsible for their husband's deaths and left with no means of support. The Creighton-Freeman Christian Hospital was established to serve these widows. Male doctors did not routinely attend women due to cultural and religious restrictions.

When Mary Agnes arrived, there was no running water and no electricity. Emergency surgery at night was accomplished by flashlights and an extension from a car battery. Most of the water wells contained brackish water, and drinking water had to be brought in from more than half a mile away, and even then it had to be boiled over wood or charcoal fires. Mary Agnes played a role in improving both of these through her fundraising efforts. She also obtained funds from Jamestown friends for X-ray equipment. The facility grew from a small outpatient dispensary to a 125-bed hospital for women, later serving men as well. It included a school of nursing and a postgraduate course in midwifery, as well as a Christian ministry, a school and a girl's orphanage.

In Brindaban, Mary Agnes met Elda Mae Barry, already serving there as a nurse. They became lifelong friends and companions. Elda Mae was born in Meridan, Kansas, on September 7, 1904. She had been very ill in her early teens and then felt a call from God to nursing and missionary work. Obtaining a nursing degree from Bethany Methodist Hospital, she served in Brindaban for thirty-six years. During her leaves from missionary work, she furthered her education in midwifery. She taught at the Creighton-Freeman Christian Hospital's school of nursing, established the graduate school of midwifery and served as its superintendent until her retirement in 1964.

India gained its independence from Great Britain in 1947. Mary Agnes served there throughout World War II, when supplies and medicines were often scarce. She was honored by King George VI in December 1944 with the Kaiser-I-Hind Silver Medal for her services to the women and children of India. She spent twenty more years in devoted service to the poor, retiring in December 1964 from her missionary post.

Mary Agnes returned to the United States not ready to fully retire. She accepted the post of college physician at Western College for Women in Oxford, Ohio, a post she held for five years. She was joined by Elda Mae Barry, who had also retired from her service in Brindaban. The two women settled in Jamestown in 1971, and Mary Agnes was appointed to the WCA Hospital medical staff, retiring four years later. They continued to live full lives, were involved in a number of community volunteer activities and traveled extensively to visit family and their many friends. They also hosted travelers who visited Jamestown. Eventually, they moved to the Dibert Home and then to Heritage Village Health Care Center. Mary Agnes died on February 16, 1996, age ninety-four, and Elda Mae died on October 7, 1997, age ninety-three. Both lived long lives, spent in service to a suffering humanity, to God and to their strong Christian faith.

Burchard, Charles and Virginia. Personal letters and photographs. Private collection.

Monroe-Cassel, Margaret, Reverend. Personal interview, contact with family by author.

Thompson, B. Dolores. "Dr. Mary Agnes Burchard." *Jamestown Post-Journal*, March 2000.

YWCA of Jamestown, New York, record books.

Researcher and author: B. Dolores Thompson, Jamestown Branch

MARY Q. CHAPIN

1933–
LABOR ARBITRATOR/HISTORIAN/AUTHOR/
ACTIVIST

Proud resident of the Mohawk Valley, Mary Chapin has assisted and educated the community in many exciting and diverse endeavors. Bringing her natural passion for honoring past events and fostering future achievements, Mary is a trailblazer who utilizes her philosophy of promoting optimum life fulfillment for women.

Mary was born in Shepherdstown, West Virginia, and raised in Washington, D.C. When asked about the origins of her activism, she stated, "The beginning of everything I have accomplished started in high school, when I attended Holy Cross Academy in Washington, D.C."

In 1954, Mary wed Edward J. Chapin Jr. After his assignment to Griffiss Air Force Base in Rome, New York, they made their home in the Mohawk Valley. Mary held a number of civic and community positions and established a career as senior personnel administrator for the State of New York. Edward became a civilian electronics engineer for the Rome Air Development Center, a distinguished position that he held until his retirement in 1985. Ed and Mary have three children: John Edward Chapin, J. Patrick Hopkins and Susan Q. Chapin (who passed away in 1980).

Mary is a retired State of New York employee with a distinguished career in personnel and labor relations. She was on the panel of labor arbitrators for the American Arbitration Association for six years. She is a magna cum laude graduate of Binghamton University in peace studies and conflict resolution. Mrs. Chapin served a six-year term as a Governor Pataki–appointed member of the Mohawk Valley Community College Board of Trustees, becoming a trustee emeritus in 2002. She is a past president of the U/R Metro League of Women Voters and past vice-president of the Mohawk Valley Branch of the American Association of University Women, during which time she led a Coalition of Community Organizations in holding a "Sister to Sister Summit" for girls ages eleven through fourteen from school districts in Rome, Utica, New Hartford, Whitesboro and New York Mills.

Honors include the Conservator of Women's History Award from the National Organization for Women (NOW) in Syracuse and the Service to Women Award from Zonta. She was instrumental in securing a $46,000 grant for the YGIRLS in 2009. She also received an Outstanding Women Award from the YWCA. Mary received the New York State Woman of Distinction Award in 2007, and she is included in *Who's Who of American Women* and *Who's Who in the World*.

Mary considers as her most notable achievement, among many, the spearheading of the six-year campaign to establish a Day of Commemoration for Susan B. Anthony. With other members of the Mohawk Valley Women's History Project, Mary helped collect more than seventeen thousand signatures from the diverse community members of thousands of cities in more than forty-seven states. On November 5, 2005, the Susan B. Anthony Bill, supported by Senators Meier and Alesi and Assemblypersons Destito and Townsend, was signed into law by Governor George E. Pataki, marking an annual statewide commemoration of Susan B. Anthony Day.

Mary was the first female host of the longest-running WUTR-Utica television program, the popular *Mohawk Valley Seniors*. Fostered by her eclectic background, she compassionately crafted a format that spoke both to seniors and their families about contemporary issues in their lives. With weekly guests, Mary presented programs that were issue-oriented and touched on difficult topics in a natural and easy-to-understand language.

She is the author of *Women's Suffrage: A Dream of Full Citizenship*, presented at Seneca Falls for Celebrate '98. She has lectured on "Women of the Mohawk Valley Who Changed History." Mary authored significant works and performed as a "Living Legend Performer" in *The Life of Alice Paul, Susan B. Anthony-Up Close and Personal* and *Susan B. Anthony's Work for Abolition of Slavery*. These compelling performances were delivered to a wide variety of captivated audiences and have been highly acclaimed. She has also developed a program series centered on "Women at Ground Zero: Stories of Courage and Compassion," by Susan Hagen and Mary Carouba.

Mary teaches courses on Women Leaders of the World, Women of History and Environmental Awareness at the Mohawk Valley Institute of Learning in Retirement (MVILR) at the State University of New York, Institute of Technology. Her environmental work has focused on issues that threaten childbearing women and their families and the impact of hydrofracking on air, water and land. Mary was one of the first upstate activists. She is a member of Citizens for the Protection of Health and the Environment and has been a tireless advocate for three years. She serves as project consultant for Hydro Relief Web. She writes prolifically on all of these important topics. She is also preparing an eight-week course to be taught at MVILR. A devoted historian, Mary is currently completing her latest book, *Susan B. Anthony and George Francis Train in Kansas, 1867: A Love Story*.

Mary is a woman for all women.

Mary Q. Chapin's 2011 autobiography, Greater Rochester Area Branch. Former member of the Mohawk Valley Branch.

RHEA DOYLE ECKEL CLARK

1903–1985
EDUCATOR/COLLEGE PRESIDENT
"SAVIOR OF CAZENOVIA COLLEGE, NEW YORK"

Rhea Doyle was born in Binghamton, New York, on January 19, 1903, studied piano and earned a scholarship to Ithaca College. When she learned that Ithaca College didn't give a teaching degree, she transferred to the Crane School of Music State Teachers College in Potsdam, New York. Her first teaching job was in Solvay, New York. She started the first band, with instruments donated by Solvay Process (Allied Chemical). She later became director of music for Solvay schools. While there, she married Jacob E. Eckel, an architect and Notre Dame graduate, and together they had four children. Jacob passed away in 1969.

The donation of instruments was just the beginning of her talent and ability to motivate people and to raise money, which she did for Cazenovia College. She did much volunteer work and was on several school boards, including the Cazenovia Board.

In 1957, when Cazenovia College was dying and had fewer than fifty students and thirteen faculty members, she was asked to be interim president for three months. She saw a great need for a small two-year college for girls and decided to stay. She persuaded women from Syracuse and Cazenovia to make curtains for the dormitory to replace the paper ones, to donate furniture and to recruit students. It paid dividends. In the fall of that year, Cazenovia College opened with more than two hundred students. The college started to grow.

She saw the need for more classroom and dormitory space. Through her energy and enthusiasm, thirteen buildings were erected in the thirteen years of her serving. The school has about one thousand students today. She retired in 1971. After Eckel retired from Cazenovia College, Governor Nelson Rockefeller appointed her director of the New York Office for Aging. She worked in Albany and spent weekends at Presidential Plaza.

In 1974, she married Dr. Wesley C. Clark, who had been director of journalism at Syracuse University.

She was the recipient of three honorary degrees: St. Lawrence University, Doctor of Human Letters, 1966; Wheaton College, Norton Massachusetts, Doctor of Human Letters, 1965; and LeMoyne College, Syracuse, New York, 1961.

She received so many appointments and recognitions and served on so many boards that they are too numerous to mention. When she died on January 23, 1985, after heart trouble and cancer, her obituary made the front page of the *Syracuse Post-Standard*, as well as several local papers. Senator Tarkey Lombard said, "She was one of Onondaga County's first ladies, a woman whose smile was always warm and remembering." County executive John Mulroy stated, "She was one of the most outstanding women I have ever met." The college is deeply indebted to her.

Baker, Robert A. "Rhea Eckel Clark Dies; Longtime Area Leader." *Syracuse Post-Standard*, January 23, 1985.

Researcher and author: M. Edwina Norton, Syracuse Branch

Ruby Cohn

1922–2011
Author/Educator

Ruby Burman Cohn, world authority and close friend of Samuel Beckett, died at the age of eighty-nine on October 18, 2011.

Ms. Cohn was born on August 13, 1922, in Columbus, Ohio, and grew up in Brooklyn, where she lived with her mother and grandparents. Her mother, an attractive lady of Russian descent, had been widowed, remarried and divorced. Ruby was enrolled in public school as Ruby Hopkins and used that name until she married in 1946.

Ruby and I met in Junior High School. She was beautiful and brilliant and had a personal magnetism that attracted everyone. I invited her to a tea party at my house with a group of close friends. We formed a club, the PPP (Planning, Preparing, Producing). We spent the week doing homework together. On Saturday, we ate Chinese food and went to the movies. After the movie of the week, we came home, rewrote the script and presented the play for our friends in my backyard; Ruby was Robert Browning, and I was Elizabeth Barrett. At our junior high school graduation, we did scenes from *A Midsummer Night's Dream*.

We attended Franklin K. Lane High School. Ruby and I were reporters on the staff of our school newspaper. She suggested that, in addition to this, we should start a school magazine for creative writing. We got Mrs. Stock, our English teacher, to be faculty advisor and ran a contest to determine the title of our new magazine. The students voted, and since our school was in the middle of a cemetery, it was decided that *The Spook* would make a great title. (This was in the mid-'30s; this title would never be accepted in today's culture.)

By September 1938, Ruby and I were students at Hunter College. We loved our college years. Ruby was bright, pretty and popular. She had many boyfriends and many dates. I was married at nineteen, and Ruby was in my wedding party. The year 1942 brought graduation and World War II, and Ruby joined the service. She became an officer in the Women Accepted for Volunteer Emergency Service (WAVES), a women's division of the navy. She learned to install radar on battleships. I worked for Western Electric as a junior engineer trouble-shooting radar equipment.

After the war, my husband and I started a family. Ruby went to Europe, where she completed the first of her doctorates. In Paris, she became acquainted with the work of Samuel Beckett. The play she was most excited about was *Waiting for Godot*. Little did she realize then that this would turn out to influence her life's work.

In 1946, Ruby married Melvin Cohn, a microbiologist. (He was one of the boys in our old group of friends.) They moved to St. Louis, where Melvin taught. They divorced in 1962.

At Washington University in St. Louis, Ruby earned her second doctorate, with the theme of "the Comic Gamut." This would establish the reputation of "absurdist" theater.

The years from 1949 to 1954 found Mrs. Cohn in Paris. In 1969, she joined the faculty of the California Institute of the Arts. In 1972, Ruby (or Professor Cohn) moved to University of California–Davis. A recipient of Fulbright and Guggenheim fellowships, Ruby was selected by her colleagues as "Faculty Research Lecturer." She retired from UC-Davis in 1992. In a memorial article published by the *Enterprise*, it was noted that Ruby Cohn was the author or editor of more than twenty monographs and anthologies on modern and contemporary United States, British and Continental drama, among which was the first of many influential books on Samuel Beckett.

Of Samuel Beckett, Ruby Cohn wrote, "A postwar Frenchman in his artistic concern with man's metaphysical situation, an irrepressible Irish man in his comic astringency, a disillusioned student of the intellectual disciplines of the classical Christian legacy, Beckett conveys alienation as the human heritage."

Ruby Cohn left a legacy of major criticism and analysis in theater and literature.

American Society for Theatre Research. "In Memoriam: Ruby Cohn." www. astr.org/component/content/article/14-necrology/275-in-memoriam-ruby-cohn-1922-2011.

Cohn, Ruby. *Just Play: Beckett's Theater.* Princeton, NJ: Princeton University Press, 1980.

———. *Samuel Beckett: The Comic Gamut.* New Brunswick, NJ: Rutgers University Press, 1962.

Davis Enterprise. "Ruby Cohn." Special to the *Enterprise*, October 27, 2011. www.davisenterprise.com/obits/ruby-cohn.

Weber, Bruce. Ruby Cohn Obituary. *New York Times*, October 31, 2011.

Researcher and author: Lillian Goldson, Islip Area Branch

JANE COLDEN

1724–1766
BOTANIST

At a time when there were no female scientists, Jane Colden was the first American female botanist to successfully use the Linnaean system of classifying plants in English.

Jane Colden was born on March 27, 1724, in New York City to Cadwallader Colden, a man well known for his writings in mathematics, botany, medicine and history. He was also lieutenant governor of the New York colony and wrote one of the first history books, *History of the Five Indian Nations Depending on New York*. Jane's mother, Alice, came from an upper-class English family and received the best education a woman could have at that time. It is believed that she educated her daughter.

In 1728, when Jane was four years old, the Coldens moved to three thousand acres of land located ten miles west of Newburgh, New York. They called their land, which was one of the most remote and wild areas of the New York colony, Coldenham. There, Jane grew to love the plants, trees and flowers. By the age of six, she already had a keen interest and knowledge of indigenous flora. Using simple English words, her father taught her the Linnaean system of plant classification, which is based on plant parts.

Jane succeeded in describing and drawing 340 different types of flora that existed in colonial New York. Her work's consistent use of the Linnaean system was so accurate that she was considered a leading botanist in her time. It also promoted the idea that botany was a science suited to women because plant life was so delicate—just like women, as it was thought at the time. This accomplishment made her instantly famous. The idea of a female botanist was a real curiosity to the scientific community of that era.

Besides listing and identifying plants, Jane also wrote about their medicinal uses, knowledge she acquired from Native Americans. For example, a tea made from mountain mist leaves was used for stomach pain and the bark from the prickly ash shrub could help with coughs. Jane continued her work in botany until 1759, when she married Dr. William Farquhar. It is thought that she gave up her work in order to devote herself to her husband and family.

Thanks to the botanist Joseph Banks, Jane Colden's book is in the British Museum of Natural History. Her manuscript will always remind us of two important facts—that the first female American botanist came from Rockland County, New York, and that many of the same trees, shrubs and plants that you see everyday in Rockland County were once new and exciting botanic discoveries.

Colden, Jane. *Botanic Manuscript of Jane Colden, 1724–1766: First Woman Botanist of Colonial America.* New York: Chanticleer Press, 1963.
Imprints on Rockland County History: Biographies of 12 Women. American Association of University Women, New City Branch, New York, 1984.

Researcher and author: Elizabeth Palombella Vallone, Rockland County Branch

EILEEN COLLINS

1956–
ASTRONAUT

Eileen Collins is a woman of great accomplishment. While serving in the air force, Eileen worked hard to broaden the roles of women in the military. In 1979, she became a T-38 instructor pilot, later an aircraft commander and also an instructor in C14 cargo jets. She graduated from the United States Air Force Test Pilot School in 1990 and was selected by the National Aeronautics and Space Administration (NASA) as an astronaut in 1991. She secured her place in history when she became the first woman to pilot the space shuttle in 1995 and then to command the space shuttle in 1999 and again in 2005. As significant as these accomplishments are, equally important was the path she followed to attain her ultimate success.

Eileen Collins grew up in Elmira, New York, where her parents struggled to make ends meet. She "dreamed about space" and "admired pilots, astronauts, and…explorers of all kinds." She was determined to make these dreams come true. She worked hard in school, but after she graduated from high school, there was not enough money to send her to college. Rather than give up, she put herself through Corning Community College. She worked full time to pay for her education and also took flying lessons to bring her dreams closer to a reality. She then was granted a scholarship to Syracuse University, where she earned her BA in mathematics and economics. She continued her education at Stanford University and Webster University. She became one of the first women to go directly from college into air force pilot training, an area previously reserved for men. Her willingness to work hard and study hard won her the respect of her instructors and her peers. Many people would have given up their dreams when barriers like insufficient money or gender bias stood in her way. Instead, Eileen Collins simply worked harder to achieve her goals.

Eileen Collins retired as an astronaut, but not before she blazed a new trail for women to travel. She shattered the glass ceiling in NASA and became a role model for girls and women everywhere. In her words, "I want to do well because I know that I'm representing other women, other pilots, military pilots as well as civilian pilots who are hoping to come here to NASA and be pilots themselves for the space shuttle." Eileen Collins is truly a pioneer in the field of space aviation, and she has earned the respect and admiration of us all.

Encyclopedia of World Biography. "Collins, Eileen." www.notablebiographies. com.

National Aeronautics and Spaces Administration. "Astronaut Bio: Eileen Collins," May 2006. www.jsc.nasa.gov/Bios/htmlbios/collins.html.

StarChild. "Eileen Collins." http://starchild.gsfc.nasa.gov/docs/StarChild/ whos_who_level1/collins.html.

Photography courtesy of Chemung County Historical Society, Elmira, New York.
Researcher: June Ford, Elmira-Corning Branch
Author: Julie Biviano, Elmira-Corning Branch

RUTH J. COLVIN

1916–
LITERACY ADVOCATE/FOUNDER OF LITERACY VOLUNTEERS OF AMERICA

Ruth Johnson Colvin has devoted her life to literacy as a global issue, as well as locally in Syracuse, New York. At the age of ninety, she traveled to Haiti to launch an adult literacy program by using materials that she wrote herself.

Born in Chicago, Ruth studied at Moser Business College and later obtained a BS in business administration from Syracuse University. Through her church, she learned of literacy work in overseas missions. Upon learning in 1962 that eleven thousand adults in Syracuse could not read or write, she began a literacy program in her own home.

This program developed into Literacy Volunteers of America (LVA) and was incorporated in 1967 as a national, educational, nonprofit organization that trained volunteers to teach Adult Basic Literacy and English to Speakers of Other Languages. In 2002, LVA merged with Laubach Literacy International (also in Syracuse) to become ProLiteracy Worldwide, now having more than 1,200 affiliates across the United States and partnering with more than fifty groups worldwide. It has completed a national accreditation system to ensure top-quality training, management, assessment and accountability.

Over the past ten years, Mrs. Colvin has concentrated on writing books and giving training in local language literacy. She has been sensitive to native cultures and traditions in developing countries, such as in Madagascar, Papua New Guinea, Guatemala, Pakistan, Haiti and countries in Africa. Research and experience suggests that if one is illiterate in one's own native language, it is more difficult to learn a second language. Mrs. Colvin is experimenting with teaching basic Spanish literacy to immigrants in the United States who cannot read/write Spanish as a first step toward teaching English. She is also experimenting with teaching Af Maay to illiterate Somali-Bantus immigrants as a first step and concurrent with teaching English.

Mrs. Colvin and her husband have traveled to sixty-two countries, giving training in twenty-six of them. Her most meaningful experiences have been where she encouraged practical grass-roots ventures. She works with top professionals in the literacy field and stresses the importance of a "learner-centered, collaborative approach" to teaching.

Ruth has written several books. *Tutor 8* (8th edition, 2009) is a training and text for volunteers to teach basic literacy in English. *I Speak English* (4th edition) is a training text for volunteers to teach English to Speakers of Other Languages (ESOL). *In the Beginning Was the Word* teaches reading and writing through the Bible. She also wrote *A Way with Words* (a story of literacy) and many native literacy books.

In 1987, Mrs. Colvin was given the highest award for volunteers in the United States: the President's Volunteer Action Award. The recipient of nine honorary doctorates, she was inducted in the National Women's Hall of Fame in 1991. In 2006, she received the Presidential Medal of Freedom, the highest award given to a civilian.

Colvin, Ruth. "Introduction." *Tutor 8*. 8th ed. Syracuse, NY: New Readers Press, 2009.

Notes obtained from Ruth Colvin (Ruth Johnson Colvin, curriculum vitae, 2009) by Nancy Clausen.

Syracuse Post-Standard. August 13, 2007.

Researcher and author: Nancy E. Clausen, Syracuse Branch

MINNA ANTHONY COMMON

1882–1950
NATURALIST/ARTIST/VOLUNTEER

Minna Anthony Common (1882–1950) was an extraordinary woman who left an imprint on the North Country that is still visible and viable today. Born in 1882, Minna's mother, Margaret, died of diphtheria when Minna was only five weeks old. Her father, Paul Anthony, brought her to Watertown, New York, to be raised by her paternal grandmother, Amelia Brown Anthony. Young Minna attended the local grammar school and graduated from Watertown High School in 1899. She served as high school librarian through her four-year course there and then completed a postgraduate year. For the next four years, she was a first-grade teacher in the Brownville–Glen Park school. During that period, she commuted from her home in the city, riding her bicycle in favorable weather and traveling by trolley in inclement weather. At that time, she began tutoring children. This interest in educating children continued throughout her life.

After her marriage to James Allison Common in June 1904, she and her husband resided in Potsdam, New York, and then in the city of Watertown. The Commons had six children: Faith, Robert, June, Catherine, Ruth and Vera. All of them received bachelor's degrees and three received master's. In the summer, Mr. and Mrs. Common lived at Thousand Island Park (a village on Wellesley Island in the St. Lawrence River). Mrs. Anthony, her grandmother, was one of the first residents of this summer resort. While a cottage was being built for the Commons, Mrs. Common lived in a tent on the site. Minna Anthony Common first became interested in studying nature at Thousand Island Park, where summer courses were conducted. One of her teachers was the late Anna Botsford Comstock, a professor at Cornell University, and it was from her that she received her formal instruction in nature studies. After many summers, she laid out a one-and-a-half-miles-long nature trail on a densely wooded hill behind her cottage. The Rock Ledges Nature Trail has had visitors from all over northern New York and still exists today more than seventy-three years later.

Another talent that Mrs. Common possessed was developed from early youth: painting in several media. She had no formal art training, but a neighbor, the art teacher at the high school, worked with her, teaching her painting techniques and taking her along on numerous sketching expeditions. From another teacher she received lessons in pen and ink sketching, and from a local artist she learned the art of china painting and watercolor work.

In 1947, she wrote and illustrated her first articles for the "Farm and Garden" section of the *Watertown Daily Times*. Each week until she died, she contributed two articles, one on birds and one on flowers. For the previous twenty-five years, her nature articles had been published in the *Watertown Daily Times*, as well as the *New York Times*, the *Herald Tribune*, the *Christian Science Monitor* and magazines such as *Bird Lore* and *Audubon*. For the twenty-four years before her death, Mrs. Common had been the official federal bird observer for the Jefferson County area and kept the National Fish and Wildlife Service informed of bird migrations. She also conducted the yearly local bird census for the Audubon Society and the North Country Bird Club, which she founded.

Mrs. Common was very prominent in the activities that preceded the expansion of the Watertown School System, and she worked with the Watertown Improvement League to promote the new high school. Mrs. Common was a member and active worker of the First Presbyterian Church. Other memberships included the LeRay de Chaumont Chapter of the Daughters of the American Revolution, the Federation of Women's Clubs, the Outlook Club, the Jefferson County Historical Society and the Watertown Garden Club. After her death, the nature center in Wellesley Island State Park was named for her.

We can see the influence of this extraordinary woman on the life of her daughter, Catherine Common Johnson. The legacy endures. Northern New York has been uniquely blessed by the lives of these two women. Their vision, their creative energy and their persistence has left an indelible mark that will endure and continue to inspire a whole region of New York State.

Watertown (NY) Daily News. "Mrs. J.A. Common, 67, Dies, Rites Tuesday." January 23, 1950.

Researcher and author: Margaret Coe, Jefferson County Branch

CLARA COMSTOCK

1879–1963
TEACHER/PLACEMENT AGENT FOR THE ORPHAN TRAIN

Clara Comstock is one of the amazing women of our area whose story needs to be told. She gave to her community and to her society a generosity of time and energy above the mere earning of a livelihood. Clara came from a farming family near Hartsville, New York. She was born in Hartsville in 1879 to Charity E. Oakes Comstock (1854–1926) and Charles Comstock (1854–1922).

Clara graduated from Canisteo Academy in 1895, took a teachers' training course for several years in Canisteo and then started teaching at the Brace Farm School for Boys in 1903. Here we must take time to look at Charles Loring Brace, Clara's employer at the Brace Farm School, because she was to work with Reverend Brace for most of her life. Charles Loring Brace founded the Brace Farm School for Boys in 1894 in Valhalla, New York. In 1853, as a young minister, he had started the Children's Aid Society (CAS), which gathered up homeless children and found homes for them, usually on farms, because Reverend Brace believed in "the redemptive power of rural life." By the time Clara Comstock began to teach at the Brace Farm School, the society ran the Brace Orphanage in New York City, where homeless children were taken in and fed, clothed, checked medically and prepared for new lives.

After teaching at the Brace School, Clara became a placement agent for Reverend Brace's Children's Aid Society. To make sure that the children were given to caring parents who could support them financially and emotionally, the CAS had agents like Clara, who visited every family of prospective parents. Of course, when the CAS sent the children to their new homes by train, Clara Comstock and the other placement agents went with the children to care for them on the way and stayed with them until they were sure that the new family and the child were compatible.

These trips became known as the famous Orphan Trains. It boggles the mind to think how many miles Clara logged on trains between New York and the prospective homes of her children throughout the East and Midwest. In an article on Briomag.com, "A Home Long Forsaken: The History Behind the Story of the Orphan Trains," it is noted that "between 1911 and 1928, Clara oversaw seventy-four orphan trips west." Orphan Train baby Richard Call said that "Clara Comstock placed more than 1,200 children and kept track of them until they came of age."

She then made follow-up visits to make sure that the children were treated well and were happy in their new lives. These placement agents, like Clara Comstock, made the Orphan Trains a true finding of new homes and not the slave market that some organizations achieved with their indentured servant operations.

Of course, Clara put in not only her time but also the extra caring that came from her belief in the goodness of her work. In her book *Minding the Children: Child Care in America from Colonial Times to the Present*, Geraldine Youcha wrote, "Clara Comstock, who traveled west with groups of children from 1911 to 1928, put it this way: 'On my first trip with a party of children to West Point, Nebraska, I thought it was the most incredible thing imaginable to expect people to take children they had never seen and give them a home, but we placed them, and never failed to accomplish it. The home is always there, it is for the worker to find it.'" Clara felt she had done a good job in choosing the homes and thought that the children soon forgot their past lives. She was quoted by Youcha as saying, "They rarely showed any desire to return to New York and soon forgot they ever lived there. I do not remember but one boy who wished to return, he was a boy of twelve and wanted to become a fireman in New York."

This undoubtedly tells us more about Clara Comstock and her skills and pure motives than it does about the reality of the success of the entire placement process. Clara and a few like her were likely the exceptions. Youcha wrote that the number of orphan children placed out by various agencies during the years from 1854 to 1929 was a staggering 250,000. She noted that the society's own records show that 42 percent returned to the city. This makes Clara Comstock's achievement that much more important. She made sure that her charges found good homes and were happy there. With her mentor and employer Charles Loring Brace, she believed that they were doing good and successful work. Brace, as Youcha put it, believed that institutions were not the solution to saving the lives of homeless children; instead, they needed "a close relationship with caring adults." His farm school and Orphan Trains were his way of achieving this. Youcha wrote of Brace, "Instead of orphanages, Brace proposed 'the family as God's Reformatory' and sent the children first to nearby farms in New Jersey and New York and then west on trains that were then making the wide-open spaces accessible."

Women like Clara Comstock ended the era of the big orphanage and moved to a more humane care: the new family. In 1957, a fund dedicated to the education of needy children was established in her name. She died in 1963 and is buried at Hornellsville Rural Cemetery.

Briomag.com. "A Home Long Forsaken: The History Behind the Story of the Orphan Trains." October 2008.

Call, Richard. *Crooked Lake Review* (Spring 1999).

Youcha, Geraldine. *Minding the Children: Child Care in America from Colonial Times to the Present.* Boston: Da Capo Press 2005.

Researcher and author: Martha Treichler, Bath Branch

ELIZABETH A. CONNELLY

1929–2006
NEW YORK STATE LEGISLATOR

On September 6, 1952, Elizabeth Ann Keresey and Robert Connelly were married in Christ the King Roman Catholic Church in the Bronx, New York. Two years later, they moved to Staten Island to buy a house and raise a family. This was "before the bridge" (the Verrazano Narrows Bridge linking Brooklyn to Staten Island and spanning the Hudson River, completed in 1964) and before Staten Island became urbanized, and they probably regarded it as an idyllic place for their children to grow up. Mrs. Connelly settled down and became "an ordinary housewife."

Her history to that point was fairly straightforward. She was born in Brooklyn in 1929 and grew up in the Bronx during the Depression era. She graduated from Walton High School in 1946 and then went to work as a secretary in Manhattan, where she met the man she would marry.

Fast-forward fifty years. On May 25, 2006, the funeral for Elizabeth Ann Connelly was attended by hundreds, including city and state officials, judges, councilmen and local residents, as well as family. Her passing was mourned by thousands on Staten Island and throughout New York State who had come to regard her as their champion and friend. She was highly regarded and she was well loved by many. She had received many honors, and a number of public facilities had been named for her.

What happened in those intervening years to evoke such acclaim? Well, in addition to running her sprawling colonial home in a quiet North Shore neighborhood and raising four fine children, Mrs. Connelly made a political career for herself that no one could have predicted. She started by doing volunteer work for the Democratic Party and later became secretary for the club. Her career officially began in 1973, when she won a special election for the North Shore's Sixty-first Assembly District seat. She became the first woman ever to be elected from Staten Island to the New York State Assembly. Her career was marked by many firsts as she went on to serve twenty-seven remarkable years in the assembly.

Mrs. Connelly became well known statewide as a champion for those most in need. Her mission seemed to be to make government serve those whom others ignored but who most merited her efforts. She devoted her time to improve the lives of the mentally ill, the disabled, women and many others who needed her intervention. It was primarily due to her efforts that the infamous Willowbrook State School on Staten Island—which housed the mentally ill, the developmentally disabled and sometimes the merely unwanted in deplorable, abusive conditions—was finally exposed and closed down. This was a first step in her vision to provide community-based care—medical, social and educational—for all those who were previously ignored and neglected. She was tireless in her efforts to educate the public to the then novel idea to provide humane, localized care and treatment for all the disabled.

Her efforts were recognized when, in 1977, she became the first female Democrat to chair an assembly standing committee. She was appointed chair of the Assembly Committee on Mental Health, Mental Retardation, Developmental Disabilities, Alcoholism and Substance Abuse. These areas defined much of her service in the assembly. Under her leadership, there were vast improvements in the mental health community, including a reorganization of the State Department of Mental Health. Over the years, these changes and reforms reverberated throughout the state.

Among her remarkable accomplishments, Mrs. Connelly sponsored a law and secured funding to help establish the first halfway house in the New York metropolitan area for female alcohol addicts, the Amethyst House, which still operates on Staten Island at this writing. She also aided victims of brain injuries and their families with a statute to start a treatment and education center for them. She sponsored a law to recognize the rights of female veterans. She was central to developing the law for traffic to stop for standing school buses, and this became statewide law. She authored the law establishing the "Stop DWI" program, a law to establish treatment programs for compulsive gamblers and another to assist those suffering from AIDS. Suffice it to say that, although we can't enumerate all her work in this space, her impact on individual lives in New York State was enormous.

In 1993, Mrs. Connelly racked up another first when she was appointed chair of the Committee on Standing Committees. She topped this in 1995 when she had the high honor of being named Speaker Pro Tempore of the assembly, making her the then highest-ranking woman in the history of the New York State legislature.

Mrs. Connelly, known to many as "Betty," was a lovely woman, tall and stately in appearance yet always approachable, with a ready smile and a tireless ear for those in need. Her devotion and compassion for those least able to help themselves seemed boundless. Mrs. Connelly was soft-spoken yet always succinct in her remarks, and her presence commanded attention. Her appeal transcended party politics, class or gender. She was reelected for twenty-seven years of glorious service. She was supported and assisted in her efforts by her equally compassionate, kind and capable husband, Bob Connelly, but that's another story that needs telling.

We would do well to remember Mrs. Connelly, her character and her career and to learn from her unflagging, forthright efforts, her can-do attitude and her enormous goodwill and compassion. We are so much better for having had Betty Connelly in our midst. She deserves to be remembered with great honor.

Hart, Rob. *Staten Island Advance*. Advanced Albany Bureau, May 2006.

Helvesi, Dennis. "Elizabeth A. Connelly, 77 Longtime Assemblywomen, Is Dead." *New York Times*, May 26, 2006.

Randall, Judy. *Staten Island Advance*. Advanced Albany Bureau, May 26 and May 31, 2006.

Staten Island Advance. "Elizabeth Connelly Was First Woman Elected on Staten Island." March 26, 2011.

Researcher and author: Beatrice Ramirez, Staten Island Branch

BARBARA CONNOR

1956–
NEPHROLOGIST/EMERGENCY CARE PHYSICIAN

In a shrinking world, the paradigm urging us to live and work locally but act globally takes on a more immediate and powerful meaning. Such an ethic is exemplified by Dr. Barbara Connor, emergency room physician, an altruist both in her community and in the Third World. Barbara lived and worked in Skaneateles and Auburn, New York, for more than twenty years. She now lives and practices medicine in Christ Church, New Zealand. Still, her humanitarianism takes her to some of the poorest, most disadvantaged places in the world.

Barbara Connor, born in 1956 and raised in the suburbs of Detroit, Michigan, didn't need to know that the advent of the women's movement a decade later would further validate her goal to become a doctor. Her sights were always set on becoming a physician as a child. In a family of three children, she was the only girl and sibling to follow the medical career paths of her father (a pediatrician) and her mother (a registered nurse). In high school, she volunteered as a candy striper since this was an excellent opportunity to gain experience in the healthcare field. After graduating from a girls' boarding school, Barbara was accepted at Wellesley College in Massachusetts, the same four-year college from which Hillary Clinton had graduated ten years earlier. Barbara found this unisex education to be very supportive and stimulating. She especially loved and took advantage of the many intellectual and cultural events both on and off campus since her school was so close to Boston. She played the flute with the Massachusetts Institute of Technology student orchestra.

Four years later, with her BS degree, Barbara's application to medical school in Syracuse, New York, was accepted. This was Barbara's first-choice school since her father successfully had completed his studies there. After finishing four years of medical school in 1982, she was well on her way to becoming a physician. She went on to a three-year residency program and another two-year fellowship, with a specialization in nephrology.

By the time she began her professional practice as a nephrologist, she had married and become a mother. Her first son, born in 1987, and a second son, born three years later, caused Dr. Connor to reevaluate her priorities. She recognized that parenting was equally important, if not more so, than her passion for her work. As a specialized physician, her work schedule was too demanding, so she struck a better balance between her work and home life and opted to go into emergency medicine. For twenty-four years, Dr. Connor performed this role at the Auburn Hospital and raised two bright, successful young men, now in college. She also found time to be the president of the world-renowned Skaneateles Chamber Music Festival for three years and was on its board for seven years.

Barbara's devotion to her local professional duties as an emergency care physician has broadened over the past six years, as she has responded to a call to serve others beyond our borders. In 2003, in cooperation with a local church, she offered her expertise to help with the expansion of a mission program in El Salvador. For six years, Barbara joined a team of health professionals delivering basic and preventive healthcare to patients of all ages living in remote, impoverished villages surrounding the capital of San Salvador. One of her young patients, diagnosed with severe rickets, was brought back to Syracuse for six months in order that her badly deformed legs could be operated on and rehabilitated. Today, at age eleven, she can walk normally. Another positive outcome of her service has been the creation of a small, profitable cottage industry, made up of village women who embroider scrubs and send them back to the States to be sold.

Medical outreach work and her love of people and other cultures proved to be such good medicine for Dr. Connor that within a few years she was actively involved in the building and staffing of a new clinic in southern Sudan. With the resettlement of some of the "Lost Boys" of Sudan in her own church, she came to know and be inspired by the vision of John Dau, author of the book *God Grew Tired of Us*. Grateful for the many opportunities he was given to further his studies and better his life, John shared his hope of building a clinic in the area of southern Sudan, where he grew up until he had to flee. It took three years for his dream to become reality with the help of his congregation at the Skaneateles Presbyterian Church and the guidance, input and support of Dr. Connor and her medical team. In March 2009, Barbara made her second trip to the clinic, which had been up and running since 2007. When she is not on the ground there, she maintains contact with the clinic on a regular basis through teleconferencing and solar-powered Intelsat, advising, diagnosing and lending whatever help is needed.

The exhaustion of two full days of travel and sleeping in a tent for two weeks, with only gas-generated power, for two hours during the day, does not deter Barbara from wanting to continue her involvement and support of the clinic. For her, the determination and will of one of her pregnant patients—who walked twelve hours for prenatal care—is reason and reward enough.

The Skaneateles, New York Branch of the American Association of University Women is so proud to have Barbara as one of its many members—a woman making an outstanding mark on the lives of others both locally and globally.

Information obtained from Dr. Barbara Connor by Gail van der Linde, March 2009.

Researcher and author: Gail van der Linde, Skaneateles Branch

EVELYN MEYERS CURRIE

1921–
EDUCATOR/VOLUNTEER

Evelyn Meyers Currie was born on November 21, 1923, in Gloversville, New York. Known to everyone as "Evvie," she has led a very active and productive life. She graduated from Gloversville High School in 1941. Evvie pursued her college education at the University of Rochester and graduated with a Bachelor of Science degree in English in 1945, followed by a Bachelor of Music in voice and music education at the Eastman School of Music in 1946. After graduation, Evvie married Robert R. Currie in 1946, and since he worked for General Electric, they moved to a variety of locations, including Rochester, New York; Pittsfield, Massachusetts; Scotia, New York; and Somers, New York. They raised two children, a son and daughter, with whom they are very close.

Always eager to learn, Evvie continued to pursue her education as a student of Robert Shaw at Tanglewood during the summers of 1947 and

1948. In 1966, she was awarded a master's degree in American studies at Union College and took graduate courses in English at Western Connecticut College in 1977. Evvie taught vocal music and was the choral director at all levels from kindergarten through college during a thirty-year span in New York in Rochester, Schenectady, Ballston Spa, Scotia and Somers, as well as in Detroit, Michigan.

Evvie's motto is found on the calendar she keeps on her desk and in her purse: "God can do tremendous things through the person who doesn't care who gets the credit!" She has spent her life in service to others. With an exceptional work ethic and an ability to organize and lead others, Evvie has been an invaluable contributor to a number of organizations.

Upon retirement, Evvie and her husband settled in Burnt Hills, New York, where Evvie could pursue her interest in a variety of musical/performance opportunities in the Capital District. She is a fifty-year member of the New York State School Music Association and the Music Educators National Conference. Her activities, positions and memberships in groups related to her love for the arts include Saratoga County Arts Council, Place for Jazz, Proctor's Restored Theatre (Schenectady), League of the Schenectady Symphony Orchestra, vice-president of the Schenectady Arts Council, chair of the New York State Arts Decentralization in the Albany-Schenectady and Saratoga areas and Saratoga Performing Arts Center (SPAC), where she is a sponsor and volunteer usher.

In addition, Evvie has been involved in other community groups such as the League of Women Voters, Planned Parenthood, the Burnt Hills Methodist Church, New York State United Teachers and Sunnyview Hospital Auxiliary, and she served as president of the board of managers of the Schenectady Day Nursery. She is a member of a committee of six who serve on the steering committee of the New York State Task Force on Tobacco-free Women and Girls, sponsored by Roswell Cancer Center and the New York State Department of Health. During the months of February and March, she and her husband have also worked as Elderhostel coordinators for the University of South Alabama at the Gulf Shores State Park.

Evelyn has received a number of special recognitions. In 2005, she was honored with the University of Rochester's Reunion Service Award for sixty years of chairing university reunions. In 2005, she was elected to a three-year term on the National Women's Hall of Fame Board in Seneca Falls, New York, and was reelected to another three-year term in 2008. In that same year, she also received the Eastman School of Music Medallion for sixty-two years of support of this school.

Evvie Currie's involvement with the American Association of University Women has been extensive and varied. She is a paid life and honorary life member and has served in a number of capacities. At the local level in various branches in New York and Michigan, she has been program vice-president, recording secretary, hospitality chair, cultural arts chair, Legal Advocacy Fund chair and executive vice-president. She was president of the Schenectady branch from 1994 to 1996 and was named grant honoree of this branch in 1997. At the state level, Evvie has been a member of the Educational Foundation State Committee, a nominating committee chair and cultural interests director on the New York State Board of Directors. She was the state Legal Advocacy Fund director from 1998 to 2002, when New York was recognized for the second-highest Legal Advocacy Fund contribution in the country, $31,423. In 2001, she was presented a Certificate of Appreciation from the American Association of University Women Legal Advocacy Fund Board for her commitment to its mission in the branch, state and community. She was recognized by a special Legal Advocacy Fund named in her honor, the Evvie Currie Giving Circle, to which member contributions could be designated. Evvie served as president of the American Association of University Women New York State from 2002 to 2004, and from 2004 to 2005, she was advisor to the New York State president and chair of the state nominating committee.

Currie, Evelyn. Interview recorded by Gerri Pinkerton and Pam Haller, winter of 2009. Written information was also provided to Pinkerton and Haller around this time.

Researchers and authors: Gerri Pinkerton and Pam Haller, Schenectady Branch

VINNI MARIE D'AMBROSIO

19??–
POET/EDUCATOR

Vinni Marie D'Ambrosio remembered her great-grandmother as a poet, chanting her poems and ballads before a fig tree in her Brooklyn garden while one of her sons strummed a guitar in accompaniment. Vinni's two grandfathers also had a flair for imaginative storytelling and plenty to tell. One had been a prison warden stationed all over Italy (and a swordsman), and the other had been a sailor in his youth whose thumb had been cut off in India in a horrible brawl. Her own father was somewhat literary-minded too, a rhymester at large family Sunday dinners, raising his wine glass in witty couplets to toast each seated diner, even the children. So, of course, she diligently wrote down "poems" in a notebook that she still possesses. With practice, the poems got better and better, and thus her first poems were published in *National Scholastic* magazine when she was thirteen and fourteen. She received her first fan mail as a result, letters from Germany and the Philippines.

In high school, on the first day, she was elected president of her home room. She had no idea why. She soon became editor of the school newspaper, which under her editorship won the Columbia University Journalism Award. She also achieved the highest grade average in the history of the school. She certainly was having fun. The art department gave her a solo exhibition in the faculty room. These things were interesting delights. She was also a cheerleader, though it was not so interesting to her. In her senior year, the dean had her apply for a scholarship at Smith College. The dean warned her that she might find some discrimination at college. "Why?" Vinni asked. The dean told her that it was because she was Italian American, a Roman Catholic and a Brooklynite. This was astounding to her.

At Smith, on the very first day, Vinni found a surprise: a sweet welcoming letter from her high school dean. She had been assigned to live with thirty-four young women in one of the language houses, La Casa Española, and there, in the first week, she was elected house representative for the freshman class. Her love for Spanish had been strong in high school (her grade in the NYS three-year Regents Exam was 100 percent), and the love grew at Smith. But she majored in what most fascinated her: American studies. She minored in the history of art and took as many courses in creative writing as she could. As a junior, she founded a barbershop double quartet that sang in hospitals around the campus for two years. In her senior year, she was elected to Alpha Phi Kappa, a national honorary society for the creative arts.

After graduation, she spent a year as a clerk and storyteller in the New York Public Library. In the parks, during spring and summer, dozens of children would come to hear the "Story Lady." She was offered a fellowship by the New York Public Library to go to Library School at Columbia University, but she decided instead to take on a PhD program at New York University in English and American literature. Meanwhile, she founded and directed the "Sunday Afternoon Poetry Readings" at the Brooklyn Museum, running it for twelve years. (Allen Ginsberg once attracted an audience of five hundred there.) She was at the same time teaching as a full-time instructor at Brooklyn College (lasting for twenty-four years, ending as a full professor); facilitating a poetry workshop in her home (for seven years); playing piano in a Dixieland jazz band (for seven years); and leading "Reading Poetry Aloud," a program at the American Association for University Women (for twenty-five years). She became poet-in-residence at San Diego State University and received two month-long summer fellowships from a writer's colony. She was elected president of two international organizations: Pen and Brush Inc. in Greenwich Village, New York, a 125-year-old society for women in the arts (the first of its kind), and the T.S. Eliot Society, St. Louis, Missouri, because her New York University dissertation subject was T.S. Eliot.

Her involvement with poetry had a strong effect on people. As a teacher for twenty-five years, she regularly had her students buy a paperback anthology of poetry, and she began every class session, no matter what the subject was—drama, short stories, the novel or remedial writing—with a seven-person reading of one poem; the same poem was read seven times! No discussion was required, but usually the students insisted. At the end of each semester, the students would tell her that the one book they would not sell was the anthology and that they found themselves reading from it on the subway. Vinni feels that the same strong influence occurred at the Brooklyn Museum. People opened up to poetry readings there, sometimes in crowds. Newspaper publicity helped. She herself has given more than one hundred poetry readings all over the United States and in Canada—at colleges, libraries, coffee shops and bars, as well as on radio and television.

Vinni brought up a wonderful daughter, Cynthia, who has a wonderful son, St. John, while also becoming a poet, essayist, translator, editor and author of four books, three of them of her poetry: *Life of Touching Mouths* (NYU Press); *Mexican Gothic* (Blue Heron Press, a book with art by Karen Kune, now in worldwide collections, including the Victoria and Albert Museum, London); *An Italian Morning* (Waterside Press); and the fourth book, a cultural study concerning the unexpected influence of Omar Khayyam's *Rubaiyat* on T.S. Eliot (New York University Press). Her poems have won dozens of awards and have appeared in anthologies, journals, textbooks and newspapers in the United States and in translation abroad.

Vinni is a member of the PEN American Center, an active board member of the American Association of University Women of New York City and professor emerita of Brooklyn College of the City University of New York. She is listed in multiple *American Who's Who* books, as well as several *Dictionary of Writers* books. She firmly believes that the arts, through the empathy they invariably invoke in us, have the power to lead to an empathy that spreads far and wide and can help to save the world from wars. A big idea? She says yes.

Information obtained from Vinni Marie D'Ambrosio by Julie Kleszczewski. Vinni Marie D'Ambrosio, PhD. "About the Poet/Scholar." www.vinnimarie. com/index_files/Page4168.htm.

Researcher and author: Julie Harrison Kleszczewski, New York City Branch

SARAH LYON DAVENPORT

1847–1929
VOLUNTEER/PHILANTHROPIST

Sarah Lyon Davenport was born to James and Harriet Robie Lyon on February 19, 1847, in the village of Bath, Steuben County, New York. She had a younger brother, Reuben, and a younger sister, Harriet. The Lyon and Robie families were wealthy and influential members of the community, having helped in the early development of Bath, carved out of the wilderness in 1793. Her grandfathers and father were the original entrepreneurs, dealing in real estate, holding positions as village president, bank manager and postmaster and helping to found the library, the churches and the Steuben County Agricultural Fair. They are memorialized in Bath by Lyon and Robie Streets.

Sarah's mother was said to have had a fulfilling life in her home, family and church, enjoying many friendships, but we know very little of Sarah's personal life. In 1879, at age thirty-two, she married John Davenport, who was forty-four. The Davenports were even more wealthy and influential than the Lyons and Robies, and John and his brother, Ira Jr., ran the widespread family business. After a world-tour honeymoon, John and Sarah resided in the forty-eight-room family mansion, Riverside, with Senator Ira Davenport Jr. Sarah was soon appointed a trustee of the Davenport Home for Orphan Girls, founded by Ira Davenport Sr. and supported by the family.

It is not known when her dedication to causes began, but her public interest became evident with membership on the State Charities Aid Association in

1884 (Resolution 1). In 1895, Sarah Davenport was appointed by Governor Morton to the Prison Commission and was perhaps the first woman to hold such an office. She was dedicated to ensuring humane treatment and decent accommodations for all prisoners. When the Prison Commission was reorganized to become the State Commission of Correction, she was again appointed and then reappointed every year until her death. She was a member of the Steuben County Board of Child Welfare, the National Association for the Study and Relief of Epilepsy, the Commission for the Care of the Insane, the Willard State Hospital Board of Visitors and the American Prison Association.

After John Davenport died in 1895, Sarah purchased a large brick residence on Haverling Street and became an arbor enthusiast, filling the eight acres with trees and shrubs from around the world. When she traveled abroad, taking her car, chauffeur and other staff, they would return with plants and cuttings for her estate, named Eight Acres.

Sarah continued her many interests and was also an active member in the Baron Steuben Chapter of the Daughters of the American Revolution, the National Society of the Daughters of Founders and Patriots and the American Scenic and Historical Preservations Society. In 1917, she became an organizer, board member and benefactor of the Bath Chapter of the American Red Cross. Her philanthropy and kindnesses were legendary. She was known as the "Grand Old Lady of Steuben County."

When Sarah died in 1929 at age eighty-four, the *Steuben Courier* reported, "Her activities and influence were state-wide, her home was the center of many organization functions and her passing has caused universal sorrow in our village." In 2005, Sarah Lyon Davenport was inducted into the Steuben County Hall of Fame.

Steuben County legislature. "Presentation of the Names of Persons Selected for Induction into the Steuben County Hall of Fame and Confirmation by the Steuben County Legislature." Archives of the Steuben County Historical Society, Magee House, Bath, New York, 2005.

Treichler, Martha. "Sarah Lyon Davenport." *Crooked Lake Review* (Spring 2004): 43–47.

Researcher and author: Mary E. (Betty) Langendorfer, Bath Branch

VIRGINIA OLIVER DEAN

1896–1989
EDUCATOR/COMMUNITY LEADER

Educator, school administrator, voracious reader, world traveler, feminist, volunteer and philanthropist are just some of the words used to describe Virginia Dean.

She was born on April 9, 1896, in Oswego, New York, the only child of Charles and Margaret Oliver Dean, who were prominent members of the community. After attending local schools, she went to Wells College in Aurora, New York, and graduated with a Bachelor of Arts degree in 1917. Later she earned her Master of Arts degree, with election to Phi Beta Kappa, from Syracuse University.

Dean began her career as a Latin teacher at Oswego High School in 1917, and in 1940, she became principal of Fitzhugh Park School (elementary and junior high combined) and director of Junior High and Elementary Education for the district. Former colleagues and students have fond memories of this remarkable woman as a very good teacher and administrator who was bright, professional and fair-minded. She retired in 1959 after serving in a variety of positions with the Oswego School District for forty-two years. During that time, her top priority was devotion to the schools.

A constant student, Dean traveled extensively throughout six continents and made friends all over the world. When 982 refugees of the Holocaust were housed at Fort Ontario in Oswego between 1944 and 1946, 60 of them were students in Fitzhugh Park School. She commented that she was glad that she had been to Europe and could understand some of their customs.

An avid volunteer in the Oswego community, she served twice as chairman of the Women's Division of the Community Chest. She also was a member of the American Red Cross Board of Directors and spent fifty years volunteering at Oswego Hospital as a member of the Women's Auxiliary. Other memberships included those in the Women's City Club, Zonta International, Women's Civic Council, the Westminster Club of the Presbyterian Church and the American Association of University Women (AAUW). In the Oswego Branch of AAUW, she was chair of the local student loan fund for twenty-five years and was honored in 1967 by the branch when a monetary gift was presented to the National Fellowship program in her name. She played tournament bridge and was a life master in the American Contract Bridge League. Honors include a listing in *Who's Who of American Women* and the Zonta Club Award as Outstanding Woman of the Year in 1975.

As an educator with great vision, she left a sizeable donation in her will to the Oswego Public Library and other community organizations, and so her legacy continues.

Dean, Virginia. Personal interview recorded by Lawrence Baron, November 19, 1983, Oswego County Oral History Program.
Fulton (NY) Valley News. Obituary of Virginia O. Dean. June 22, 1989.
Oswego Palladium-Times. "Zonta Club of Oswego Honors Retired Educator." August 25, 1975.
"Virginia Dean Legacy Leaves Indelible Mark on Oswego Community and Oswego Public Library." Unpublished document in the archives of the Oswego Public Library, Oswego, New York.

Researcher and author: Marilynn J. Smiley, Oswego Branch

KAREN DECROW

1937–
WOMEN'S RIGHTS ACTIVIST/ATTORNEY/LECTURER/AUTHOR

Karen DeCrow was born on December 18, 1937, in Chicago, Illinois. She went to Northwestern University and later moved to Syracuse, New York. She became a writer and editor for a New York City publishing company.

At age thirty-two, she attended Syracuse University School of Law. In her first year at law school, she was the first woman to run for mayor in Syracuse. She became a nationally recognized attorney, author and lecturer and one of the most celebrated leaders of women's movements. From 1974 to 1977, she served as the national president of the National Organization for Women (NOW), for which she was instrumental in obtaining significant legislative and legal gains for women. She timelessly advocated on behalf of the Equal Rights Amendment (ERA).

Karen became a worldwide lecturer on such topics as law, gender and equality. She wrote several books, including *The Young Women's Guide to Liberation, Sexist Justice* and *Women Who Marry Houses: Panic and Protest in*

Agoraphobia. She has written several articles that appeared in the *New York Times*, *Los Angeles Times* and *Washington Post.*

As a lawyer, she has specialized in constitutional cases and fought for civil liberties law. She has taken on gender and age discrimination cases. The equal rights act gave a foothold to a movement that was already gaining strength. When she was a young woman, most American careers were all but closed to women. They rarely became engineers, doctors, lawyers, politicians or CEOs. A young girl could aspire to become a teacher, a nurse or a clerk but not much else.

After abortion became legal in New York State in 1970, she spent time escorting women who came to New York for abortions. She was also cofounder of the World Women's Watch in 1988.

On the day of her induction into the Women's Hall of Fame in Seneca Falls, New York, on October 10, 2009, she received a standing ovation after her speech. Her plaque was on the wall with such other known women as Hillary Clinton, Sandra Day O'Connor, Betty Friedan and many other well-known women. She said, "I was familiar with them, but now they are my peers." The Women's Hall of Fame is the oldest organization dedicated to honoring and celebrating the achievements of American women. Seneca Falls is the birthplace of the American women's rights movement. It's the site of the first known women's rights convention, held in 1848.

DeCrow now resides in the town of Pompey, New York, about thirteen miles from Syracuse, and has a private law practice.

About.com—Women's History. "Karen DeCrow." http://womenshistory. about.com/od/second-wave-feminists/a/Karen-DeCrow.htm.

DeCrow, Karen. "Feminism Lives!" *Post-Standard*, March 28, 2010.

Kirst, Sean. "The Transformed World of Karen DeCrow: A Girl Can Dream of Anything." *Post-Standard*, October 12, 2009.

National Women's Hall of Fame. "Karen DeCrow." www.greatwomen.org/ women-of-the-hall/search-the-hall-results/details/2/229-DeCrow.

Researcher and author: M. Edwina Norton, Syracuse Branch

CORINNE DiSOMMA

1957–
PUBLIC SERVICE/VOLUNTEER

Corinne DiSomma has been a lifetime resident of the town of Babylon, and since 1999, she has been the town of Babylon receiver of taxes.

Ms. DiSomma graduated from the Lindenhurst Senior High School with a regent diploma, and while working as a secretary, she earned enough money to pay for her own college education. She received a degree in business administration from Suffolk Community College. Ms. DiSomma was also able to get her real estate certificate.

She was already interested in local politics as a young woman. Ms. DiSomma was interviewed for the deputy tax receiver's position in 1978, beginning a career in public service to her community that continues to the present day. In 1999, she made her first run for an elected position and won a landslide victory for receiver of taxes, running unopposed ever since. As receiver of taxes, she has instituted many programs to increase efficiency and streamline services, including a method by which taxpayers can use their credit cards to pay their taxes.

Ms. DiSomma is involved in many professional affiliations, such as the New York State Tax Receivers and Collectors Association, the New York State Government Finance Officers' Association (NYS GFOA), the Lindenhurst Kiwanis Club and the Suffolk County Girl Scout Council, as well as being secretary treasurer of the Babylon Conservative Club, to mention just a few.

During Ms. DiSomma's many years of public service, she has been involved in many volunteer activities, such as the Great New York Read Aloud Program, the Babylon Breast Cancer Walk-a-Thon, the Suffolk County Bay Scout Council Phone-a-Thon, West Babylon Parent-Teacher Association fundraisers, the Muscular Dystrophy Association's Shining Star program and so on. Ms. DiSomma also volunteered to participate in the America Association of University Women Islip Branch's program on women in government, where she was well received.

Corinne DiSomma, during her many years of public service, has been the recipient of numerous awards and recognitions, including the West Babylon

Athletic Club Woman of the Year Award, the Gertrude Van Kirk Woman in Government Award and, in 2007, the New York State Women of Distinction Award by the New York State Senate.

Ms. DiSomma is married and has two children.

Town of Babylon. Elected Officials—Tax Receiver. www.townofbabylon. com/electedofficials.cfm?cid=7.
Town of Babylon publications, various.

Author: Marlene Cvetkovic, Islip Area Branch

CAROLYN JOSLIN DONOVAN

1939–
VOLUNTEER

Carolyn Joslin Donovan was born in 1939 in Newton, Massachusetts, into a family with a long tradition of concern for the welfare of others. Her grandfather and father were internationally known in the medical field. Her mother was active in the community. By her teen years, Donovan had established her activist priorities through chairing the student Social Welfare Committee and attending the Model United Nations as a delegate. In 1956–57, the Joslin family welcomed Barbel Sohr, a German (American Field Service) student into their home. The girls became close friends, and the relationship sparked Donovan's interest in foreign languages and culture. During her undergraduate years at Vassar, she majored in German and French; subsequently, she earned a master's degree in German literature and a master's degree in curriculum at Virginia Polytechnic Institute and State University. Marriage to Arthur Donovan, a history of science professor, introduced her to faculty life at several American universities. At the same time, she continued to pursue her career, teaching German, French and English as a Second Language.

The many strands of Donovan's personal and professional values and skills have culminated in a unique and remarkable leadership style. As a member of AAUW since 1980 and president of the North Shore, Long Island Branch (1997–98), she has been unassuming and gracious, welcoming of divergent opinions and positions yet clear and firm in moving discussions and projects forward productively. As president, she increased the membership of minority women, encouraged men to join and helped to organize the North Shore Branch's 1998 conference, titled "Women and Girls Worldwide; What Happened Since Beijing, 1995." The conference featured a "Showcase of Action." Besides her leadership in the North Shore Branch, Donovan has served AAUW at the state and national levels.

Donovan's commitment to social justice and women's rights found a new focus in 2000 when she became AAUW's representative to the United Nations. In that capacity, she served as a member of the association's International Affairs Committee and was an AAUW delegate to the International Federation of University Women (IFUW) Triennial held in Perth, Australia, in 2004.

When Donovan's work at the UN introduced her to Martha Beck of Yaounde, Cameroon, a new and exciting partnership was created. Together, the two women raised funds and made contacts to support girls' education and women's political rights and teach about the UN in Cameroon. A key project was the training of urban Muslim girls for employment as health aides and seamstresses. The resulting income enabled the girls to stay in school rather than drop out to raise dowry money.

In 2007, the United Nations Commission on the Status of Women had as its main theme ending discrimination and violence against girls. For Donovan, who was serving as vice-chair of the Working Group on Girls (WGG) of the UNICEF NGO advisory committee, it was the "Year of the Girl." The group's goal was to ensure that governments implement commitments to young women made through international declarations and conventions, such as the Beijing platform for women. Donovan's work entailed urging many of the ninety NGOs involved to register young women as delegates. These girls identified issues of discrimination and violence that they wanted their governments to address more vigorously, lobbied during meetings and returned home as advocates for making girls visible in their own communities and nations.

Donovan serves as a member of the Steering Committee of the WGG and oversees communications and publications. One of the group's slogans, "Today's Girl Is Tomorrow's Woman...Don't Leave Her Behind," acknowledges "the central truth and challenge facing the group—that without educational opportunities and equal rights for girls, the next generation of women will continue to suffer political and economic discrimination, and their societies will squander the potential of half their populations." Thus, lobbying for inclusion of girls' rights in the work of the UN is crucial.

In 2006, Beaver County Day School recognized Donovan as one of its outstanding alumnae with a Social Responsibility Award for her efforts at the UN. In an interview for the school magazine, she explained her personal philosophy of moderating political activism with patient understanding:

> *Some would find the political complexity and glacial pace of working within the U.N.'s channels frustrating and discouraging, but not Donovan, who manages to remain hopeful and to see incremental progress. She describes herself as "very process-oriented"—a likely result of Beaver's progressive approach to learning—and says this trait is essential in her work. As Donovan points out, "Americans are used to a responsive government. Our democratically-elected senators and congressmen are forced to listen to their constituents. That's not true in many other countries. Although the U.N.'s 60th General Assembly recently adopted the girl-child resolution, some governments cannot sign on because their laws cannot be changed." Those that do sign on are monitored by non-governmental organizations like the AAUW and must report to the U.N. every four years on their progress.*
>
> *As an example of the unfinished battle, Donovan points out that it has been more than a quarter of a century since the U.N. adopted the Convention of the Elimination of All Forms of Discrimination Against Women (CEDAW), often described as an international bill of rights for women. "The basic human rights, including property rights and health rights, that American women take for granted are those that women in other countries are still fighting for," Donovan stresses. Her role at the AAUW is to press governments to keep their promises to women by passing laws that ban early marriage, sexual harassment, and sex-trafficking, and that give women access to public education, family benefits and fair wages.*

Beaver Country Day School magazine (Spring 2006): 26.

Interviews with the following AAUW members: Catherine Ellison Moore, president, North Shore Branch, 2004–6, currently IFUW representative to the UN; Diane Dutton Haney, president, North Shore Branch, 2000–2002, and president, New York State AAUW, 2006–8; Carolyn Lippmann, secretary, North Shore Branch.

Researcher and author: Trudy Ruchman, North Shore Branch

CRYSTAL EASTMAN

1881–1928
FEMINIST/LAWYER

Crystal Eastman was born in Marlboro, Massachusetts, on June 25, 1881. Her family lived in Elmira, New York, from 1889 until 1894. For two of those years, the family lived in Park Church. The living quarters are now used as Sunday school rooms.

Annis Eastman, Crystal's mother, fostered her daughter's feminism at an early age. As a matter of fact, both parents nurtured Crystal's independence. When she was fifteen, Crystal attended a summer symposium, organized by her mother. She composed and read a paper at this meeting "because the only way to be happy is to have an absorbing interest in life which is not bound up with any particular person. No woman who allows husband and children to absorb her whole time and interest is safe against disaster."

She graduated from Vassar in 1903 and returned to teach at Elmira Free Academy for a short time. She received her master's degree in sociology from Columbia University. Crystal then graduated second in her class at the New York City University School of Law in 1907.

New York State governor Charles Hughes appointed her to a commission studying industrial accidents, unemployment and farm labor. At this time, Crystal drafted the nation's first workers' compensation law. Crystal was a very progressive thinker; she wrote and spoke concerning the results of death or serious injury to a husband on the job. These often left widows and children with no or very little income.

In 1913, she along with Alice Paul and Lucy Burns formed the Congressional Union for Women Suffrage. They organized demonstrations and daily picketing of the White House. Many women were arrested for loitering.

A very independent woman, Crystal divorced her first husband in 1915 and refused alimony. She said that alimony was "nothing less than an admission of financial dependency on men."

She and Emma Goldman worked diligently to advance the concept of birth control and legalize abortion and free speech during war times. During this time, 1919–21, due to the "Red Scare," they were "classified as enemies of America and came under surveillance of the newly formed FBI. Crystal and many other prominent women were blacklisted."

She became an advocate of civil liberties and promoted the right of dissenters and conscientious objectors. She also helped establish the National

Civil Liberties Bureau in 1917. In 1919, Crystal organized the First Feminist Congress. She also founded the U.S. Woman's Peace Party. Jane Addams was the national president, and Crystal was the leader of the radical New York branch. In 1921, the party was renamed the Women's International League for Peace and Freedom, which today is the nation's oldest women's peace organization.

Crystal was one of the Equal Rights Amendment's four authors. This amendment was introduced first in 1923. She said of this amendment, "This is a fight worth fighting even if it takes ten years." Little did she know how long the fight would take.

A woman decades ahead of her time, Crystal died in 1928 in Erie, Pennsylvania. A quote from her obituary reads, "She was for thousands a symbol of what the free woman might be."

Britannica Online Encyclopedia, "Crystal Eastman." www.britannica.com/EBchecked/topic/177433/Crystal-Eastman.

Byrne, Thomas E. *Chemung County, 1890–1975*. Elmira, NY: Chemung County Historical Society, 1976.

Elmira Star-Gazette, miscellaneous articles.

Spartacus Educational. "Crystal Eastman." www.spartacus.schoolnet.co.uk/USAWeastman.htm.

Researcher and author: June Ford, Elmira-Corning Branch

SUSAN ECKERS

1942–
EDUCATOR/VOLUNTEER

Although I was born in Yonkers, I never really lived there. My parents were living in the Bronx. When I was about a year old, we moved to Hollywood. My mother realized this was not a place she wanted to live, and so we moved back to New York. Since my mother grew up in Manhattan, her mother had a summer place in a village called Sea Cliff.

As far as I am concerned, Sea Cliff is where I began, as I have no memories of life before Sea Cliff. I started school at the Sea Cliff school (a kindergarten through twelfth-grade building). Just after beginning second grade, we moved into a house in the neighboring town of Glen Head. Little did I know that by the time I entered seventh grade that the three communities Sea Cliff, Glen Head and Glenwood Landing would merge into one school district, and I would go back to Sea Cliff school for eighth and ninth grades, on split session no less. When I entered tenth grade, the new North Shore High School was close enough to completion that we could begin school there.

Our consolidation experience was unique in that we chose our school colors, maroon and white; wrote a new school song; and came up with the nickname for our teams, the Vikings, and our yearbook, the *Talieson*. It really made the early student body feel a certain connection to this school. I graduated from North Shore High School in Glen Head, New York. From this little town I went to the big city. I was lucky enough to gain admittance to both New York University and admittance to the women's housing right on Washington Square in Greenwich Village.

My course of study was to become a teacher of Industrial Arts or shop. I was perfectly happy with this choice, even though it meant I was one of two females in a class of about thirty males. Not only did I learn in my classes, but I also learned a lot about living on my own. After all, I had New York City as my campus.

While at New York University, I got in a part-time job at the student center doing lighting for the building. Our crew was involved not only in doing lighting for the drama department but also in any shows that were put on in the building. This included professional entertainers who came to perform, art shows, fashion shows, poetry readings, etc. I also joined the amateur radio club, did engineering for the school radio station and for one year was on the swim team as a diver. While I was on the swim team, I discovered that there was a bowling team and switched to that team for my junior and senior years.

After graduation, I began my career as a teacher. In 1965, Industrial Arts was taken by the boys only. I was the only female shop teacher that I knew of in Nassau or Suffolk Counties.

In the spring of 1965, I married Steve Eckers, a classmate from the Industrial Arts program at New York University.

My second year of teaching found me in a different school system, where I stayed for four years and achieved tenure. Parents were shocked when they came to open school and found out that their son had a female shop teacher.

What was even more surprising was that this was their sons' second year with me. The boys just took it in stride and never bothered to tell their parents. I then left teaching with the intention to start a family.

Before I could do that, I had an opportunity to get a job at an outdoor museum, Old Bethpage Restoration Village (OBVR). My job was to demonstrate cooking in a fireplace and interpret village life of the mid-nineteenth century. It was through my job at OBVR that I learned of the existence of a group of antique tool collectors. That started my involvement in the Early Trades and Crafts Society. I left OBVR after the birth of my second daughter.

During my time as a "stay at home mom," I always seemed to find some way of earning "babysitter" money. For a while, I was the secretary of the bowling league, and I taught an after school elementary woodworking class. Then I got a job as an office manager for the local locksmith shop, an ideal position for me. I could make my own hours. If I needed to be home for the girls, I could. This job lasted until my older daughter graduated from high school.

I soon found a job as an assistant bookkeeper. After about two years, I switched to another company, where I was accounting clerk. That job didn't work for me, so I quit and signed up with an accounting firm to take temporary assignments. I did very well; all my one- or two-week jobs turned into three- and four-week assignments.

Then I was discovered to be very ill with heart disease. After a triple bypass operation, I returned to the last company I worked for as a temporary worker. As I finished that assignment, my husband mentioned that his school was short of substitute teachers. Since I had a valid teachers license, I offered to help them out. I was so happy doing sub work, and they were so happy with me that I continued as a substitute teacher until my retirement in 2002. After retirement from teaching, we both became judges with the Odyssey of the Mind competition at the local level. Since then, we have judged at the state level and at the international level.

I continued my involvement with Girl Scouts even after both my daughters graduated. Now I am the historian for the Girl Scouts of Suffolk County, head the history committee for Girl Scouts of Suffolk County, am a member of the local service unit team and maintain their website (serviceunitone.org). Girl Scouts will be celebrating their hundredth year on March 12, 2012. I will be involved in many ways as head of our PATH (the history committee).

As a coronary bypass patient, I am a resource for others going through the procedure.

In addition, I also volunteer with the Huntington Lighthouse Preservation Society and the Huntington Historical Society. In 2010, I worked with a committee for our fiftieth high school reunion, which was a *huge* success. After our reunion, we self-published a soft-covered book called *Class of 1960, 50 Years Later*. It has been well received by my classmates.

Susan Eckers's 2011 autobiography.

GERTRUDE ELION

1918–1999
SCIENTIST/INVENTOR

Gertrude Elion was a female inventor. She was one of only ten women awarded a Nobel Prize when she received hers in 1988 for medicine. She was also one of very few to receive this honor without a doctorate. In 1944, she was the first woman to be inducted into the National Inventors Hall of Fame.

Gertrude's interest in science and specifically cancer research centered on her beloved grandfather. His painful death from cancer when she was only fifteen led to her career choice. Together with her research partner Dr. George Hitchings, they developed drugs that fight childhood leukemia. She has received more than forty patents for her inventions. She also invented a drug that makes it possible to have kidney transplants between unrelated donors; the drug known as AZT, which helps AIDS patients; and a drug that relieves the side effects of chemotherapy.

Gertrude entered Hunter College in New York City in 1933 at age fifteen and graduated with highest honors in 1937. Without any financial aid, she was not able to attend graduate school. She decided to stay in New York, work as a teacher and get a degree in chemistry. After saving some money, she was able to attend graduate school at New York University in the fall of 1939. She obtained her Master of Science degree there in chemistry in 1941. Although she was unable to complete her doctoral studies at the Brooklyn Polytechnic Institute, she later received several honorary degrees. During World War II, when male chemists were in the war, she was able to work in a laboratory and achieve the successes already mentioned.

Gertrude Elion died on February 21, 1999, in Chapel Hill, North Carolina.

Altman, Lawrence K. "Gertrude Elion, Drug Developer, Dies at 81." Wellesley College, February 23, 1999. www.wellesley.edu/Chemistry/chem227/news/obit-elion.html.

Energy Quest. "Super Scientists: Gertrude Elion," 2006. www.energyquest.ca.gov/scientists/elion.html.

Nobelprize.org. "Autobiography." www.nobelprize.org/nobel_prizes/medicine/laureates/1988/elion.html.

Researcher and author: Marion Mahoney, Islip Area Branch

MARIA L. ELLIS

1949–
BUSINESS/VOLUNTEER

Maria L. Ellis is a graduate of the Harvard Business School Owner-President Management Program, and she has a bachelor's degree in business administration and a master's in business administration from the University of Massachusetts–Amherst. Maria worked at a variety of financial institutions, including Bank of America, Citibank, the MONY Group and Northwestern Mutual. Throughout her twenty years of career experience in advising and counseling investment clients, she has become highly skilled in understanding and interpreting clients' specific real estate needs and objectives, as well as the substantial impact this has on their financial well-being and lifestyle. As a former investment advisor and financial planner, she has specialized in converting client needs and objectives into successful action plans.

Having sensitivity to one's needs and the financial tools to identify the right deal is not enough though. It takes a seasoned negotiator and deal closer to deliver the results that one expects and deserves for such lifestyle- and wealth-affecting transactions. Maria has successfully negotiated dozens of high-stakes transactions—ranging from medium income to the high seven figures—and she knows what it takes to close a win-win deal for both individuals and corporations. Additionally, through Citi-Habitats Relocation Services, Maria can offer additional specialized services through Settling-In Services and Citi-Furnished. She also has exclusive relationships with Manhattan's apartment landlords.

Maria's background includes leadership in many charitable causes, community activities and social events. She received the Woman of the Future Award, sponsored by the American Association of University Women and the New York Women's Agenda. Maria currently serves on the following nonprofit advisory boards: the Virginia Gildersleeve International Fund, a leading authority on small grant funding to empower women and girls in developing countries (vgif.org); the College of Mount Saint Vincent, which offers excellent academic and professional programs to more than 1,800 undergraduate and graduate students (mountsaintvincent.edu/about. php); the American Association of University Women of New York State, which advances equity for women and girls through advocacy, education, philanthropy and research (aauw.org); and the Real Estate Academic Initiative at Harvard University (REAI), an interfaculty interdisciplinary program focused on real estate research and education across the University. REAI is overseen by the Office of the Provost and is led by a Core Faculty Committee representing five Harvard schools: the Graduate School of Design, the Faculty of Arts and Sciences, the Kennedy School of Government, the Harvard Law School and the Harvard Business School (reai.harvard.edu).

Maria L. Ellis's 2011 autobiography. North Shore Branch, Westchester Branch.

KAY ERWOO

1936–
EDUCATOR/VOLUNTEER

Kay Erwoo was involved with St. Mark's Church from childhood on. At age nine, she was inducted into the Rummage Sale as a volunteer helper. Of course, her mother and her sister,

Gloria, were already leading Rummage chairman and hard workers. This followed for the rest of her life in every way—choir, Sunday school teacher, Episcopal Church Women, warm accessories for Outreach for January and so on. Chair of this or that, she's still at it—a loving volunteer life.

Kay joined the Islip Chamber of Commerce as a resident member in about 1975 and helped with every community project, was chairman of the 1983 reenactment of the Town of Islip Tercentenary Celebration, was chairman of the Main Street Mural in 1987, spent twenty-five years on the board of directors, worked on beautification flower boxes and so on.

Kay became a teacher assistant in the reading department in 1974 at Commack Road Elementary School. She had a wonderful experience there and started many programs in the reading room and throughout the school. A well-known activity was pairing up the school's reading children with folks in the Little Flower Nursing Home. They bonded with these folks, and there was a free bus that often took those involved for a morning visit. The kids made easy games to play out of oatmeal containers, and there were large-print books the children would read to their friends. They went all year but never at the holidays, for there were plenty of Scouts and such at that time. It was a huge success. Kay was the first person in the entire district to receive the Pride of Islip Award, and I believe that this heartwarming project was the reason.

Kay began the Beatrix Potter Author Study and High Tea program after a worrisome student told her that his grandmother, with whom he was living, wouldn't make him a cup of tea after school. He was a heartbreaking youngster, so began the tea program after reading about Potter's life and her lovely books. Every staff member wanted to be included in these festive tea parties. Kay was blessed in her twenty-five years to have had the best principals. Whatever she would suggest, they would say, "Just do it!"

After seventeen years, Kay moved up to the Islip Middle School when reading monies ran out. She was positioned in the library, which was a joy. There Kay began a Read-a-Thon. She had so many friends in the chamber and all over town that she invited to come with certain favorite authors, books or poems. The students were split into groups of fourteen, and each guest sat with his or her kids for about thirty minutes. They then had refreshments with all the guests throughout the huge library. It was a blast.

Having visited Islip, England, and made lifelong friends, Kay decided that it would be a great idea to create a "friends across the sea" program. The Islip to Islip Pen Pal Program was born. She began with a group that was matched up, and the American kids had pen pals in Islip England. That also worked out splendidly.

A fun program that Kay also began at the middle school was called Lunchtime Lectures. The principal loved this one, too. Every Tuesday, the sixth graders would bring their lunch to the library, and she would have a different speaker each week from every walk of life or experience. As speakers, she had politicians, rotary exchange members, veterans, a fireman, a health food store owner, a local fishing industry representative, older residents, the postmaster, town board members, female lawyers, nurses, collectors, artists, historians, a *Titanic* movie actor, photographers and so on.

Around this time, Kay was notified that her name along with Charles Webster had been tapped to become Keep Islip Clean commissioners. It would be a spinoff of Keep America Beautiful. Kay has been a commissioner for twenty-one years, working on every Earth Day, cleaning up and restoring Islip Beach, removing graffiti, recycling and so on. The program is now being carried on all these many years later very successfully. Kay's dream came true for now there is an Islip High School KIC Club to which the students can move up.

Kay is a charter member of and on the board of directors for the Historical Society of Islip Hamlet. The members are working for the enlightenment of Islip Hamlet's history. It involves collecting artifacts and helping with fundraisers.

She has been a Seatuck environmental volunteer from the beginning and would volunteer over at the Webster estate early on. Kay had a Beatrix Potter Tea for children in October 2010 at the New Suffolk Environmental Park on South Bay Avenue (the Seatuck/Scully Center). Potter was an environmentalist and naturalist all of her life. Kay is also a member of the Islip School District's Standards of Excellence committee and a member of the district's Community Council. Her favorite volunteer work comes on Mondays at the thrift shop. She almost never misses the day. Kay is involved with Suffolk Literacy, which does very worthwhile work. She was a spokesman for the organization at the volunteer program she puts on at West Islip Library.

She was selected a few years ago to be the Suffolk County Woman of Distinction from the entire Suffolk County area. She also received the Islip Town Women's History Month Award.

Mostly she is wife, mother, grandmother, sister and daughter. Kay says that she is best at these jobs.

Information obtained from Kay Erwoo, 2010.

Researcher and author: Nancy Mion, Islip Area Branch

JOANN FALLETTA

1954–
ORCHESTRA CONDUCTOR/CLASSICAL MUSICIAN

When JoAnn Falletta was hired by the Buffalo Philharmonic Orchestra in 1998, she became the first woman to serve as the music director of a major symphony orchestra.

Born in 1954 in Queens, New York, she was taken regularly by her parents to concerts in New York City. The gift of a guitar for her eighth birthday sparked her musical ambitions. Being intrigued with the person on the podium at the concerts she attended, she decided at age ten to become a conductor. She began her musical career as a guitar virtuoso and mandolin player, and as a teenager, she was often called on to perform with the Metropolitan Opera and the New York Philharmonic when a work required a mandolin or guitar obbligato.

In 1972, she began studying classical guitar at the Mannes School of Music, and despite the school's doubts about a female conductor, she was allowed to study conducting for her undergraduate degree (BM). Falletta pursued further study in orchestral conducting at Queens College (MA) and in 1989 became the first woman to earn a doctorate in conducting from the Juilliard School of Music (MM and DMA). She studied conducting with Jorge Mester, Semyon Bychkov, Sixten Ehrling and others, including master classes with Leonard Bernstein.

JoAnn Falletta has served as associate conductor of the Milwaukee Symphony Orchestra (1985–88) and as music director of the Queens Philharmonic Orchestra (1978–88); the Denver Chamber Orchestra (1983–92); the Women's Philharmonic in San Francisco (formerly the Bay Area Women's Philharmonic, 1986–96); the Long Beach, California Symphony Orchestra (1989–2001); the Virginia Symphony Orchestra (1991–); and the Buffalo Philharmonic Orchestra (1998–). She is acclaimed as one of the finest directors of her generation.

During her tenure at Buffalo, she has brought the Philharmonic to a new level of national and international prominence. Besides programming the traditional orchestral repertoire, she has branched out by also selecting artistically important but seldom-heard works by contemporary composers from various countries, American composers and female composers. Under her leadership, the Buffalo Philharmonic has made an unprecedented number of highly acclaimed recordings, resulting in several Grammy Awards and a contract with Naxos, a major commercial recording company. The orchestra has also taken tours and made frequent radio broadcasts on National Public Radio and internationally throughout the European Broadcasting Union.

Under her direction since 1971, the Virginia Symphony Orchestra has been recognized as one of the nation's leading regional orchestras. She has scheduled world premieres, broadcasts on National Public Radio, recordings and performances at the Kennedy Center and New York's Carnegie Hall.

As an internationally known director, she has been invited to conduct orchestras throughout the United States, Europe, Central and South America, Asia and Africa and to participate in many music festivals (Tanglewood, Interlochen and Brevard, to name a few). Some of her honors have included the Seaver/National Endowment for the Arts Conductors Award; the Stokowski Competition; the Toscanini, Ditsori and Bruno Walter Awards for conducting; and awards from the American Symphony Orchestra League and the American Society of Composers, Authors and Publishers (ASCAP). The president of the United States appointed her to the National Council on the Arts. The JoAnn Falletta International Guitar Concerto Competition has brought international attention to the classical guitar and to Buffalo, and she has received recognition by becoming a member of the Western New York Women's Hall of Fame and as an advocate of female composers.

Falletta has made history as a conductor through the exceptional quality of her work, charisma, choice of repertoire, world premieres, innovative programming and promotion of her orchestras through concerts, recordings, broadcasts and tours.

Barber, Charles, and Jose Bowen. "Falletta, JoAnn." *The New Grove Dictionary of Music and Musicians*. 2nd ed. Edited by Stanley Sadie. Oxford, NY: Oxford University Press, 2001.

Buffalo Philharmonic Orchestra. "Music Director: JoAnn Falletta." www. bpo.org/meet/director.php.

Burns, Kristine H., ed. *Women and Music in America Since 1900: An Encyclopedia*. Westport, CT: Greenwood Press, 2002.

Lecky, Karen S. "Women Conductors: A New Phenomenon?" A Senior Honors Project. Rollins College, Winter Park, Florida, 2007.

Lee, Raya, and Edward Yadzinski. *Buffalo Philharmonic Orchestra: The BPO Celebrates the First 75 Years*. Buffalo, NY: Buffalo Heritage Unlimited, 2010.

Twenty Seasons, Twenty Vignettes: Behind the Scenes with JoAnn Falletta and the Virginia Symphony. Norfolk, VA: Signature Printing, 2011.

Researcher and author: Marilynn J. Smiley, Oswego Branch

GINNY FIELDS

1946–
LEGISLATOR/ASSEMBLYWOMAN/ENVIRONMENTALIST

Ginny Fields, a Democrat, was a NYS assemblywoman who represented the Fifth Assembly District on Long Island. She was elected to the Assembly in a special election on March 9, 2004, and served until she was defeated in the election of November 2, 2010.

Ginny Fields was first elected to the Suffolk County legislature in November 1999 and served two terms. As a county legislator, she voted to save Suffolk taxpayers $115 million and authored legislation directing Suffolk County to complete the Smart Growth Master Plan. A strong, civic-minded leader, Fields cofounded the Oakdale Civic Association and served on the Sayville Chamber of Commerce Board of Directors.

Fields was committed to providing children with the education they will need to compete for the best jobs. A mother of two sons, a former PTA member and a Cub Scout den mother, Fields advocated for more state aid for local schools, for increased parental involvement and for keeping college affordable.

She is the former chair of the Suffolk County legislature's Health Committee. She also enjoyed a thirty-seven-year career as a healthcare administrator. She was concerned with many aspects of governmental involvement in healthcare.

Involved in her community, Ginny Fields worked as a grass-roots leader and activist for many years. As an environmentalist, she has been concerned with wetlands, habitat and open space and served as president of the Great South Bay Audubon Society. In 1999, she championed the acquisition by the State of New York of Benton Bay, comprising 127 acres of wetland, after working for ten years to facilitate preservation of the parcel.

Fields ran for Town of Islip supervisor in 2003 but lost. However, the winner's quote that appeared in local newspapers calling her a "bimbo" caused the American Association of University Women and other organizations to rally to defend her and other women in government. She won the next election.

Fields took a stand against higher taxes—the result, she believed, of high salaries for educators. The Teacher's Union campaigned to defeat her and did.

She was always available to her constituents and worked to solve their problems. She was a crusader and a caring person who made a difference in the lives of New York State Long Islanders.

Fields, Ginny. Interview by Nancy Mion, 2010.
Wikipedia. "Ginni Fields." http://en.wikipedia.org/wiki/Ginni_Fields.

Researcher and author: Nancy Mion, Islip Area Branch

CAROLYN FISH

1945–
ACTIVIST/VOLUNTEER/EXECUTIVE DIRECTOR

Carolyn Fish (also known as Carolyn Fink) is an acknowledged leader in the movement against violence directed at women. Her activism began in the early 1970s when she joined the Rockland County Branch of the National Organization of Women and soon became its vice-president of programming. In that capacity, she convened the first countywide forum to bring the concerns of battered women to public attention. This led to her becoming a founding member of the Rockland Family Shelter and subsequently assuming responsibility as its executive director in 1980. Under her leadership, what began as a grass-roots initiative expanded into a multiservice agency and a model for serving survivors of domestic violence and sexual assault by acknowledging the intersection of sexism, racism and other oppressions in the domination of women. She has been recognized locally and nationally for her activities and efforts to realize the mission of the Rockland Family Shelter: to create a society in which all individuals can live with dignity and equality, free from fear, violence and oppression.

She joined a "consciousness raising" group in the early 1970s, and by 1973, she had volunteered for various feminist activities, including co-chairing several of Rockland County NOW's highly successful conferences. In the early 1970s, Rockland County NOW established a crisis hotline. It revealed that the major problem facing the female callers was that they were victims of abuse by their partners and had nowhere to turn. This led a group of feminists, social workers, nuns, battered women, religious and community leaders and government officials to create the Rockland County Coalition Against Domestic Violence. The coalition was incorporated as the Rockland Family Shelter, and Fish joined the staff in 1979, initially as the assistant director. Today, Carolyn serves as the executive director of Rockland Family Shelter, a position she has held for more than thirty years.

Carolyn Fish has been a keynote speaker and workshop leader and trainer at numerous local, state, national and international conferences. Her article "Women Abuse: The Role of the Health Care Provider" was published in the *American Journal of Gynecologic Health* (May/June 1989).

She was a board member and served as co-president of the New York State Coalition Against Domestic Violence. She was a member of the New York State Crime Victims Advisory Board, the New York State Anti-Trafficking Advisory Committee and advisor to the New York State Justice Task Force. She was a member of the governor's Task Force to Create the NYS Model Domestic Violence Polices for Counties and is the co-chair of the STOP FEAR Coalition. She has been honored for her work by numerous organizations, including the Rockland County district attorney's office, the New York State Crime Victims Board and the Rockland County Police Chief's Association and received the New York State Senate's Distinguished Women of the Year Award in 1999. Her biography is included in the anthology *Feminists Who Changed America, 1963–1975* (University of Illinois Press, 2006).

Carolyn Fish was born in 1945 and is married to Irvin Fink. They have two daughters, Amy and Lori Fink, and three grandchildren, Brianna Fink, Benjamin and Mariah Seymann. Carolyn holds a BA degree from Queens College of the City University of New York (CUNY).

Carolyn Fish's April 2012 autobiography.
Submitted by Patricia Deacon Cropsey, Rockland County Branch.

LOUISE FLOOD

1929–
EDUCATOR/COMMUNITY LEADER

Louise Flood said that she was a rather timid child, hesitant to ask questions in school. Those who meet her casually now at the age of eighty might not notice anything extraordinary about her. However, anyone who has worked with Louise on her various community endeavors knows well that she is no longer timid and is far from ordinary.

Born in Kingston, New York, in 1929, Louise still lives in the same house in which she grew up, a twenty-eight-room home dating from the 1850s that was at one time an inn and at another time a boardinghouse. Her grandfather bought it in 1910 because he needed the spring on the property to provide water for his property across the road. Her father eventually settled his family there and used an outbuilding for automobile repair and sales during the Depression, with her mother acting as the bookkeeper for the business.

After earning a BA degree in Latin, which included certification to teach, the only Latin teaching job she could find was in California. Because the baby boom in the early 1950s caused a teacher shortage, she was able to take a six-week emergency elementary teacher training program and accepted a job teaching kindergarten in Cairo, New York. The public school class was held in a church facility due to lack of other space, and she taught forty-five children with no aides, including serving them lunch and assisting with forty-five snowsuits and boots during the winter. She attended the State University of New York–New Paltz full time during two summers, took extension courses in the evening and completed a thesis to obtain a Master of Education degree in early childhood education. After four years in Cairo, she was offered a kindergarten position in West Hurley, closer to home.

The mother of one of her students suggested a double date, with a blind date for Louise with a man who was widowed and had two children. When this man, Jack, later became her husband, she left her teaching position to take care of her two stepchildren and set up a nursery school in her home. She later had two children of her own and did substitute teaching for grades from kindergarten through high school. Children of European parents on temporary assignment to IBM in Kingston provided the opportunity for Louise to tutor Latin so they could continue their studies at home, and she enjoyed getting to know many of their parents as well.

Starting right after college, Louise became a Girl Scout leader, continuing an involvement with Scouting that began in her youth. Over her sixty-six years in Scouting, she was a leader for many years, a trainer of leaders, a camp counselor and an active member of many committees, and she held various neighborhood offices. She was instrumental in sponsoring an exchange program with European Girl Guides. With two others, she spent hundreds of hours going through and archiving the local council's material stored in the basement of the council building. She is still a registered Scout but is no longer active since the local council merged with others in the area, and the office moved to Westchester.

In 1975, Jack joined the Kingston Rotary Club, the motto of the international Rotary organization being "Service above self." Louise participated in the wives' group, the Rotary-Anns, as women were not allowed in the club until the late 1980s, and worked on many service projects. The Floods hosted participants of the Rotary's Group Study Exchange, groups of five young businesspeople from other countries who came to the United States to learn more about Americans and the way they do business. After Jack died, Louise was invited to join Rotary herself, and she is now both secretary and historian of the local club.

Louise has also been the regent (chapter leader) of the Wiltwyck Daughters of the American Revolution, a service organization dedicated to promoting patriotism, preserving American history and securing America's future through better education for children. She provided leadership to the Kingston chapter at a time when the chapter was floundering. The chapter owns a stone house in uptown Kingston that dates from the late 1600s. As regent, Louise oversaw remodeling of the upper floor, previously used only for storage, including refinishing the floor and installing cabinets to hold many research materials and historical artifacts. It is now a lovely room where research can be done. She currently serves on the board of directors, is a house tour docent and is one of the trustees of the incorporated society that cares for the building.

Continuing her interest in foreign exchange programs, Louise has been a very active member of American Field Service (AFS) Intercultural Programs, hosting an exchange student from Switzerland for a school year and acting as the liaison to support other locally placed AFS students. Using both letters and e-mail, she corresponds with many of the exchange students and people from the Rotary Group Study Exchange, extending her impact around the world.

After having been on the board of the local Big Brothers/Big Sisters program for eight years, a few years ago Louise became a big sister to a thirteen-year-old girl with disabilities. She thinks that this match is a particularly good fit and continues to spend more than the recommended time with her little sister.

Many people with as many interests and activities as Louise would be just participants, with their names on many rosters. People who work with her, however, insist that she is a valuable asset to all teams, giving 110 percent to any project or group with which she is involved. Louise herself said that one of her goals in all her activities is to help build strong women because they can be valuable participants in their communities, thus expanding the difference she makes.

Louise Flood. Interview by Sheila Beall, October 27, 2009.
Stedge, Pat. Phone interview, October 26, 2009. Pat also provided input from Marilyn Powers.

Researcher and author: Sheila Beall, Kingston Branch

MARGARET FULLER

1810–1850
AUTHOR/JOURNALIST/PHILOSOPHER

Margaret Fuller, an American writer, journalist and philosopher, was part of the transcendentalist circle that also included Ralph Waldo Emerson, Henry David Thoreau, Louisa May Alcott and others. She was born on May 23, 1810, in Cambridge, Massachusetts. When she was just three years old, her father, a Harvard-trained lawyer and congressman, decided that it was time for her to begin her classical education: Latin, Greek, grammar, history, mathematics, music and modern languages. By age six, she was translating Virgil. She lived in a time when women were expected to be wives and mothers only and were not even admitted to colleges. Highly intelligent and educated, she did not fit in well with her peers. At one point in her life, she wrote, "I now know all the people worth knowing in America, and I find no intellect comparable to my own."

When her father died in 1836, as the oldest in the family, Margaret became financially responsible for the family, even though control of his estate went to an uncle. At this time in history, no woman was allowed to have control over money, even if she may have inherited it. A natural teacher, she found employment in several schools, where she developed her own Socratic style of teaching. She also began her "Conversations," or educational salons, for women, which attracted about two hundred prominent women. Elizabeth Cady Stanton later wrote that these were "a vindication of women's right to think."

She traveled, published books and essays and worked as a journalist for the *New York Tribune*, writing investigative articles and critiques of the arts. She judged works on their aesthetic merits rather than on moral values, as was common at that time. Before joining the *Tribune*, she traveled to the Great Lakes and wrote about sleeping in a barroom, shooting rapids in a canoe and witnessing the suffering of native people and pioneer women in her 1844 book *Summer on the Lake*. Later that year, after joining the *Tribune*, she spent a night in Sing Sing Prison, gathering a group of female prisoners in dialogues similar to her Boston Conversations. During her twenty months at the newspaper, she wrote about 250 bylined articles, plus many unsigned columns and reviews. Her investigative pieces took her into New York's hospitals, asylums and slums. She critiqued race and class issues, often from the perspective of women. In 1845, she published *Woman in the 19th Century*, now considered an early feminist classic. This was three years before the celebrated Seneca Falls Convention, which began the formal effort for women's suffrage.

In 1846, friends offered her passage to Europe in exchange for tutoring their son. She spent four years in England, France and then Italy, where she married and had a child at age thirty-eight. Returning to America, their merchant ship ran aground off Fire Island on July 19, 1850. She and her family perished. Today, scholars increasingly see Margaret Fuller at the very heart of transcendentalism, perhaps more so than Emerson and Thoreau. She can also be seen at the very heart of the women's equality movement, exemplified by these words: "What woman needs is not as a woman to act or rule, but as a nature to grow, as an intellect to discern, as a soul to live freely, and unimpeded to unfold such powers as were given her when we left our common home."

UU World. www.uuworld.org.

Photograph from the Library of Congress.
Researcher and author: B. Dolores Thompson, Jamestown Branch

MATILDA JOSLYN GAGE

1826–1898
WOMEN'S RIGHTS ACTIVIST/AUTHOR/EDITOR/THEORIST/HISTORIAN

Matilda Joslyn Gage was born on March 24, 1826, in Cicero, New York. An only child, she was raised in a household dedicated to antislavery. She married Henry Hill Gage, and they eventually settled in Fayetteville, New York, where they raised four children. Their home was offered as a station on the Underground Railroad. She challenged the laws of her nation, risking arrest and imprisonment by helping fugitive slaves escape to freedom. During the Civil War, Gage was an enthusiastic organizer of hospital supplies for Union soldiers. In 1862, she predicted the failure of any course of defense and maintenance of the Union that did not emancipate the slaves.

Although occupied with both family and antislavery activities, Gage was soon drawn to a new cause: the women's suffrage movement. Her life's work would become the struggle for the complete liberation of women.

Gage was one of the "triumvirate" of leaders of the National Woman Suffrage Association. As chair of the Executive Committee, Gage ran the day-to-day operations with Susan B. Anthony and authored the organization's major documents with Elizabeth Cady Stanton. Together, Gage and Stanton wrote the *1876 Declaration of Rights of Women*; risking arrest, Gage and Anthony presented it at the nation's centennial celebration, directing their action "to the daughters of 1976." Gage played an integral part in preserving the incredible record of the suffrage movement by coediting the first three volumes of the *History of Woman Suffrage* with Stanton and Anthony. She also authored the influential pamphlets *Woman as Inventor* (1870), *Woman's Rights Catechism* (1871) and *Who Planned the Tennessee Campaign of 1862?* (1880).

In the 1870s, Gage spoke out against the brutal and unfair treatment of Native Americans and supported treaty rights and native sovereignty. She was adopted into the Wolf Clan of the Mohawk nation and given the name Ka-ron-ien-ha-wi (Sky Carrier). Inspired by the Six Nation Iroquois Confederacy's form of government, where "the power between the sexes was nearly equal," this indigenous practice of women's rights became her vision. Influenced by the egalitarian Haudenosaunee culture, she influenced the utopian feminist vision of her son-in-law, L. Frank Baum, in his fourteen *Oz* books.

In 1871, Gage was one of the many women nationwide who unsuccessfully tried to test the law by attempting to vote. When Susan B. Anthony successfully voted in the 1872 presidential election and was arrested, Gage came to her aid and supported her during her trial. In 1880, Gage led 102 Fayetteville women to the polls when New York State allowed women to vote in school districts where they paid their taxes.

Discouraged with the slow pace of suffrage efforts in the 1880s and alarmed by the conservative religious movement that had as its goal the establishment of a Christian state, Gage formed the Woman's National Liberal Union in 1890 to fight moves to unite church and state. Her book *Woman, Church and State* (1893) articulates her views on this.

Gage died in Chicago, Illinois, on March 18, 1898. Her lifelong motto appears on her gravestone in Fayetteville: "There is a word sweeter than Mother, Home or Heaven; that word is Liberty."

Wagner, Sally Roesch. *She Who Holds the Sky*. Aberdeen, SD: Sky Carrier Press, 1998.

Researcher and author: Nancy E. Clausen, Syracuse Branch

WILMA GITCHEL

1939–
COMPUTER SALES/FINANCIAL ADVISOR/ARTIST/VOLUNTEER

"Explore Your Opportunities—The Sky's the Limit!" A conference for seventh-grade girls is held yearly at the College of Mount St. Vincent in the Riverdale section of the Bronx. This conference became a reality because of the vision of Wilma Gitchel. She wanted to give today's girls the encouragement she had not received as a young girl to pursue nontraditional careers. The conference introduces the students to women working in the fields of science, technology, engineering and mathematics.

Wilma was born on September 8, 1939, in Kearney, Nebraska. Her father was a teacher who worked for the Bureau of Indian Affairs and taught in several schools on the Pine Ridge Indian Reservation in South Dakota. Her mother taught private music lessons. She has a sister nine years older and a brother two years younger. When Wilma was about three years old, the family moved to Flandreau, South Dakota, where her father taught in a boarding school for high school Native American students. Since then, Wilma has always had an interest in Native American concerns.

A career guidance test given to students in high school indicated that her interests were musical, artistic and mechanical. Music had always been a part of her life, as she studied piano and flute. She was a member of her high school band. She wanted to take advanced math courses so that she could become a mechanical engineer but was blocked. Further, she was told by many that these interests were not suitable for girls. She came to believe that the world did not want her and essentially gave up.

Wilma did graduate as valedictorian from Flandreau High School. She won a National Merit Scholarship and enrolled in Macalester College in St. Paul, Minnesota. However, she had not recovered from the perceived rejection in high school. She dropped out of college after a year and a half, giving up her scholarship. She had a baby boy whom she gave up for adoption.

She met and married a man from India who had come to the United States as an undergraduate at the University of Minnesota. She had a job as a secretary on campus. He convinced her to go back to school. She enrolled at the University of Minnesota as a pre-social work major (an interdepartmental major) and graduated in 1963.

She persuaded her husband to move to New York, as that was where she believed there were many jobs. She worked as a secretary for two attorneys at the National Patent Development Corporation. They obtained licenses for inventions overseas and marketed them in the United States.

Secretarial work was unfulfilling, and she became determined to pursue the mechanical engineering degree. Meanwhile, in 1956, she saw an IBM brochure for the position of systems engineer. A line drawing of both women and men was on the cover. This was a revelation! She phoned the IBM personnel department and obtained an interview. Notwithstanding her lack of a technical degree, she secured the position, largely because of her musical background. The work was as technical support within the computer sales department. She worked in Manhattan and Brooklyn.

Wilma soon noticed that sales representatives had more prestige and earned more money. Even though all the sales reps were men, she made that her goal. IBM policy called for a performance review every six months.

During this review, the employee was asked to state his or her career goals and objectives, which would be part of the record. Despite consternation expressed (nonverbally) by the managers, Wilma always stated that she wanted to be a sales rep. Eventually, Wilma was given the opportunity to be a pre-sales technical rep and worked with two male sales representatives. Her business card now read "Marketing Representative." The two men left IBM, and Wilma was asked what she wanted to do. She promptly said, "I want my own territory, of course." She was given the job and was the first woman at that time to have full territorial responsibility in her particular region of the company. This was in mid-1970. She was quite successful.

Wilma resigned from IBM and went to India with her husband in mid-1971. They shipped their car to Antwerp and drove from there to India. They bought a farm in the Punjab. They had fifty acres and raised rice in the summer and wheat in the winter. They planted nine acres, but the rest of the land was too alkaline for raising crops. Much time and energy was spent in discovering ways to remedy the alkalinity in the soil. She helped develop an inexpensive, successful variation on a known method to treat the soil. However, Wilma decided that this life was not for her, and she returned alone to New York.

She looked for work in computer sales but found a job in technical support at the *New York Times*. She got her MBA from Pace University and was promoted to manager of Technical Support. Ultimately, she decided that she preferred the sales environment. The rest of her computer career was in sales at Datapoint, Sperry Univac, and she returned to mainframe computer sales at Tandem Computers.

Next, she became a financial advisor and worked at this from 1992 to 2006. She now concentrates on painting—producing the "Conference," a video editing project featuring 8mm movies made by her parents while living on the Pine Ridge Indian Reservation—and in writing her story for her son. She is indeed a woman of many talents.

Wilma married Harry Leeds in 1994. In 2005, she was reunited with her son. She was thrilled and noted that he exhibited many of the same talents as she. She has three grandchildren, two stepdaughters and three stepgrandchildren.

Wilma was president of the Westchester American Association of University Women branch from 2000 to 2003 and before that was program co-vice-president. She has made a difference with her leadership as president. She brought many programs to the branch to further understanding of diversity. One such program was "Courageous Conversations," a film and discussion group to combat racism. Another outreach effort was made in cosponsoring an annual lecture and discussion event with UN-USA in Westchester. She also arranged for AAUW to be a part of "We Are Westchester," a loose coalition of Westchester-based nonprofit organizations and community groups dedicated to social, economic and racial justice. Through this group, we cosponsored with Pace University a series of three films on green America and the American Indian. Wilma also takes responsibility for sending out alerts for members to advocate for public policy issues and to respond to action calls on pending legislation.

Perhaps most personally meaningful to Wilma has been the "Exploring Your Opportunities" conference, which became a reality due to her persistence in finding the tools and people to implement the plan. It has nurtured girls' interest in science, math, technology and engineering and encouraged them to consider related careers. It has provided role models and hands-on experiences for them. The students are encouraged to take prerequisite courses in high school in order to keep their career options open.

Wilma has an optimistic attitude that believes that anything is possible. For many young girls, she has opened possibilities that were denied to her. Indeed, "The Sky's the Limit!"

Information obtained from Wilma Gitchel, 2009 and 2012.

Researcher and author: Phyllis Zekauskas, Westchester Branch

Manna Jo Green

19??–
ACTIVIST/ENVIRONMENTALIST/NURSE

Manna Jo Green has been a lifetime activist for peace, social justice and the environment. She is currently the environmental director for the Hudson River Sloop Clearwater and a contributing editor to the *Hudson Valley Green Times*. She has served with the Hudson Valley Green Building and Renewable Energy Working Group, on the board of the Hudson Valley Materials Exchange and with the Hudson Valley Biodiesel Cooperative. She is an active member of the League of Women Voters and numerous other civic organizations. She has also served as chair of the Rosendale Environmental Commission; has served on the Hudson Valley Regional Packaging Task Force, the NY State Battery Task Force and the NYS Roundtable for Consensus on Tire Management; and for five years hosted a weekly environmental call-in radio show, the *Recycling Hotline and Environment Show*, on WGHQ. She was recently reelected as councilperson for the town of Rosendale.

Manna actively promotes green building and landscaping practices and has built a model solar-powered Sustainable Living Resource Center to house a large collection of information on sustainability-related projects. It includes a resource library and a meeting space for seminars, workshops, movement and meditation and uses 80 percent less energy than conventional construction and generates one-third of its own electricity.

Manna graduated in 1963 from Stamford High School in Connecticut. At the age of eighteen, while living in Bridgeport, Connecticut, she met Dr. Martin Luther King Jr., who came there to help organize the local chapter of the Congress of Racial Equality (CORE). Manna volunteered to serve as secretary of the Bridgeport chapter and was sent to Washington, D.C., to lobby for the Civil Rights Bill, which made racial discrimination illegal. At times, lobbying was a frightening experience. Certain congressmen openly booed and harassed the supporters of the bill. When the bill passed, she joined with leading civil rights organizers, including Dr. King, Andrew Young and Jesse Jackson, in giving thanks and singing "We Shall Overcome." She said that she felt empowered for life by this inspiring experience.

Manna earned an associate's degree in nursing from Ulster County Community College in 1976 and received a Bachelor of Arts degree in biology (pre-medicine) from the State University of New York (SUNY) at New Paltz, magna cum laude, in 1986. While studying for her degree in biology, she became intensely interested in the environment. She has completed coursework toward a master's in environmental studies at Bard College. Manna was also a critical care nurse at Benedictine Hospital, Kingston, New York, for twenty-two years. During her outstanding career, Manna helped to organize two union campaigns, one with the New York State Association of Nurses (NYSNA) and the other with New York State United Teachers (NYSUT). As a result, conditions for patients, nurses, other healthcare providers and support staff greatly improved. Manna served for more than ten years as recycling coordinator/educator for Ulster County. Before that time, she started the current recycling programs in Rosendale, New Paltz and SUNY–New Paltz.

Manna supports collaborative land use planning and problem solving. Working with Cornell Cooperative Extension and the Hudson Valley Sustainable Communities Network (now Sustainable Hudson Valley, or SHV) to promote sustainable agriculture and green building and landscaping practices, she helped create the Finding Common Ground process to restore a healthier working relationship between area farmers and environmentalists. This resulted in a Hudson Valley Harvest "buy local" campaign and a genuine shift in agriculture in the region.

As a sustainability educator, Manna teaches communities how to balance environmental preservation, economic prosperity (based on quality of life indicators) and social equity using effective communication. She is a trainer for the Natural Step Framework, a sustainability methodology for businesses and institutions. In 2004, Manna wrote a New York State Energy Research and Development Authority grant to fund a ten-kilowatt solar system that was installed on the pavilion at the Rosendale Recreation Center in May 2005 at no cost to the town. When the sun shines, the meter spins backward, and the town saves money. Currently, she is helping to initiate a "transition town" in Rosendale, which proactively addresses peak oil, climate change and economic instability by creating strong, resilient economies that meet their community's essential needs locally to the greatest extent possible.

Manna's work at the Hudson River Sloop Clearwater includes protecting the ecology of the river from the impact of power plants and industrial pollution. For more than ten years Manna has been actively involved in getting General Electric to clean up the PCBs in the Hudson River, for which dredging finally started in May 2009. Clearwater has recently initiated an environmental justice campaign that combines Manna's passion for social justice and environmental protection.

In February 2003, Manna made a trip to Iraq for three weeks with two other women as peace delegates in the Hudson Valley Peace Brigade of the Iraq Peace Team/Voices in the Wilderness. They wanted to prevent the war and hoped to bring a message of peace and friendship to the people of Iraq and, in return, to bring the faces of the people of Iraq, their hopes and dreams, to the people of the Hudson Valley.

For relaxation, Manna practices yoga and enjoys dancing, kayaking and spending time with friends and family. She has two grown sons. Ivan is a world-class rock climber in New York City. Solomon manages a foundation that helps prevent or address the problems associated with subprime mortgages.

In 1996, Manna was nominated as Woman of the Year by the Ulster County YWCA. She received the prestigious Spirit of the Universe Award in 1997 for her commitment to the planet and to her community. In June 2000, she was honored to receive the Mohonk Consultations Award for Distinguished Service and Environmental Sensitivity. She is indeed a person who has made outstanding contributions in using technology appropriately to promote the best way to live in our environment and to understand, improve and protect it. She is committed to the beliefs that humans can live in harmony with one another and the planet and that if your cause is just and you are persistent, you will eventually triumph.

Green, Manna Jo. Interview by Patricia Stedge, 2010.

Researcher and author: Patricia Stedge, Kingston Branch

LOUISE HALL

1926–
HISTORIAN/PRESERVATIONIST/VOLUNTEER

The Smithtown Historical Society, founded in 1955, had a devoted volunteer director for twenty-three years. Louise Hall was a longtime resident of St. James, New York, the community that was named for its Episcopal church. Many buildings in the area were original to the colonial period, and the Setauket Spy Ring was valuable to General George Washington in the Revolutionary War. Farmers were persecuted and their homes invaded by the British troops who occupied Long Island.

Louise lived in a historic home that was built by Caleb Smith, a man of the family who founded Smithtown in the early 1600s. She worked tirelessly to research and record the identified historic buildings, completing the "blue forms" necessary for NYS protective legislation. She assisted in the establishment of the historic district along Route 25 in downtown Smithtown that preserved fifteen acres along with several historic buildings and a row of "ship-mast" locust trees from destruction by developers. The merger of the Smithtown Historical Society and the Branch Preservation Association made it possible to link resources to accomplish the historians' goals.

In the 1980s, Louise served as a trustee of the Stony Brook Museum. When the museum changed its programs and was divesting looms and spinning wheels, Louise acquired the pieces for educational programs at the Judge Lawrence Smith Homestead, the Epenetus Smith Tavern and the

Franklin Arthur Farm. She implemented very successful school programs in which fourth graders who study colonial history can get hands-on experience dipping candles, spinning and weaving. Programs are offered on farm life in early America, innkeepers and nineteenth-century Long Island.

Louise was alert to possibilities for funding and support. Over many years, she personally supervised fifty Boy Scout candidates who needed projects for Eagle awards and were willing to build ramps, paint, restore and landscape the historic properties, which are always in need of maintenance. The Rotary Club installed new bathrooms, which were essential.

Not all buildings can be saved, but the Brush Barn is a success story. Frank Brush was town clerk for many years, and his family barn was used for storage of the wagons and horses of the fire department. When it became available, Louise arranged for a carpenter to dismantle part of the building so that it could be transported several blocks and rebuilt in the historic district. It was refurbished, heated and made available for community meetings. It is used often and has added much to the town.

In 1988, the Smithtown Historical Society was given a portrait by the Platt family. Louise embarked on a three-year search and was assisted by Dr. William Oedel at the National Portrait Gallery in Washington, D.C. The painting is of Jonas Platt (1769–1834), whose family left Long Island after the Revolution and founded Plattsburgh. The painter is Joseph Wright, a prominent English artist (1756–1793) who died in Philadelphia of yellow fever; the portrait was done in the early 1790s and is very valuable. Jonas Platt was a congressman and a member of the New York Senate. Louise Hall is personally responsible for the authentication of this treasure.

Today, there is a paid director of the Smithtown Historical Society, who organizes events and oversees the annual Heritage Country Fair, and a part-time curator, who organizes exhibits and catalogues the collection of artifacts. There is a board of directors, and many members contribute their time and talents. The mission is the same: to keep history alive.

Because of Louise Hall, there are eight buildings; twenty acres; documents and artifacts; a collection of furniture, costumes and fabrics; photographs; and works of art. Although Louise has retired, she still lives near Smithtown and is a presence in the historic community. Her guidance and dedication were invaluable, and she leaves a wonderful legacy to future generations in Smithtown.

Smithtown Historical Society Whisperings 1, no. 3 (November 2008): 3.

Researcher and author: Phyllis Anderson, Smithtown Branch

FAITH W. HALLOCK

1919–2008
ACTIVIST

Faith Hallock was a woman who lived her life as a champion of women's rights. Her zest for life and her unwillingness to accept the traditional limits placed on women earned her the admiration and respect of women of all ages.

Faith was born in a time when the scope of possibilities for women was much narrower than it is today. She saw the value of education as an avenue toward equal opportunities and went to Middlebury College in Vermont. There she joined Pi Phi, the first women's fraternity in the country. At Middlebury, she became one of two women to be accepted into the United States Civilian Pilot Training Program. She opened doors for future women like Sally Ride and Eileen Collins when she became one of fewer than two hundred women to earn a pilot's license in 1940. After college, she worked for American Airlines at the Chemung County Airport. In the 1970s, Faith broke another barrier by becoming the first female probation officer at the Elmira Correctional Facility, again opening doors for the many women who followed her in this field.

After retiring from the correctional facility, she became involved in several community organizations and in many activities that furthered the rights of women. She served as president of many of these organizations. Zonta, Chemung County Council for the Aging and Region IV PEF Retirees were among the groups that flourished under her leadership. She was also active in Business and Professional Women, Brand Park Association and the Finger Lakes Health System Southern Tier Advisory Council. As if her involvement in all these organizations did not keep her busy enough, she spearheaded the efforts to place two Elmira women in the National Women's Hall of Fame in Seneca Falls, New York. She nominated Crystal Eastman, a local women's rights activist, three times and organized an extensive letter writing campaign until she was finally successful in gaining a place in the Hall of Fame for Ms. Eastman. Faith was also instrumental in the induction of Eileen Collins, the first female to pilot the space shuttle.

Faith Hallock was presented with many awards honoring her efforts for advancing women's rights. She received the Crystal Eastman Award in 2006 from the Chemung-Schuyler Labor Assembly for her work on behalf of all working people. She was presented with the Athena Award in 2007 by the Chemung County Chamber of Commerce for her efforts in fostering opportunities for women. Both of these honors were richly deserved for the time and energy that Faith dedicated to improve the lives of both men and women in her community.

Faith's life was a life well lived. She was an enthusiastic supporter of a woman's right to forge her own destiny, and she let no barriers stand in the way of achieving her goals. She is truly a role model for us all.

Elmira Star-Gazette.
World War II Teach In. "Faith Hallock: The Pilot." sites.google.com/site/ teachworldwarii/faith-hallock.

Researcher: June Ford, Elmira-Corning Branch
Author: Julie Biviano, Elmira-Corning Branch

PRISCILLA HANCOCK

1938–
EDUCATOR/VOLUNTEER/HISTORIAN

Priscilla Hancock has been honored for her community service since her teenage years in Hempstead High School, when she received the Daughters of the American Revolution Award in 1956 for Outstanding Citizenship and Service. Along with being president of the largest high school Future Teachers of America Club in the United States in 1956, she traveled to Long Island high schools helping to establish their Future Teachers of America clubs.

Teenage leadership was evidenced in her serving as president of her sorority and Junior Debs of the local Women's Club, as managing editor of her high school newspaper and in officer positions in the scholastic honor clubs. Her first time being included in a national publication was in *Who's Who Among American High School Students*

1956. Subsequent listings in *Who's Who* publications through the years included *Students in American Universities and Colleges 1959–1960, Human Services Professionals 1988–1989, American Education—Classroom Educators* 1989–1990 and *American Women 2008–2009, 2010–11.*

At Cortland College of Education (now State University of New York–Cortland), Priscilla graduated cum laude with a BS in elementary education in 1960. She held leadership positions in the service organizations, the board of governors and Cardinal Key, as well as being a residence counselor in the dormitories and a member of Alpha Sigma Sorority and Kappa Delta Pi (national honor society in education). She was selected to do her practice teaching in the Campus School at the college. Priscilla met her husband, Robert G. Hancock, at the college. They were married on August 6, 1960.

She began her teaching career in 1960 in the Farmingdale, New York public schools. Until 1963, she was a teacher of third graders. During summer vacations, she was an arts and crafts instructor in the Farmingdale Youth Council Program (1956–63).

Leaving teaching temporarily, her career as a mother began with the birth of her son, Gregory Scott Hancock. While living in Brightwaters, New York, and raising him and his sister, Kimberly Beth Hancock, and brother, Glenn Edward Hancock, she became a parishioner of St. Patrick's Church of Bay Shore.

Priscilla became a member of the Islip Area Branch (Long Island, New York) of the American Association of University Women in 1967 and later became a life member. AAUW participation highlights included serving as vice-president for membership and the New York State membership representative for Long Island and the Metropolitan New York Area; as treasurer in raising funds for the Educational Foundation and for the branch's first named gift; as creative arts chairperson in teaching many workshops on embroidery and other needlework skills and creative crafts; in organizing and hosting the branch's first and other Children's Craft Fairs; and in serving on the branch board (twelve years) and hosting Summer Socials.

As a member of the Embroiderers' Guild of America (from 1967 through 1980s), she led workshops and was a speaker on her "Recycling of Vintage Needlework."

Priscilla's teaching career later continued in the Bay Shore, Long Island, New York School System, in which she taught fourth grade at the Gardiner Manor School until 1994. She taught workshops for teachers, coordinated her students' exhibits with the Bay Shore Garden Club (1985–87) and organized historical field trips for all the fourth-grade classes. Early interest in Long Island history was evidenced (when she was an eighth grader) in her first prize–winning essay "Historical Spots on Long Island" in the essay contest at the Long Island Fair in 1951.

Past organizational membership have included the Bay Shore Classroom Teachers Association; Friends of Long Island's Heritage; New York State United Teachers; Bay Shore Student Financial Aid Fund (1974–75); cofounder of Mothers' Auxiliary of Boy Scout Troop 153 (1976); and Music Sponsors of the Bay Shore Schools, co-chaired Bay Shore's First Invitational Marching Band Competition (October 25, 1981).

Priscilla is a charter member of the Bay Shore Historical Society (founded in 1985) and was honored as an Outstanding Member in 2010. Other memberships since 1994 have included those in the Bay Shore Garden Club, the Bay Shore Retired Teachers' Association and the Summit Council of Bay Shore/Brightwaters and Bay Shore Beautification Society.

Upon retirement from teaching in 1994, Priscilla continued her interest in history by establishing the Historical Reference Library for Bay Shore at the circa 1820 Gibson-Mack-Holt House of the Bay Shore Historical Society at 22 Maple Avenue, Bay Shore, New York. She has continued maintaining the library since its founding seventeen years ago. Historical materials have been donated to the library (which has doubled in size) through her presentations to the chamber of commerce and Bay Shore/Brightwaters Summit Council (since 1995).

Priscilla's research projects in the community have included the erection of a permanent sign, "The Historical Bay District," in Dr. George King Park, Bay Shore, New York; historical slide shows; scores of pictorial exhibits, including Brightwaters Centennial Exhibit (2007), Bay Shore's Tercentenary Exhibit (2008) and Bay Shore-Brightwaters Public Library's Centennial Exhibit (2001); the creation and narration of the Historical Bus Tours of the community as part of the Preservation and Restoration Committee and the Society; a booklet, *Historical Bay Shore*, a chronology published by the Bay Shore Schools that was a part of a New York State award (2008); and a DVD, *Bay Shore of Yesteryear*, with 140 vintage scenes of Bay Shore, which she also narrated (2009).

In being a founding member of the Bay Shore Historical Society and serving as vice-president/membership chairperson of the historical society for fifteen years, Priscilla has received recognition for her service. Honors she has received have included the Distinguished Service Award from the Town of Islip, Women's History Month (2002); the Decade of Community Service Award from the Summit Council of Bay Shore/Brightwaters

(2004); the First Annual Historical Preservation and Restoration, Peter Fox Cohalan Award from the Town of Islip (2009); and the Bay Shore/ Brightwaters Distinguished Citizen Award (along with her husband and the Bay Shore Historical Society) from the chamber of commerce and Business Improvement District (BID) on May 20, 2010.

Pricilla and her husband, Bob, reside in Brightwaters, Long Island, New York, and volunteer at the Gibson-Mack-Holt House of the Bay Shore Historical Society in Bay Shore, New York.

Further Honors

Certificate of Special Recognition from the U.S. House of Representatives (2010)
Joint Legislative Resolution from the New York Senate and Assembly (2010)
Two proclamations from the Suffolk County legislature (2010)
Proclamation from the Suffolk County treasurer (2010)
Citation of Commendation from the Town of Islip (2010)
Certificate of Special Commendation plaque from the Bay Shore Board of Education (2010)
Certificate of Special Honor plaque from the Summit Council of Bay Shore and Brightwaters (2010)

Information obtained from Priscilla Hancock, 2010 and 2011.

Researcher and author: Marlene Gilliam, Islip Area Branch

Elinor Hare

1928–2012
Humanitarian

Reverend Dr. Ruby Elinor Hare, born on January 8, 1928, in Jamestown, New York, did not find her life's work until she was in her middle years. She epitomizes the phrase "only she who attempts the absurd can achieve the impossible." "Absurd" is a word she heard many times as she pursued her goal of helping incarcerated women.

Elinor had planned to enter nursing school when she graduated from high school, but due to family circumstances, she married and subsequently had three children. The marriage did not work out, and Elinor depended on public assistance for a few years. She was granted a license by the New York State Cosmetology Board, and she and her friend, Rose, opened a successful business in their home. However, she yearned for more and earned degrees from Jamestown Community College and the State University of New York–Fredonia. She had taken a course in religion, during which she felt God's call to the ordained ministry, a field not really open to women at that time.

Elinor persevered and enrolled in Union Theological Seminary in New York City. In 1973, Rose found employment and moved with her. Elinor's seminary training included a trip to Chicago to monitor a jail program. One day, she visited the court pens and could not believe what she encountered. That night, she felt a strong call from God to minister to women who are being held in court pens while awaiting their court appearances.

Elinor returned to New York City determined to establish an advocacy program for women incarcerated on Rikers Island. No such program existed. She had to design it, sell it and find funding for it. Along the way, she heard the word "absurd" many times. She received her Master of Divinity degree in 1977 and then a master's in criminal justice in 1983, the year her Women's Advocate Ministry (WAM) became a reality. She completed her Doctor of Divinity degree in 1988.

The WAM program is nonjudgmental. Elinor had realized that its focus should not be on what the women had done but on what they presently needed. Of great concern to them is their children, who are sometimes left to fend for themselves, often too young to understand where mom has gone. The great majority of the women are mothers—especially from minority populations—are heads of the households, have a history of alcohol and drug abuse and are poor, unskilled and uneducated. Most have committed economic crimes rather than violent ones and were emotionally, physically and/or sexually abused as children. What they need most is a friend who will listen or just be there. Elinor understood this and knew that this was God's plan for her life.

Elinor turned over the reins of WAM in 1993. The program relies mainly on volunteers and survives mostly on grants and donations. A significant number of the women turn their lives around, thanks to the compassion, friendship and nonjudgmental acceptance they receive from WAM. Elinor has maintained contact with a number of those with whom she advocated. She and Rose returned to Chautauqua County in 1999. Elinor has continued her advocacy work, visiting prisoners in the county jail. She initiated the Visitors Center at the Lakeview Shock Incarceration Facility in Brocton, New York. She also serves as associate pastor at the Lakewood United Methodist Church.

Elinor has been honored by the State of New York for her work on behalf of women through her Women's Advocacy Ministry. In 2002, she received the Woman of Distinction Award at a celebration in the Well Legislative Office Building in Albany.

Hare, Dr. R. Elinor, Reverend. Doctor of Divinity thesis 1987–88. Drew University, Madison, New Jersey.

———. Interview by B. Dolores Thompson, 2003.

Headley, Barbara Eyvonne. *Wise Women Bearing Gifts*. N.p.: Judson Press, 1988.

Thompson, B. Dolores. "Reverend Doctor Elinor Hare." *Jamestown Post-Journal*, March 2003.

Researcher and author: B. Dolores Thompson, Jamestown Branch

Ruth S. Harley

1902–2005
College Administrator

Ruth S. Harley, a longtime member of the Garden City Branch of the American Association of University Women, is honored by the university center that bears her name on the Adelphi University campus. Born in Brooklyn on May 21, 1902, Ms. Harley was an icon of the university community until her death on July 4, 2005. She is warmly remembered at Adelphi as the "First Lady of the University."

Ruth, a graduate of Erasmus Hall High School in Brooklyn in 1920, had planned to go to Vassar but was late in her application. The Vassar officials suggested that she go to Adelphi, then a women's college in Brooklyn, for a year. She took courses at Adelphi, performed well and was accepted at Vassar for her sophomore year. She said, "No thank you," stayed at Adelphi and became more involved. That stay lasted until the end of her life.

Ruth's transition from Adelphi student to staffer came shortly after her graduation in 1924. A Latin major, Ruth taught the language for a year at Adelphi Academy. During afternoons, she worked in the college endowment office. She was soon hired full-time as the assistant in the registrar's office. In 1932, she was appointed registrar, a position that she held for a decade. She then earned a master's degree in personnel administration from New York University. In 1942, she was named dean of women, a post that she held for almost three decades, longer than anyone in the school's history. Ruth witnessed much change in Adelphi: the growing college's move from Brooklyn to Garden City in 1929, financial setbacks in the 1930s that necessitated massive fundraising, admission of African American women in the 1940s and the acceptance of Japanese American women from United States internment camps after World War II.

In 1946, Adelphi returned to its coeducation roots when the women's college opened its doors to returning servicemen. Ruth welcomed the new students and became especially involved in the sports program. She was known to attend every basketball game.

She had remained engaged with her alma mater after retiring as the university's dean of women in 1970. She served on the Alumni Association Board, on the President's Advisory Council and with the Friends of the Adelphi Library. Ruth also was guest speaker at an American Association of University Women Sister-to-Sister Summit at Adelphi in 2001. She was an active member of the American Association of University Women and at her Baptist church, the Church in the Garden. In June 2003, she suffered a debilitating stroke and passed away two years later.

Dr. Marsha Tyson Darling, who had interviewed Ruth for an oral history project, stated that her story is important as a primer on a woman's rise in a time when female leaders were few and far between. Early on, she stepped forward during a young institution's moment of need. With that came "the invitation to do more."

Ruth always referred to the university center as "her edifice." Her influence and good works are evident also in the impact she had on so many people in the Adelphi community. The Garden City Branch is very proud of this outstanding member—truly a woman who made a difference.

Adelphi University magazine (Summer 2002): 16–19.

Researcher and author: Joan Stafford, Garden City Branch

CATHERINE DICKES HARRIS

1809–1907
HUMANITARIAN (UNDERGROUND RAILROAD)/NURSE/MIDWIFE

Catherine Dickes Harris was one of the few black women to shelter fugitive slaves for the Underground Railroad. Catherine was born on June 10, 1809, near Meadville, Pennsylvania, into a racially mixed family. A widow, she came to Jamestown in 1831 with her infant daughter and built a small frame house at 12 West Seventh Street. She quickly established herself as a nurse and midwife, with knowledge of herbal medicines. She worked also as a domestic to support herself and her daughter. She was described as "tall and slender with a refined and intelligent face" and as possessing a happy, generous, thoughtful and unselfish disposition.

Her home, only sixteen feet in length, sheltered many fugitive slaves who were making their way to Canada through the Underground Railroad system. In a 1902 interview, she stated that at one time seventeen runaways were brought all together to her home. Village citizens also brought "eatables… for me to cook and feed them." Catherine's knowledge of healing salves and medicines was often needed. A New York State historical marker was placed on the site in 1936.

Catherine is credited with founding the Blackwell Chapel African Methodist Episcopal Zion church in 1881. The small congregation met in her home in its earliest years. The current church edifice was constructed from 1898 to 1902. A parsonage was constructed on the site of Catherine's home. Catherine died on February 12, 1907, and is buried at Lakeview Cemetery.

Thompson, B. Dolores. "Catherine Dikes Harris." *Jamestown Post-Journal*, March 1984.

Researcher and author: B. Dolores Thompson, Jamestown Branch

HELEN HAYES

1900–1993
ACTRESS/HUMANITARIAN

Helen Hayes was known throughout the world as the famous actress of stage and screen, but in Rockland County, she was Mrs. MacArthur, the library aid, PTA mother and tireless advocate for the handicapped. Through her efforts, the Rehabilitation Hospital in Haverstraw, New York, which was later named for her, became a state-of-the-art facility. She launched the endowment fund that assists today in maintaining the hospital's reputation as being of the finest rehabilitation hospitals in the Hudson Valley.

Helen Hayes Brown was born in Washington, D.C., to Francis Van Arnuin Brown, a wholesale meat dealer, and Catherine Estelle Hayes, an actress. Both parents were often away from home because of their professions. Helen was placed in the care of loving females: her grandmother, her Aunt Mammie and her Aunt Annie.

In spite of their frequent absences, both parents had a profound effect on Helen. Her father instilled in her an appreciation for the beauty of nature, and she was an avid gardener until she died. From her mother, she received the love of the theater. In her book *On Reflections*, Miss Hayes wrote, "The reaching out for excellence and the need to be the best at what I was doing, I learned from my mother and father. My father did his small job well and with humility, which taught me how to survive success. Success came too easily, too early, and too quickly. I never yearned to be an actress—because I always was one. I never dreamed of a career—I always had one."

At age five, Helen made her professional stage debut in Washington. At age eight, she was on Broadway in the musical *Old Dutch*. Her mother's ambition fostered Helen's talent. While they traveled and performed together, Helen continued her education and graduated from Sacred Heart Academy in Washington in 1917.

After having the lead in *Pollyanna* in 1917–18, Miss Hayes performed with William Gillette in *Dear Brutus*. Later, she was recognized for her talent by the Broadway producer George C. Tyler, who commissioned plays for her. Working for Mr. Tyler was difficult and unpleasant because of the long hours and poor working conditions.

In the meantime, her friends were organizing Actors Equity to protect performers from unfair employers and agents. Helen refused to join; she felt obligated to Mr. Tyler and did not want to be disloyal. However, when she found out that he had refused a part for her that she desperately needed, she broke with Mr. Tyler and joined Actors Equity.

At age twenty, Helen Hayes was a star—a veteran actress—but was far from professional. Realizing this, Helen took lessons in boxing, fencing and interpretive dance while investigating all the schools of acting. She concluded that there were only two styles of acting—good and bad.

Although Helen commanded a larger-than-life appearance on stage, in reality she was very shy. Once, as she sat in a fashionable gathering, a handsome young man came and sat next to her. With Charles MacArthur, Helen could talk for hours. She had made a connection with this man that she had never had before. They both knew immediately that they were in love and meant for each other. In 1928, they married and bought Pretty Penny, their home on North Broadway in Nyack, New York.

Both Helen and Charles had very successful careers, she as an actress and he as a playwright. He is most famous for *Front Page* and several other plays. He wrote the script *The Sin of Madelon Claudet* for Helen, and she won an Oscar for her 1932 performance. Through the years, Helen Hayes garnered forty-three honorary doctoral degrees, two Oscars, two Tony Awards and an Emmy.

In 1930, her precious daughter, Mary, was born. Like her father, Mary lived on the edge of laughter and couldn't take anything seriously. Both had a passion for justice and a talent for loving. When Mary was five, her parents adopted her infant brother, James Gordon MacArthur. Mary defended his every fault as they grew and were great friends. Both were demonstrative, eager to love and be loved. One day, when Helen and her daughter were in a summer stock production, Mary came down with what they thought was a cold. When she became excessively fatigued, she was hospitalized. Polio was her diagnosis, and she remained hospitalized for weeks in an iron lung. Mary died at the age of nineteen. Her cheerful and persevering attitude during her illness was an inspiration to her mother. After her death, Helen vowed to help paralyzed and helpless children. Also, after Mary died, Jim was a great comfort to his parents.

Miss Hayes joined the National Foundation for Infantile Paralysis and accepted the national chairmanship. The Mary MacArthur Fund helped build a twelve-bed ward at Boston's Children's Hospital. With Helen as chairperson, the National Foundation was instrumental in financing Dr. Jonas Salk's research to develop the vaccine for poliomyelitis.

Seven years after the death of Mary, Helen's husband died. The impact of Charles's death led Miss Hayes to consider retiring from her acting career. She felt the demands of stardom were relentless. Nevertheless, she was persuaded to perform in *Anastasia*.

Miss Hayes continued to work and used the television to lobby for the rights of the handicapped, the aging and abandoned children. In October 1983, she hosted the radio show *The Best Years*, a program for the elderly. At that time, she was also working on community projects, including the restoration of the Tappan Zee Playhouse.

When she died on March 17, 1993, she was remembered as the "First Lady of the American Theater" and by Rocklanders as the "First Lady of Rockland County."

Alexander, Ron. "A Party Benefits School Fund." *New York Times*, November 12, 1983.

American Association of University Women, New City Branch. *Imprints on Rockland County History: Biographies of 12 Women*. New York, 1984.

Eaton, Anne. "Helen Hayes Endures Hell to Portray Legendary Sleuth." *Rockland Journal News*, October 16, 1983.

Hayes, Helen. *A Gathering of Hope*. Philadelphia, PA: Fortess Press, 1983.

———. *A Gift of Joy*. New York: M. Evans & Company, 1965.

———. "Only Nyack—A Reconciliation." *Rockland Journal News*, October 9, 1983.

———. *On Reflection: An Autobiography.* New York: M. Evans & Company, 1968.

Laudor, Richard. "Friends, Thank Miss Hayes...." *Rockland Journal News*, October 24, 1979.

Moritz, Charles, ed. *Current Biography—1956*. New York: H.W. Wilson Company, 1956.

North, Steve. "For Helen Hayes 'Golden Years' Abound." *Rockland Journal News*, December 24, 1978.

Savell, Isabelle K. "Miss Helen Hayes—Rockland's Special Treasure." *Rockland Journal News*, October 9, 1983.

Uglow, Jennifer S., ed. *The International Dictionary of Women's Biography.* New York: Continuum, 1982.

Who's Who of American Women, 1983–84. 13th ed. Chicago: Marquis, 1983.

Photograph from the Library of Congress.
Researcher and author: Elizabeth Vallone, Rockland County Branch

BESSIE M. HILLE

1887–1971
SOCIAL WORKER/MISSIONARY

Bessie M. Hille was born on October 28, 1887, to Louie Charles and Charlotte Fitch Morrison Hille near Bonny Hill, Bath, Steuben County, New York. She was one of four children. Bessie as a young child was interested in religion and enjoyed going to the neighborhood Wesleyan Methodist church, where her father sang in the choir. The depression of 1892 forced the family from their farm, and her father became head farmer at the Davenport Home for Orphan Girls in Bath. The family first attended the Bath Baptist Church and then transferred to the First Presbyterian Church, where Bessie was baptized. At the age of ten, she met a missionary who had served in India, and she decided that she also wanted to become a missionary.

In 1905, she graduated from Haverling High School as valedictorian, and then in 1910, she graduated from Northfield Seminary in Massachusetts, where she studied religious education. Her religious zeal increased, and she longed to go to China, but her parents were reluctant to let her go, so she worked in New York City's east side as a social worker for three years. This experience served her well in her future endeavors.

After that time, the Hilles consented to her wishes, and on November 3, 1913, at age twenty-six, the new missionary sailed from San Francisco on the steamer *Siberia*, arriving in China on December 8, 1913. Bessie spent the next one and a half years learning the language. Her first assignment was to the South Gate area of the old city of Shanghai. For five years, all by herself, she taught Christianity and did settlement work in a region that covered three villages, two cities and the surrounding countryside. She traveled by wheelbarrow, narrow-gauge railway, houseboat and sampan.

Bessie was one of the founders of the Nantao Christian Institute, China's first slum neighborhood house. She also organized a Christian church in Shanghai that by 1950 had 1,500 members. When Japan invaded China in 1932, she was allowed to stay, but in 1943, she was arrested as a prisoner of war and spent eight months in a concentration camp in Shanghai, after which time she was repatriated to the United States, arriving in New York on December 3, 1943.

She used the time at home to recuperate and then do graduate work at Cornell University. She was a sought-after speaker for the Presbyterian

Board of Foreign Missions in western and central New York State. In 1946, she returned to China to help with mission relief work and the establishment of schools for Chinese children. By 1951, Communist activity had made her realize that she was an embarrassment to her Chinese community and that she might again be imprisoned. Having served as a missionary for thirty-eight years, she returned home in April 1951.

Bessie served as acting treasurer of the Presbyterian Mission Board in New York City until February 1952, when she returned to Bath. For the next twelve years, she was very active in her church and community and always had a full schedule of speaking engagements. In 1953, she was visited by one of the three Chinese sisters she had adopted in China at the request of their dying father.

In 1964, Bessie moved to a home for retired Presbyterian missionaries in Duarte, California, and died there on February 15, 1971, at age eighty-three. She is buried in the Hille family plot at Grove Cemetery in Bath, New York. Bessie M. Hille was inducted into the Steuben County Hall of Fame in 2005.

Brink, Helen Kelly. "Bessie Morrison Hille." Supporting information for Steuben County Hall of Fame Nomination, submitted on December 27, 2004.

Researcher and author: Mary E. (Betty) Langendorfer, Bath Branch

ALICE HOFFMAN

1952–

AUTHOR

Alice Hoffman was born in New York City on March 16, 1952. She grew up on Long Island and attended Adelphi University. She has an MA from Stanford University and currently lives in Boston.

Her mother was a social worker, and her parents separated when she was quite young. She grew up in the working class and was surrounded by women. A passionate reader as a child, she grew up missing role models and feeling that she was an outsider and was misunderstood. She has said,

"The only women who ever appeared in the curriculum were British and dead." As a struggling writer, she felt confused until she found that women could write about their lives and produce work deserving to be honored. Ms. Hoffman has honored Grace Paley and Tillie Olson as fine writers and political activists who inspired her. She has described a story as "not a glass half full or half empty but as a beautiful object which can be filled with most anything."

She wrote her first published novel at twenty-one and is still writing, having published nearly thirty books to date. Besides novels, she has written short stories and books for children. Her most popular novel, *Practical Magic*, was made into a movie starring Sandra Bullock and Nicole Kidman. At first, she supported her novel writing by writing screenplays, mostly for Warner Bros. Her books have often appeared on the *New York Times* bestseller lists, as well as "best books of the year" lists by various publications. *Here on Earth* was a selection of Oprah's Book Club.

She describes herself as more optimistic as a writer than as a person. She starts with an image rather than a plot and maintains that she is the last to know what the book is about. At one time, she used to paint her office "the color of the book." She is famous for her book openings.

"What we give back is as important as what we publish," she has said. She herself is a breast cancer survivor who established the Alice Hoffman Breast Cancer Center at Mount Auburn Hospital in Cambridge, Massachusetts, and has frequently spoken about it. She has also often given advances for her books to causes such as the Hoffman Center, Amfar, PEN's People with Aids Fund, the Grand Street Settlement House and Girls Inc.

Alice Hoffman's website. "Biography." http://alicehoffman.com/bio/biography.

Hoffman, Alice. "On Being a Woman, a Writer, and a Citizen of the World." Keynote speech at the PEN Hemingway Awards, John F. Kennedy Library, Boston, March 30, 2008.

Researcher and author: Diane D. Haney, North Shore Branch

PATRICIA SCHRACK HOGEBOOM

1937–
EDUCATOR/AUTHOR/VOLUNTEER

Pat was born and grew up in Buffalo, New York, where she attended school. She became a public speaker at an early age, entering and winning a number of public speaking contests, such as the Voice of America and Voice of Democracy Contests, from the time she was an eleven-year-old elementary school student. During those years, Pat was the first girl to ever win any of those contests. She was also a student of dance, and with her speaking and dancing skills, she became a young actor, performing in summer stock shows locally and even, at the age of eighteen, traveling with a visa for work in summer stock in Canada, where she performed in Toronto. But she was always interested in the larger community, and she was a leader in the teen girls' organization of her church and also a local young teen group called Triangle Girls. They were the daughters of members of the Masonic organization. That was the first of her experiences running meetings and learning to guide others to serve the community.

She was accepted into Syracuse University's School of Speech and Dramatic Arts after her graduation from high school in the top 5 percent of her class; however, she worked a year before entering Syracuse University on grants-in-aid and scholarships. She continued performing and teaching dance as she paid for the remainder of her tuition and all of her room and board through her four years of college, graduating cum laude in 1959.

In the following years, she married Bill Hogeboom, whom she met at Syracuse, and they moved to Long Island, where he would continue his studies. Pat reinvented her life as a volunteer in her church, a part-time teacher of English and, eventually, a guidance counselor. However, since her main goal was to have and raise a family, when their sons, Christopher John and Matthew Patrick, were born, Pat preferred not to work full time. Instead, she used her skills to continue to work in local theater and summer stock, for which she was a choreographer, actor and even director for more than fifteen years.

During those years, Pat also joined the organization that was to form the basis for her next educational focus. In 1965, she joined the Islip Branch of the American Association of University Women (AAUW) and soon became its president, always grateful to have an opportunity to know and be influenced by "like-minded people." She was a named honoree in 1982 and has served the national office on committees as well. During those years, she also went to the AAUW offices in Washington, D.C., and learned how to lobby for women's rights.

When it was time for her to get a master's degree at C.W. Post to become a guidance counselor, she once more created another job for herself: a teacher of bread baking, working out of her home. Pat also received a grant from AAUW. She would always say that her master's degree was paid for by AAUW and many loaves of bread. In the years she devoted herself to that occupation during the 1970s, Pat presented and taught her classes in stores such as Macy's and also wrote articles for publication in *Newsday* and the *New York Times*. She became a consultant for the Islip Township Senior Citizen Division; in her forties, she created the Volunteers Serving Seniors volunteer organization and built it into active service for the township's seniors with more than six hundred volunteers.

In 1990, Pat finished her master's degree and was able to get her first full-time job in education. She also became the president of New York State AAUW. That job took her all over her state and fulfilled her dream to help other women have the courage to move forward in their lives. One of the greatest skills Pat was to learn as an executive-level volunteer for AAUW was in training its leaders in human-resource skills. She was so well trained that she did indeed do human-resource training for forty years. In fact, when at the age of forty-nine she got her first full-time work as a guidance counselor, it was because her work had come to the attention of educators. She was asked to set up group workshops in her district for parents. She created workshops for students in grief counseling, one called Making the Move, as students moved into a new district, and also one for children of divorce.

Pat also used her skills during the '90s when the AAUW program for teen girls presented Sister-to-Sister conferences across Long Island. In fact, Pat produced and participated in the training itself for three of these conferences. Then, as other members became more familiar with leading this opportunity that reached out to girls to help them improve their own futures, she mentored two more full conferences—seeing to it that they were advertised, that the schools knew about them and that the group leaders were well trained for the job. These conferences were a culmination of the work that AAUW has done for young women for more than one hundred years.

As the years have progressed, Pat continues to evolve. Although she has lost her husband of forty-five years and is also a cancer survivor, she is still active. Her early writing efforts led to the publication of two historical novels, *The Hope Chest* and *Idle Hours: The Grace and the Glory*. The first is inspired by the early journals of her aunt, a teacher on the Nebraska plains at the age of seventeen. The second is the only book about Consuelo Vanderbilt as a child. Consuelo was raised at her family's estate in Oakdale, New York, where Pat also raised her own family. Consuelo was to become the Twelfth Duchess of Marlborough in 1895. Pat now gives programs on the development of her stories all over Long Island. For nine years, she has also written a monthly column for a literary magazine called the *Great South Bay Magazine*. Her column is titled "Luvpats" and focuses on the history and recent events on her home ground, Long Island, one of the earliest parts of America settled by English colonists in the 1600s.

Pat's greatest pride, however, is in her two grandchildren by her oldest son, Christopher. Kyle, twelve, and Kasey, nine, give her life the joy and focus that she and her husband, Bill, once gave to their own two boys.

Pat's professional work has been recognized in *Who's Who of American Women* and *Women in Education*.

Information obtained from Patricia Hogeboom, 2011.

Author: Marlene Gilliam, Islip Area Branch

KATHLEEN HUDDLE

1948–
ARTIST/PHOTOGRAPHER/WRITER/JEWELRY
MAKER/PEACE AND SOCIAL ADVOCATE

Anyone who enters the Huddle Art Studio in Elmira, New York, is immediately captivated by its welcoming charm and the presence of Kathleen Huddle's angelic creations. A seven-foot-tall, freestanding painted angel, displaying an ornate banner on which "peace" is written, beckons the visitor to explore. There is more evidence in the cozy, well-organized studio that angels are a favorite subject of artist Kathleen Huddle, as are children and women of all ages. Each theme appears to correlate with an important event in the artist's life.

Kathleen was born in 1948 in Sayre, a small town in the northern tier of Pennsylvania. As a child, she loved to draw and often preferred sketching to studying in school. She graduated from Sayre High School in 1966, and due to financial circumstances, she postponed going to college for a while. Instead, she attended the School of Surgical Technology at the Robert Packer Hospital in her hometown. After graduation, she worked at St. Joseph Hospital in Elmira, New York, assisting in the operating room. This experience familiarized her with human anatomy, a skill she was later able to apply to her figure drawings. She met her future husband, Robert Huddle, and they were married in Elmira in 1970. After their daughters were born, Kathleen decided to fulfill her earlier ambition of going to college. In 1980, she began attending Elmira College on a part-time basis while raising four young daughters, including a set of twins. She studied art history and majored in studio art. Eight years later, she graduated summa cum laude with a BA in studio art.

Kathleen's children, being natural models, have provided her with endless opportunities to put brush to canvas. Many of her paintings show tender moments of the everyday rituals of mothers and babies. In 2007, Kathleen collaborated with poet Margaret K. Menges to create "an original art book graced with poetry" titled *Children of the Sky*. The book paired the poet's words to Kathleen's oil paintings of babies at bath time. The published work was awarded Honorable Mention in *Writer's Digest*'s Fifteenth Annual International Self-Published Book Awards. Kathleen's next published work was *Mama with a Blue Face*. It was a personal memoir of her mothering career of the previous twenty years. The title is based on a painting she completed hastily on a day not filled with tender moments—a day when a fatigued, frustrated mother needed an "extra leg" to keep up with her very active twins. Kathleen is presently working on a book about angels titled *While Angels Weep*.

Kathleen's interest in painting angels developed during a 1996 trip to Italy. She experienced what she described as an "aesthetic arrest" when she first saw the Bernini angels on the Ponte Sant'Angelo in Rome. The beauty of the sculptures had a profound effect on her. The works of other great Renaissance artists, such as Raphael and Leonardo da Vinci, also influenced the direction her art would take her next. Upon her return home, Kathleen, a dedicated advocate for world peace, focused her art on a new theme: angels as messengers of peace. Her most recognizable works—two seven-foot angels painted on wood panels—have also been made into bookmark images, available to anyone who shares the artist's wish for a more peaceful world. Kathleen developed a technique for creating hand-stamped, hand-painted Old World–looking Christmas ornaments. She was very pleased when her creations were featured in the international magazines *Somerset Studio* and *Somerset Studio Gallery* (third volume).

During the course of her career, Kathleen's individual paintings and collections have been exhibited both locally and nationally. In June 2007, she received the Arts Partnership Award from the Arts Council of the Southern Finger Lakes. She also received commissions from St. Joseph Hospital Foundation in Elmira, New York. Her favorite commission for the hospital was researching and painting the seven founding nuns who started St. Joseph's Hospital in 1908. The painting, titled *Remember the Mission*, was commissioned for the hospital's centennial celebration. Recently, the Huddle Art Studio was profiled on WSKG TV's program *The Art & Soul of the Southern Tiers*. In the well-received presentation, viewers were given a private tour by the artist, as well as a demonstration of her creative skills.

The mission statement of the Huddle Art Studio includes a dedication to community involvement and participation in cultural events. Kathleen has fulfilled that promise with much time and effort. The community looks forward with anticipation each year to two community projects initiated by Kathleen. In 2003, she founded the Elmira Open Studio Tour. This project promotes the arts through a weekend tour of area artists' studios. It is free and open to the public. The participating artists display their works, demonstrate and discuss the processes used to create them. The second project developed by Kathleen is known as the Bottega Project. Its purpose is to create an opportunity for young artists to participate in the creative processes, with the goal being a completed work of art. *Bottega* is the Italian word for workshop, and high school students can apply to be part of this workshop to study in the tradition of the old masters, such as Michelangelo. Under the tutelage of a master artist such as Kathleen, the students spend hours learning about art and planning their works. Last year, the Elmira Street Painting Festival was the venue for the Bottega Project; it drew large crowds and gave the students positive feedback for their efforts. Future plans for the Bottega Project include offering student workshops in the newly renovated community arts building of Elmira.

Kathleen Huddle has a favorite quote, written by *Mythologies* author Joseph Campbell, that she likes to share: "To live in a society without the Arts is to live in a wasteland." Through her paintings, writings, advocacy for peace and devotion to family and community, Kathleen has made the world around her a better place to live.

Author House. www.authorhouse.com.
Etsy. "Angels of Peace." www.etsy.com/shop/AngelsofPeace.
Huddle Angels. www.huddleangels.com.
Huddle, Kathleen. Interview by Jacqueline Knitter, 2009.
Kathleen Huddle's website. www.kathleenhuddle.com.

Researcher and author: Jacqueline C. Knitter, Elmira-Corning Branch

MARY SHOTWELL INGRAHAM

1887–1981
VOLUNTEER

Mary Shotwell Ingraham tirelessly took on civic causes during her long life. Any one of her causes would make a successful life accomplishment; however, she worked toward many causes and gained numerous successes. And all of this happened in a time when women's roles in life were limited. She headed the Young Women's Christian Association (YWCA) and launched the City University of New York (CUNY) as a member of the New York City Board of Higher Education. She helped found the United Service Organization (USO), which was incorporated in 1941 in New York State as per President Roosevelt's goal to assist the armed forces. She was the women's adviser to the War Department and also won the Medal for Merit, the highest honor the nation could bestow on civilians for wartime service at the time.

In her personal life, she was an alumna of Vassar and married Henry Ingraham, an attorney and a founder of the Long Island College of Medicine. They lived in Brooklyn, New York, on Adelphi Street while raising four children (two girls and two boys). The family was close, and their home was full of numerous books on every subject. During evenings, while Mary sewed, Henry would read aloud to her. They were well off financially and had two other homes on Long Island. Mary and Henry raised their children in a nurturing but somewhat unorthodox manner. Their daughter Mary (Polly) did not attend formal school until eighth grade. Polly did, however, receive an education at home, reading from the family's books and observing nature at their country homes on Long Island. Polly excelled at higher education, attending Vassar like her mother. This daughter became an educator, scientist and pioneer in women's education. Polly became president of Radcliffe College and was the first woman on the Atomic Energy Commission. Polly remembered the positive atmosphere in her home and the way her father never presented a climate of diminished expectations for girls.

Encyclopedia of World Biography. "Mary Bunting Smith Biography." www.notablebiographies.com/supp/Supplement-A-Bu-and-Obituaries/ Bunting-Smith-Mary.html.

History of USO. "USO History." http://www.home.nethere.net/uso/ history.htm.

New York Times. "Mary Bunting-Smith, Ex-President of Radcliffe, Dies at 87." January 23, 1998.

Time. "Education: One Woman, Two Lives." November 3, 1961. www.time. com/time/magazine/article/0,9171,897907,00.html.

———. "Women: Well Done." September 29, 1947. www.time.com/time/ magazine/article/0,9171,80423,00.html.

Yaffe, Elaine. Publisher review of *Mary Ingraham Bunting: Her Two Lives.* Powells Books. www.powells.com/biblio/1929490267?&PID=30264.

Researcher and author: Lillian S. Robertson, Manhattan Branch

CATHERINE COMMON JOHNSON

1914–2004
ARTIST/NATURALIST/VOLUNTEER

Catherine Common Johnson—Catherine with a "C," as she would remind those who did not know—was a most uncommon woman and a most uncommon person.

Catherine was born in Watertown, New York, the daughter of James Allison and Minna

Anthony Common. Her Anthony ancestors were among the early settlers of Jefferson County, later moving to Watertown. She graduated from Watertown High School in 1931 and St. Lawrence University (SLU) in 1935, where she was an accomplished athlete. Besides field hockey, baseball, soccer, tennis, canoe regatta and "speedball," she was also a member of the news bureau and the literary and drama clubs. The university inducted her into the Athletic Hall of Fame in 1987. In 1972, she was honored with an SLU alumni citation for her contributions as a journalist, artist and member of civic and public service groups. In 1937, she received a master's degree in journalism from Columbia University in New York City and joined the *Watertown Daily Times* as a news reporter and, later, a society editor.

John B. Johnson became her husband in 1941, when he was a *Times* reporter, before succeeding his father as editor and publisher in 1949. The Johnsons' two sons are John B. Johnson Jr. and Harold B. Johnson II, both of Watertown, and their two daughters are Ann J. Kaiser of Sackets Harbor, New York, and Reverend Dr. Deborah J. Newcomb of Dexter, New York, and Virginia.

Mrs. Johnson's keen interest in nature study and the arts was inspired by her mother, Minna. In her case, as in her mother's, she was not content with the status quo but had the drive and inspiration to lead the way, and she played a major role in the creation of many groups and committees dedicated to furthering the appreciation of nature and the arts. An accomplished artist working in many media, including oil, casein, scratch-board, pen and ink, acrylics, watercolor, collage and calligraphy, she won many honors in art shows around the country and abroad. She helped create the North Country Artists Guild and was a member of the advisory board of the Frederic Remington Art Museum.

To quote a *Watertown Daily Times* tribute, "She did not interpret nature only through her art." In 1960, Mrs. Johnson was first appointed to the Thousand Islands Park and Historic Preservation Commission. She stepped down and was honored in 2000 after forty years of service. The six-hundred-acre site was purchased by the commission in 1962 to be used for a nature center on Wellesley Island and named the Minna Anthony Common Nature Center after Mrs. Johnson's mother, who had inspired much interest in the area through her observations, sketches and writings. The building was dedicated in 1969, and Mrs. Johnson was the leader in the creation of the Friends of the Nature Center, which has raised funds for and awareness of a variety of programs and projects.

Mrs. Johnson served two terms as president of the College Women's Club and was a charter member of the Jefferson County Branch of the American Association of University Women. She was the AAUW New York State Board international relations representative to a United Nations seminar and represented the AAUW at a session held by the Department of State and United States Arms Control and Disarmament Agency in 1978. As president of the branch, she was honored as a named gift honoree of the AAUW Educational Foundation.

Catherine Johnson's imprint is on many organizations in the North Country. To list a few, she was director and officer of the Young Women's Christian Association; chairwoman of the Friends of the Library; lifelong member and active participant in the North Country Bird Club; member of First Presbyterian Church; member of Governor Rockefeller's Conference on Children and Youth; member of the board of New York Casualty Company; and corporate officer and secretary of the *Watertown Daily Times.*

With all these honors and opportunities, one cannot forget that Catherine Johnson loved life, had fun and inspired others to live as she did. She loved canoeing, cross-country skiing, birding and traveling. She and her husband, John, traveled the United States, all of Europe and the Soviet Union, always looking for the perfect church to sketch for their annual Christmas card. No "plain Jane," she loved chic clothes and high-heeled shoes.

To quote the *Watertown Daily Times* tribute to her from September 20, 2004, "Mrs. Johnson advocated for equal access to education for women, equal treatment for female athletes and recognition of women as leaders of our society. She relished in the success of her daughters and encouraged hundreds of young women to seek more education to prepare for promising careers. She assured Northern New Yorkers that this newspaper would treat women's issues seriously."

Watertown Daily Times. "Catherine Common Johnson, Artist, Journalist, Naturalist, Leader." Editorial, September 20, 2004, page A4.
———. "Catherine Johnson Dies at Age 90." September 15, 2004, section D.

Author: Margaret Coe, Jefferson County Branch

MARIE-LOUISE JOHNSON

1927–
PHYSICIAN/VOLUNTEER

Marie-Louise Johnson began her education in a two-room schoolhouse, was married at twenty-two and went on to become an internationally respected dermatologist. This last came about primarily because of her work with the atomic bomb victims in Japan.

Dr. Johnson was born in New York City in 1927. Her childhood was spent there, where her father was an attorney, as well as ninety miles north in High Falls, New York. Her grandmother had a summer home, and her father bought a farm in High Falls. There were sheep, cows, horses and chickens, and Marie-Louise had a pony. There she attended the first grade at the two-room schoolhouse but then insisted on school in New York City to keep up with her peers.

At age thirteen, Marie-Louise knew that she wanted a career in medicine, but she had never been in a hospital. It was during World War II, and there was a shortage of medical help, so with the assistance of a nun at the Benedictine Hospital in nearby Kingston, she became a volunteer. They placed her in the operating room in the mornings. When she was fourteen, her love of cemeteries led her to discover a prior local diphtheria epidemic.

In 1950, while studying at Yale Medical School, she married Dr. Kenneth Johnson, who ran a cardiology clinic and had a private practice. She was an intern, studying microbiology, when she had an opportunity to join a new program in dermatology with Dr. Aaron Lerner, the discoverer of melatonin. He had come to Yale in 1955, the first dermatologist at the medical school. Six years later, Dr. Lerner took a sabbatical leave and left Marie-Louise in charge of the Department of Dermatology. She earned her PhD there in microbiology with a project in tumor growth, as well as her MD in internal medicine.

In 1964, Dr. Marie-Louise and Dr. Kenneth Johnson were sent to Japan by the U.S. National Academy of Sciences. The program had begun in 1956. Dr. Kenneth became chief of medicine and Dr. Marie-Louise the first dermatologist. She performed extensive research on the health effects experienced by survivors of the atomic bombings in 1945 of Hiroshima and Nagasaki. In addition, she was a visiting professor at the Hiroshima University Medical School and served as a consultant to Japanese dermatologists. Her off-hours of intensive study of the Japanese language enabled her to communicate directly with patients, students and colleagues. In 2009, having made some forty-eight trips back for the radiation project, she claimed satisfaction when people she met didn't bother to compliment her ability with the language.

In 1967, Dr. Marie-Louise Johnson left Japan to become director of dermatology services at the New York University–Bellevue Hospital, at the time the largest dermatology service in the United States. In 1971, she took a leave of absence to help with the transformation of the Dartmouth Medical School to an MD degree–granting institution. While at Dartmouth, she trained medics from the Vietnam War and established a dermatology department at the Veterans Affairs Hospital in White River Junction. She also set up an early interactive TV clinic for the surrounding rural area.

In 1980, she resigned from NYU-Bellevue to return to High Falls and the Benedictine Hospital in Kingston, New York. In Kingston, she opened a private practice, and she and Dr. Kenneth became instrumental in establishing the Mid–Hudson Valley Family Medicine residency program. A dozen board-certified physicians and surgeons were recruited, easing a shortage of doctors in the area. Today, the residency has grown to sixteen practitioners. Also in 1980, she returned to Yale as a clinical professor of dermatology and established a firm linkage between her practice in Kingston and the Yale Department of Dermatology.

Due to difficulties in recruiting dermatologists to practice in rural and semirural communities, Dr. Johnson decided in 2002 to create a comprehensive skin center and train her own medical dermatologists to serve the Kingston region. With Yale and the Institute for Family Health, she established a training program for board-certified primary care physicians to become expert general dermatologists. This pioneering effort—the only one in the United States made possible with personal funds—helped to meet the urgent need for dermatological services. Dr. Johnson's efforts are broadly recognized. She has authored more than one hundred scientific publications in textbooks and journals. She has received many honors: she was the first dermatologist elected to the U.S. National Academy of Sciences Institute of Medicine, the first female president of the American Dermatological Association and the first female master of dermatology of the American Academy of Dermatology. For her international volunteer services to the poor, she was awarded the Papal Cross Pro Ecclesia et Pontifice by Pope John Paul II.

Johnson, Marie-Louise. Interview recorded by Virginia Kohli, 2010.

Researcher and author: Virginia Kohli, Kingston Branch

CALISTA SELINA JONES

1823–1900
EDUCATOR/SCHOOL ADMINISTRATOR

Calista Jones was the first woman in Jamestown, New York, to be paid the same salary as a man for the same position. The exact year has not surfaced, but it occurred in the mid-1800s.

Calista was born on May 25, 1823, in the town of Ellicott, Chautauqua County. She obtained most of her early education in private schools and entered the teaching profession in 1841. When a man failed in the management of a school in one of Jamestown's districts, the school trustees asked Calista to take over. She accepted on one condition: that she receive the same salary he received. The trustees refused. Calista held her ground, and the trustees ultimately relented because they knew that she was the only one capable of assuming the position. Thus, she became the first woman in Jamestown to receive one dollar per day for her work.

Historical records indicate that Calista was instrumental in establishing the Jamestown Union School, with its graded system, and that for twenty-two years she was principal in the school's preparatory department. She was also instrumental in establishing industrial training, allegedly the first school system in the country to do so. She served as the high school librarian from 1894 until her death six years later. It is claimed that she was also the first woman in Jamestown to vote (women had the right to vote in local school elections).

Details of Calista's accomplishments are scarce; however, they have been noted by historians, who cite her "faithfulness, persistence and energy" and claim that Jamestown and Ellicott "owe more to her than to any other person their great success in all their educational undertakings." She was also referred to as "the fearless sergeant in command of the educational picket line in the struggle to subdue ignorance and vice." A bronze tablet in her honor has hung in the school administration building for many years. Calista died on January 31, 1900, after being stricken in the school library and is buried at the Lakeview Cemetery, Jamestown, New York.

Edson, Oben, Honorable. *History of Chautauqua County.* Jamestown, NY: W.A. Fergusson, Publisher, 1894. Fenton History Center Library.

Jamestown, New York Public School Annual Reports, 1899–1900, 1900–1901. Jamestown, New York Board of Education files.

Miller, Phin M. *Chautauqua County Schools and Education in 1802–1902.* Jamestown, NY: Fenton History Center Library, 1902.

Thompson, B. Dolores. "Calista Selina Jones." *Jamestown Post-Journal,* March 1982.

Researcher and author: B. Dolores Thompson, Jamestown Branch

NANCY L. KING

1953–
PHYSICIAN

In a recent conversation with Dr. Nancy L. King of Elmira, New York, she said that she "still gets goose bumps" when attending, speaking about or hearing stories about our Twin Tiers Regional Affiliate's Susan G. Komen Race for the Cure. That comment speaks volumes about Nancy as a person and as someone who was instrumental in establishing our local Komen affiliate. Nancy was not born in the Twin Tiers, but her impact on the people of this area, particularly women and men with breast cancer, is strongly felt and appreciated.

Nancy was born on September 3, 1953, in Cambridge, Ohio, and grew up in Youngstown, Ohio. As a young person, she had a natural interest in and aptitude for biology. This led her to an undergraduate degree from the College of William and Mary in biology in 1975. She received her MA in developmental biology from Washington University in St. Louis, Missouri, in 1979, with a strong research interest. However, Nancy's interests shifted when she worked in a free clinic, the Peoples' Clinic, in St. Louis, while in graduate school. The clinic's goal was to reach out to women and teach them about their bodies and how to take care of themselves, thus empowering them to take the steps to be healthier and stronger. Her work at the clinic led her to pursue a career in obstetrics and gynecology.

Nancy's MD was earned at the Ohio State University College of Medicine in Columbus, Ohio, in June 1982, with honors/letters in obstetrics, gynecology and internal medicine. She spent from July 1982 to June 1984 at Riverside Methodist Hospital in Columbus, taking electives in internal medicine, surgery, pathology and anesthesiology. From November 1984 to 1987, Nancy was at Mount Carmel Medical Center in Columbus, with a one-month elective in ultrasonography taken at Georgetown University Hospital in Washington, D.C.

Nancy received her board certification from the American College of Obstetrics and Gynecology in December 1990 and was recertified for 1997–2009. At the time, Nancy decided to give up her practice in obstetrics (but not in gynecology); she was the only female gynecologist in the Elmira area. Many women in the area are very glad that she continues that gynecological practice to this day. She frequently speaks to groups about women's health issues, including bladder function, menopause/hormones, women's cancers and so on.

Our Twin Tiers Regional Affiliate of Susan G. Komen for the Cure owes its existence, in large part, to Nancy's work. In an interview with her, she said that two things provided the impetus that led her to work toward establishing our local affiliate. First was the death of Heather Farr, a golfer who died of breast cancer in 1993. Our area hosts a Ladies Professional Golf Association (LPGA) Tournament, and local hospitals receive monies raised at this event. Heather's death prompted people involved with the golf tournament to let local hospitals provide health education displays during tournament week, and breast cancer awareness was one of the topics. The second thing that happened was that a coworker at the Arnot Ogden Medical Center, where Nancy practices, encouraged the idea of expanding on what was already being done. Education would be the main focus, but three health runs were also held at a local park. There were between 150 to 300 participants. Some ran/walked, and others attended to learn from the educational displays available.

As some hospitals lost interest in these efforts, others thought about affiliating with the Susan G. Komen Foundation. Komen National, at first, was not interested in an affiliate in the Elmira area due to its small size. However, Nancy and those who worked with her in this persisted, and they won the right to establish an affiliate in the Elmira area. It is still one of the smallest affiliates in existence.

The first local Race for the Cure was held in 1999. From educational displays at the Corning LPGA Tournament to health runs held at a local park with at best 300 participants, it is inspiring to see that the local Race for the Cure had 1,674 participants in the spring of 2009. Nancy is not as actively involved today as she was at the beginning, but she is always present when needed and is at the race every year, cheering on participants and volunteers alike and handing out awards at the end of the race.

A quiet and unassuming woman, Nancy would be the first to say that she did not do this alone—her family, friends, coworkers, local business people and community groups all played a critical role. However, many would agree that without her efforts and involvement, our community might not have the Twin Tiers Regional Affiliate of Susan G. Komen for the Cure or an annual Race for the Cure. The nine-county area served by this affiliate would not receive the monies raised for programs involving education, screening and treatment of the women and men living here who are dealing with breast cancer.

King, Dr. Nancy L. Curriculum vitae.
————. Interview by Jan Cummings, December 31, 2009.

Researcher and author: Jan Cummings, Elmira-Corning Branch

JULIE HARRISON KLESZCZEWSKI

1942–
INTERNATIONAL PROFESSIONAL/LOBBYIST/VOLUNTEER

Julie was born on March 16, 1942, in Culver City, California, a premature baby two months early. Her parents divorced when she was four, and she, her mother and her half-sister moved temporarily to her great-grandmother's home in Spring City, Utah, a town of four hundred founded by her great-great-grandfather. Six months later, they moved to her grandparents' home, a Queen Anne–style home on Utah's and Salt Lake City's historical list of homes. Julie was brought up a Mormon, a religion not conspicuous for championing women's rights, but she learned a lot about women's rights from her beloved mother, Jenniel. She is proud that her great-great-grandmother walked more than one thousand miles in the first Handcart Company to Salt Lake City, pulling a handcart in 1854. Although her given name is Allwyne, she has used her nickname "Julie" (from "Jul," meaning Christmas in Swedish) since the eighth grade, when she was mistaken for a boy by Popsicle Pete (a representative of the Popsicle Corporation), who sent her a baseball when the company ran out of rocket rings she had ordered.

At four years old, she suffered her first seizure on Christmas Day. At age thirteen, she was finally diagnosed and controlled with medication. (The exhaustion from seizures is akin to running five miles.)

While attending a pool party at the University of Utah in Salt Lake City, she met and after a brief courtship married Reverend (Dr.) Richard Arthur (Harvard and University of California–Berkeley), thirteen years her senior. They were married on September 9, 1961. They divorced in August 1966 in California.

Julie met her current husband, Nick, who was an IC2 (E5) class in the navy, at the Long Beach, California Chess Club. Before being in the navy, he had attended the University of Chicago on a scholarship. They married on December 25, 1966, and two days later, he was shipped off to Vietnam. He returned seven months later, and in October, they honeymooned in Washington, D.C. Nick represented the United States Navy in the Armed Forces Chess Tournament.

They both returned to college at California State College at Long Beach. Julie earned a BA in English literature and Nick a BA in mathematics. A baby girl, Catherine, was born when Julie was a senior. "I passed one final with a B+, after 12 hours of labor with Catherine!" she remembered. As a graduate student, ten months later, their son was born but given little chance of survival. Today, he is six feet, three inches tall. She needed to support the family at this point because college funds were sliced in half by a law signed by the governor of California.

In 1970, on the advice of a college employment counselor, Julie joined the Long Beach Branch of the American Association of University Women (AAUW) for professional development. AAUW issues have been one of the major focuses of her life. Nick became an actuary, and they moved to southern San Francisco near San Bruno. Julie began to become very involved with AAUW. She also was passionate about raising funds for the United Nations Children's Fund (UNICEF). She organized ten schools to go trick-or-treating for UNICEF, tripling the funds raised in the prior year. (The school boards approved this.)

The family moved to New York State (Port Jefferson Station, Suffolk County) in 1975. Julie was appointed educational foundation chair and elected program vice-president in the Setauket Area Branch. She studied at the Garden City Episcopal Seminary and was licensed by the bishop to bear the chalice. In 2005, she was licensed by Bishop Mark Fisk as a Eucharistic minister in the Episcopal Church. In 1978, the family was transferred to Manhattan.

Her first position in New York City was as a Young Collector manager at Macy's Herald Square (supervising 119 employees). Later, she found inspiration working with a minister who reached out to the victims of Chernobyl with hope, oncological drugs and a religious lifestyle. She witnessed the Foreign Minister of Belaruse at the United Nations speak four and a half years after the tragedy at Chernobyl. Surprisingly, since he was from a communist country, he actually quoted from the Bible. Later, she worked as a copy editor and researcher for a man who was an author, a retired professor of religion and a rabbi.

She has held many local, district, state and national leadership positions in AAUW and elsewhere with distinction. As president of the San Bruno, California Branch, her branch published two studies, one of which influenced Lippincott regarding its kindergarten books and another that protected the sunny weather in San Bruno, which would have been sacrificed had a road through the mountains been built to foggy Pacifica. During her term as president of the New York City Branch, her branch won an unprecedented number of awards (seventeen) for programming, membership and fundraising. She authored with the New York City Branch Trafficking Committee, led by the Steps to End Family Violence Coalition, a resolution passing the strongest legislation in the country to outlaw the heinous practice of trafficking. She also served as landlord and manager of the branch's 1864 brownstone in Murray Hill for two years, supervising the building with the house team during many emergencies (such as replacing the boiler in four days), renovations and restorations in addition to working effectively with tenants and initiating outside rentals to raise funds. She is proud that she won the title of Mermaid of the AAUW NYS Convention on two occasions, swimming the most laps of any one.

She was appointed by the Altrusa International president as a United Nations Non-Government Organizations (NGO) representative with the UN Economic and Social Council, continuing to serve since 2001. In 2005, she worked with the Altrusa UN NGO team to give a workshop at the Altrusa International Conference in Puerto Rico on the Millennium Development Goals. Presently, she also serves as the chair of UN Interns for an annual conference for the committee to teach about the United Nations and participates in the Commission on the Status of Women, United Nations Association and the Working Group on Girls from time to time. She also served as president of Altrusa International, New York City; Eleanor Roosevelt, Labor Secretary Frances Perkins and Dr. Lillian Gilbraith were members of the New York City Club.

At present, she serves in the American Legion Auxiliary in several capacities: as president of the Washington Square Unit No. 1212, as the leadership chair and constitution and bylaws chair for New York County, as vice-president of District 1, as legislative vice-chair for the Department of New York and as a member of the American Legion National Legislative Council. From time to time, she serves as a judge for the American Legion Oratorical Contests (Zone Level) for high school students who compete for college scholarships. In July 2012, she was elected First District president and legislative chairman (779 members).

She and her loving husband, Nick, recently celebrated their forty-fifth anniversary on Christmas Day. Nick is the adjutant for District 1, American Legion, which includes the Bronx and New York County (eight thousand members). They adore their beloved daughter, Catherine; their son, Nick; and their daughter-in-law, Maryellen. They are also proud of their four dazzling grandchildren: Jason, ten; Zoe, eight; Matthew, five; and Holly, five.

Julie Harrison Kleszczewski's April 2012 autobiography. New York City Branch, North Shore Branch.

ROSE M. KNOX

1857–1950
ENTREPRENEUR

Born on November 18, 1857, in Mansfield, Ohio, Rose Markward Knox came to Gloversville, New York, in the late 1870s. She worked in the local glove industry, placing silk stitches on the backs of gloves from her home. She met the dashing Charles Knox at a local dance, and the couple was married on February 15, 1883. They immediately left for a honeymoon to New York City. After the ceremony, Mrs. Knox commented that "the reason we went to New York was to get some expense money, for all Mr. Knox had in his pockets when we were married was $11 and our train tickets."

The young couple settled in Newark, New Jersey, where Mr. Knox became one of the highest-paid salesmen of knitted goods in the country. Their marriage was a partnership right from the beginning, as Mr. Knox always discussed business affairs with his wife.

Rose was given a fixed allowance to run the household, and as Mr. Knox prospered, this amount increased. Anything she saved was hers, and if Mr.

Knox borrowed from this fund, it was treated as a business transaction that would have to be repaid. With systematic frugality, Rose accumulated $5,000.

Wanting financial independence, the Knox family decided to take Rose's savings and strike out for themselves by purchasing a discontinued gelatin business in Johnstown, New York. At this time, gelatin was made by cooking the shinbones of cows for a long time until they fell apart, straining the liquid, recooking it and finally clarifying it with egg whites. Knox created a way to granulate this product, thus making it easier and more convenient for easy mixing. This discovery made the Knox manufacturing plant become the leading manufacturer of unflavored gelatin.

Mr. and Mrs. Knox had three children: a daughter, Helen, who died in infancy; a son, Charles, who died after reaching manhood; and another son, James, who joined the Knox plant in 1913 after completing his education.

Charles Knox was an accountable businessman, and by 1908, he owned the Spim Soap, Ointment and Tonic Company; a small hardware store; a power company; and the gelatin factory. But upon returning from a fishing trip to Canada, Charles became ill, and a heart condition was discovered. He died in June 1908.

Rose was devastated by the loss of her husband of twenty-five years, but after considerable thought, she decided to take over the running of the gelatin firm. It was unthinkable in 1908 for a woman to be active in business, so Rose informed all of her customers that her son, Charles, would take over the business. In truth, Charles was still in school, so Rose set out to run the business herself.

Rose completely revamped her husband's sales campaign. She emphasized high nutrition at a low cost, sanitary production conditions and appealing dishes. She set up test kitchens to find new uses for gelatin in business and medicine. Her work paid off, and in 1920, gelatin was used in medicine for encapsulating vitamins and medication, and the first gel caps were made.

Mrs. Knox was concerned with labor relations, and in 1913, she instituted a five-day workweek, along with two weeks of paid vacation and paid sick leave. This move helped her garner the support and loyalty of her employees. Throughout the Depression, she cut costs and laid off not one of her employees; the Knox Gelatin Company grew. In 1915, Mrs. Knox incorporated her business for $300,000, and in 1925, that was raised to $1 million. Although Charles did enter the business, he died within a few years, and James Knox became the president in 1947.

Rose gave support to the city in which she lived and worked, and she soon became the city's leading benefactor. She gave $3,000 to the Johnstown

YMCA for its swimming pool. She purchased the Livingston Mansion in 1907 and gave it to the Willing Helpers Missionary Society for use as a home for the aged. She donated bells to the St. Anthony's Church, as well as memorial chimes to the First Presbyterian Church. Her most generous gift was that of the Knox Athletic Field. After it was purchased by the board of education, Mrs. Knox donated more than $200,000 to construct and equip the field with a clubhouse, a stadium and a playground.

When the new junior high school was completed in 1933, it was named in honor of Rose Knox, who made a donation of a school library with more than two thousand volumes. Mrs. Knox honored graduates with roses after they accepted their diplomas. This continued until her death.

Rose Knox received many awards during her lifetime. In 1918, she was named by a prominent magazine as one of the country's "most successful business women." In 1937, she was listed in an award as the woman who had contributed most to American business by the New York State Federation of Business and Professional Women. In 1950, the weekly *Cavalcade of America* broadcast presented a story on her life, with screen star Virginia Bruse in the leading role.

Mrs. Knox passed away on September 28, 1950, at her home. She was ninety-two. Son James E. Knox succeeded her as chairman of the board of directors, and her grandson, John B. Knox, became president. Rose Knox will always be remembered for her determination in making good her belief that "molasses catches more flies than vinegar," both in running her business and her daily life. Her contributions in Johnstown, New York, tell the story of a truly successful businesswoman.

Honoring Women's History Month. "Women of Distinction." Sponsored by the New York State Senate, 2007. Available electronically in the New York State Library Digital Collection. http://128.121.13.244:8080/awweb.

Rose M. Knox—Biography. Information compiled by Elizabeth Cady Stanton Hometown Association member Betty Cleary. http://elizabethcadystantonhometown.org/biographyroseknox.html.

VanDusen, Ruth E., comp. "Rose Markward Knox, First Lady of Johnstown." January 1980. www.johnstownhistory.com/roseknox.html.

Wikipedia. "Rose Knox". http://enwikipedia.org/wiki/Rose_Knox.

Researcher and author: Virginia (Ginni) Mazur, Amsterdam-Gloversville-Johnstown Branch

ELIZABETH ANN LEVY

1949–
INTERFAITH MINISTER/SPIRITUAL COUNSELOR-READER/MIDDLE EASTERN
DANCER, TEACHER AND PERFORMER

Reverend Elizabeth Ann Levy is an ordained, New York registered interfaith minister. She is also a spiritual counselor and reader, certified master handwriting analyst (graphoanalyst) and performer and teacher of Middle Eastern dance in New York City.

Elizabeth was born in Trenton, New Jersey, in 1949. She came to New York City as a young adult to explore her education and career options. She started out working as an account executive in a small public relations firm, the Press Office, while she completed her studies in acting at the American Academy of Dramatic Arts, from which she graduated in 1973.

She then began to embark on her more spiritual pursuits. She graduated and received her ordination from the New Seminary in June 1987 and completed the Master Spiritual Therapy from the School of Continuing Education program at the New Seminary in June 1988. She then continued in her studies in kabbalistic healing. She has officiated at more than 150 weddings and ceremonies. She enjoys creating and putting together each unique ceremony.

Elizabeth is currently studying Hebrew. She has studied French and Spanish as well and is striving to become more conversant in these languages. She obtained her certificate from the International Graphoanalysis Society as a master Graphoanalyst in 1987.

She served as a telephone counselor and shift supervisor at Help Line Telephone Services at the Marble Collegiate Church from 1988 to 1991. She found helping callers in crisis to be a very rewarding experience.

Using her knowledge and training in astrology, tarot and numerology, she has made numerous guest appearances on radio and cable television programs, has done extensive lecturing on these subjects throughout the greater New York City area and has written several articles on these subjects, including a write-up, "Zodiac Dragnet," in the June 20, 1990 edition of the *New York Post* on the handwriting profile of the Zodiac killer.

Elizabeth is also a Middle Eastern belly dance performer and teacher. She has been teaching classes at the Lenox Hill Senior Center and St. Peter's Church in New York City since 2004. She has adopted the name Levanah as her dance identity. As an entertainer and performer, she draws on her belly dance training, her music background from college and her brief ballet and creative dance movement studies in her childhood to use in her own interpretations, methods and unique style of teaching. Her own teachers inspired her. She participated in the Sacred Dance Guild and has performed with it at the Church of the Village in the Greenwich Village area of New York City on September 11, 2011, and on December 11, 2011.

Elizabeth taught at the New York City Branch of the American Association of University Women from 2004 to 2010 to benefit the Bina Roy Scholarship Fund and the Educational Opportunities Fund, and she has performed at the New York City Branch's various holiday and special events programs. She wrote and performed the lyrics at the New York City Branch's holiday shows to one of the branch's anthems, taken from sections of the melody to the song "Tradition" from *Fiddler on the Roof.*

She was the subject of a documentary for a cable TV show and film produced by Dr. Helen Yalof, *Bellydancer Dreams: A Work in Progress*, which aired in 2004. She is currently involved in networking and assisting animal rescuers to help save and place shelter, stray and homeless pets, as well as domestic/companion animals, in the hopes that all animal shelters and pounds will become and remain "no kill."

Elizabeth is a member in good standing of the National Association of Wedding Officiants, the International Graphoanalysis Society and Professional Psychics of America. She is also a member of the Association for Research and Enlightenment Inc. She is an associate interfaith minister with the Interfaith Temple in New York City.

Reverend Elizabeth Ann Levy's 2010 autobiography, updated December 2011, New York City Branch.

MARGARET LOCKE

19??–
EDUCATOR/TRAVELER/VOLUNTEER

Margaret Locke Jr. has had a full life of varied experiences. She grew up in Pennsylvania, attending several schools there, and graduated from Westown Friends School. She received her BA in biology from Friends College. Margaret received her Master of Science degree majoring in health and physical education from Smith College.

She taught at colleges in several places, including Oakland, Tulsa, Iowa, Alabama and eventually in Springfield, Massachusetts, where she was the first woman with a doctorate degree teaching in physical education. Margaret moved to Elmira, New York, and taught at Elmira College from 1959 to 1989. During her tenure at Elmira College, Margaret spent one year teaching in India. She also traveled extensively with the faculty while at Elmira. Some of the countries Margaret visited at this time were England, France, Italy, Egypt, Thailand, Japan, Hawaii and China (in 1969); Turkey, Lebanon, Syria and Jordan (in 1974); Spain, Morocco and Senegal (in 1979); Norway, Sweden, Denmark and Iceland (in 1981); and Austria, Yugoslavia and Hungary (in 1991). She also traveled to Russia with People to People.

While teaching during her summers, Margaret worked with the American Red Cross. In 1956, the national Red Cross hired her as dean of women in the area of water safety. In this position, she traveled throughout the United States, teaching at small watercraft schools. While working for the Red Cross, she qualified for emergency medical technician work. Margaret became a member of the American National Red Cross Board of Directors. She became a field representative for the Red Cross, covering Wayne and Pike Counties. She was awarded a Distinguished Certificate for Humanity for the 100th anniversary of the American Red Cross. Stretching from 1946 to 2009, she had sixty-nine years of community service.

Margaret has received numerous awards: in 1955, Elizabeth Dole recognized her efforts for rescuing two boys during a flood; in 1997, Margaret was one of the first people to be nominated at the Athletic Hall of Fame at

Earlham College; in 1981, her name was placed in the *World Who's Who of Women* at the international register of profiles in Cambridge, England; in 1989, the pool at Elmira college was renamed Locke Pool; and in 1991, Margaret was named the New York State American Red Cross Volunteer of the Year.

Just when one thought that Margaret might be slowing down, she packed her bag again and traveled to the Antarctic and Arctic regions. In 1985–91, she traveled to Iceland and Greenland to visit the Red Cross centers. She visited Sismuit, a gathering of Greenlanders who live on or above the Arctic Circle. For this endeavor, she received a medal from the Icelandic Red Cross.

In 1992–93, Margaret boarded a Japanese icebreaker to travel to the Ross Ice Shelf. The trip was several months long and might have been even longer had the icebreaker ship not been caught in the ice and had to turn back. In 1996–97, Margaret again boarded another icebreaker with a team of six explorers, scientists and naturalists. Her job was to interview people at each station to learn about the conditions and problems, such as food shortages. All of these excursions were made for the Red Cross.

Margaret has had quite a life. She lives in Elmira and regularly attends American Association of University Women meetings.

Information obtained from Margaret Locke, 2009.

Researcher and author: Joan C. Russen, Elmira-Corning Branch

BELVA ANN BENNETT LOCKWOOD

1830–1917
LAWYER/PRESIDENTIAL CANDIDATE/ ACTIVIST/TEACHER

Belva Ann Bennett was born on October 24, 1830, to Lewis and Hannah Bennett in the Niagara County town of Royalton, New York. She attended the local public school, where she was an outstanding pupil and graduated at age fourteen. She later taught at the same school for fifteen dollars plus board per month.

In 1848, she married Uriah McPhall, a farmer, who died three years later of tuberculosis, leaving her a widow at age twenty-two with a three-year-old daughter, Lura, and little money. Leaving her daughter with her parents, she went to Genesee Wesleyan Seminary (forerunner of Syracuse University) in Lima, New York. She graduated with honors in 1857.

She taught for the next several years and was also principal at several local schools for young women. She expanded the curriculum to include courses typically taken by young men.

Belva and Lura moved to Washington, D.C., in 1866. She opened a coeducational private school (coeducation was unusual then). She took up the right of women's suffrage, but her real interests were in equal pay for equal work for men and women, as well as job discrimination.

In 1868, she married Ezekial Lockwood, an elderly Civil War veteran, minister and dentist. He encouraged Belva to study and pursue subjects that interested her. They had a daughter, Jesse, who died before she was two.

Belva applied to the Columbia Law School in the District of Columbia but was refused admittance. She was admitted to the National University Law School (now George Washington University Law School). She completed the coursework, but the school was unwilling to grant a woman a diploma. She wrote a letter to United States president Ulysses S. Grant, the institution's ex-officio head, stating that she had passed all the courses and deserved a diploma. She received her diploma and became one of the first female lawyers in the United States. She began to build a law practice with her husband's approval. He died in 1877.

Belva was not allowed to argue a case before the U.S. Supreme Court. She lobbied the U.S. Congress from 1874 to 1879 for a bill that would expand the powers of female attorneys. A bill was passed in 1879 allowing qualified female attorneys to practice in federal court. Belva Lockwood was the first female lawyer to argue a case before the U.S. Supreme Court (1880).

In 1884, Belva Lockwood ran for president of the United States. She was a candidate for the National Equal Rights Party, engaged in a full-fledged campaign and was the first woman to appear on the election ballot. She ran again in 1888. This was done before women even had the right to vote.

She was active in the National American Women Suffrage Association and belonged to the Universal Peace Union. She was a delegate chosen by the Department of State to the International Congress of Charities, Correction and Philanthropy at Geneva in 1896, and she attended peace congresses in

Europe in 1889, 1906, 1908 and 1911. Belva was not only an advocate for women's causes (believing in professional and political equality for women), but she was also an attorney who played a role in the defense of Native Americans (helping the Cherokee people win a $5 million reimbursement from the government) and defended Mormons' right to free exercise of their religion in a letter to President Grover Cleveland. She died in 1917 at the age of eighty-six and was buried at the Congressional Cemetery in Washington, D.C.

Biography.com. "Belva Lockwood." www.biography.com/people/belva-lockwood-9384624.

Encyclopedia Britannica. "Belva Ann Lockwood (American lawyer)." www.britannica.com/EBchecked/topic/345845/Belva-Ann-Lockwood.

New World Encyclopedia. "Belva Lockwood." www.newworldencyclopedia.org/entry/Belva_Lockwood.

Norgren, Jill. "Belva Lockwood: Blazing the Trail for Women in Law." *Prologue* 37, no. 1 (Spring 2005). www.archives.gov/publications/prologue/2005/spring/belva-lockwood.

Photograph from the Library of Congress.
Researchers: Ruth Spink, Jody Longeill and Helen Butterfield Engel, Oswego Branch
Author: Helen Butterfield Engel, Oswego Branch

LUCY M. MALTBY

1900–1984
EDUCATOR/CONSUMER SERVICE

An expert in the field of applied home economics, Dr. Lucy M. Maltby was the founder and director of Corning Glass Works's home economics department and test kitchen. She was recognized as one of the top home economists in the nation, and she established a valuable link between consumers and the corporate structure.

A Corning, New York native, she received her BS degree from Cornell University, her MS degree from Iowa State College and her doctorate in home economics education from Syracuse University. Before being hired by Corning Glass Works, she had seven years of experience as a home economics teacher at secondary and college levels. Dr. Maltby became the first home economist at Corning Glass Works in 1929. When she left the company thirty-six years later, she had charge of a staff of thirty-five women handling many specialized services relating to the consumer.

Dr. Maltby was a pioneer in her field at Corning Glass Works. When she took the job, she was a department of one, with no one to turn to for advice based on practical experience. She charted her own course with one major goal: to "find out what things people want so the product can be made for them at prices they think they can afford to pay." The test kitchen she established soon became the center of consumer product development activity, as she and her staff collaborated with research scientists and engineers on using Pyrex for new products, as well as on improving existing ones to better meet the needs of the homemaker.

Working with company experts in advertising and photography, Dr. Maltby and her staff enhanced the presentation of products to the homemaker by creating attractive meals—cooked in Pyrex, of course, for advertising photographs. They also produced cookbooks and recipe cards to teach consumers the principles of scientific housekeeping. Dr. Maltby oversaw the establishment of field representatives to publicize and market Pyrex to homemakers. She herself established contacts throughout the country with other home economists, teachers, newspaper and magazine editors and radio and television personnel.

Active in many professional associations and community organizations, she served as president of the New York State Home Economics Association and president of the Alumnae Association of Cornell's College of Home Economics, and she served on the Advisory Council of Cornell University's College of Home Economics. At the time of her retirement, in recognition of her long service to and membership in the American Home Economists Association and the Home Economics Women in Business Association, she was honored at an Atlantic City testimonial dinner attended by about six hundred home economists from around the world.

Other honors for Miss Maltby included the New York State Home Economics Teachers Association Award for Service, the Distinguished Alumna Award from the College of Home Economics of Cornell University, being inducted into the Hall of Fame of Home Economists in Business, membership in the Omicron Nu Society and Pi Lambda Theta honor societies and being listed in *Who's Who of American Women* and *Who's Who in the East*.

Dr. Maltby is author of one cookbook, *It's Fun to Cook* (a Junior Literary Guild selection), published in 1938, as well as feature articles for various publications and training materials for Corning Glass Works. Throughout her career, she served as visiting professor and lecturer at several universities, including Northern Illinois University, University of New Hampshire and the University of Vermont.

When she died in 1984, James R. Houghton, Corning's CEO, reiterated her contributions to the company and consumers: "She helped to break new ground in the field of corporate responsibility to the consumer. The reputation that Corning products enjoy today in the consumer housewares market is due in no small part to Lucy Maltby's unswerving adherence to integrity."

Blaszczyk, Regina. *Imagining Consumers: Design and Innovation from Wedgwood to Corning*. Baltimore, MD: Johns Hopkins University Press, 2000.

———. *Where Mrs. Homemaker Is Never Forgotten: Lucy Maltby and Home Economics at the Corning Glass Works, 1929–1965*. Ithaca, NY: Cornell University Press, 1997.

The Leader. "Lucy Maltby Brings Home-Economics to Glass Works." August 22 and 23, 1994.

Researcher and author: Onalee Nixon, Bath Branch

ANTOINETTE (ANNETTE) MARTEN

1943–
ARTIST

Culture sometimes dictates what a child shall be called. Such was the case with Antoinette Pensabene, born on September 29, 1943, in Brooklyn, New York, the eldest of three children. According to family tradition, she was named for her paternal grandmother but became known to her siblings, family and friends as Annette.

After graduation from high school, family health issues necessitated postponing advanced studies. Annette's skills as a secretary to a vice-president of a Wall Street firm filled several years before her marriage to Thomas Marten. Before the birth of her last child, she achieved her associate's degree from the College of Staten Island as a participant in the ARC program called Adults Returning to College.

Annette and Tom relocated to Huguenot, Staten Island, in 1970, where they reared their four offspring. The boys, following in their father's footsteps, achieved the rank of lieutenant in the New York Police Department. The Fashion Institute of Technology became the source of furthering the innate talent of their two daughters. Thus was woven the close-knit family that remains. Holidays mean a gathering of children, grandchildren and sometimes extended family at the Martens' home. This same familial camaraderie is enjoyed in a yearly vacation trip to Rehoboth Beach in Delaware. It's a time cherished for the memories it engenders.

As one of Staten Island's accomplished artists, Annette's interest began in her childhood with her penchant for coloring. Her interest became a desire when she admired a painting and thought, "Maybe I can do that." That she could is evidenced by her talent in many media, among them oil, watercolor, collage and printmaking, all of which were enhanced by studying oils at the College of Staten Island and printmaking at the Art Lab at Snug Harbor Cultural Center. Attendance at the Art Students League and the National School of Design in Manhattan allowed practice and refinement of her ability.

One of Annette's achievements is a first-prize award for her watercolor *Poppy and Me* in the 1999 International Year of the Older Persons. As added prestige, it has been placed in a time capsule at the College of Staten Island to be opened in the year 2049.

Stories of the presentation of the watercolors *Walkers Point, A Rainy Day at Walkers Point* and *Autumn at Walkers Point* to our forty-first president, George H. Bush, appeared in the *Staten Island Advance*. At the Texas A&M College Library, they are timeless reminders of Annette's vacation at Kennebunkport, Maine.

Her art has been used in a fundraiser for the Ronald McDonald House in Alabama, and signed, limited-edition prints of her *Bridging the Gap*, have raised donations from private parties for various Staten Island organizations, as well as $2,000 to aid the victims of the 2004 tsunami disaster.

In order to disseminate her devotion for the arts, Annette has proctored workshops at the College of Staten Island, the Art Lab at Snug Harbor Cultural Center, the Jewish Community Center and the Institute of Arts and Sciences. Located either in Staten Island or in Manhattan, the Broome Street Gallery, the National School of Design, the Staten Island Institute of Arts and Sciences and the Tibetan Museum have all exhibited her art, along with the Red Carpet Gallery and the Pen and Brush. More than eighty of her paintings were exhibited in a solo show at the Empire State College on Staten Island, New York, from September 2011 to January 2012.

Annette is an active member of several artist groups: the South Shore Artists Group, the Artists Federation, the Harbor Artist Guild, the Snug Harbor Art Lab, the Council of Arts and Humanities of Staten Island and the Staten Island Artists Association, of which she served a term as president.

On a more personal note, she has many passions other than painting, including writing memoirs, gardening and traveling. Her experience with the Writer's Workshop of the American Association of University Women has resulted in her being published in the AAUW's 2007 *Musings* and the *Poetry Festival for Seniors* from 2003 to 2008. The Great Kills Garden Club and the Staten Island Herb Society provided instruction in horticulture and flower design. The herb garden, the numerous potted plants and the floral designs found at her home are physical evidence of her sustained interest. The Martens purchased a stackable washer and dryer to provide space for Annette's easel in the laundry room. Every room in their home has become a gallery for her art.

When the children were young, her creative energy was spent knitting and sewing most of their outfits, as well as her own coats. During times of financial stress, she created draperies and fashion accessories for the home. With her family away from the nest, she has long since put her sewing machine and knitting needles away. Annette and her husband, a retired police sergeant of the New York Police Department, have traveled to European countries, Canada, Mexico and our own Southwest.

Annette has been a member of the Staten Island Astrology Guild since 1986. She enjoys doing psychic readings at charitable fundraisers for the Staten Island Heart Society, organizations benefitting the developmentally disabled and other philanthropic organizations.

Annette is a multitalented, multitasking woman who expends her time and energy in assisting in the promotion of education and philanthropy through the arts.

Antoinette Marten's 2010 autobiography, Staten Island Branch.

BARBARA MCCLINTOCK

1902–1992
GENETICIST

Barbara McClintock was born in 1902 and died in 1992. She is one of only ten female scientists in the world who have been awarded the Nobel Prize. This award was given in 1983 in the areas of physiology and medicine for her research on transposable elements as controlling factors for gene expression in the cells of the maize plant.

McClintock earned her undergraduate degree from Cornell University's College of Agriculture. Her continued interest in botany led to both a master's degree and a doctorate from Cornell. She remained at Cornell to continue her research on the relationship between chromosomes, genes and other aspects of cytogenetics.

In 1944, she was elected president of the Genetics Society of America and became the third woman named to the prestigious National Academy of Scientists, and she was also listed among the one thousand top scientists in the United States.

She held a research position at Cold Spring Harbor Laboratory on Long Island from 1942 until her death in 1992. Her research in the 1950s was not well received. However, by the 1970s, her research on transposition had become accepted, and she was showered with awards. Most of her work was done alone, without even a research assistant. Her life was filled with the joys of discovery and investigation. She was quoted as saying, "One must have the patience to hear what the material has to say to you...Above all, one must have a feeling for the organism." Barbara McClintock was a maverick in all respects—as a woman, as a scientist and as a female scientist. She did not want her work to be looked at as coming from a woman's perspective. She felt very strongly that there is no gender in science. She rejected categories and labels and lived her own scientific life, having fun with the maize plants by making their differences understandable.

Keller, Evelyn Fox. *A Feeling for the Organism: The Life and Works of Barbara McClintock*. New York: W.H. Freeman and Company, 1983.

McClintock. Barbara. "The Significance of the Responses of the Genome to Challenge." Nobel lecture, Stockholm, Sweden, 1983.

Naylor, Natalie, and Maureen O. Murphy, eds. *Long Island Women: Activists and Innovators*. Interlaken, NY: Empire State Books, 1998.

Researcher and author: Marion Mahoney, Islip Area Branch

TESS McCORMACK-RASO

19??–
COMMUNITY LEADER

In 1900, Rockland County was an area of farms and forests with a population of 32,298. With the construction of the George Washington Bridge in 1933, the population increased to 59,599. More homes were built, but it maintained its rural character. The building of the Tappan Zee Bridge, the New York State Thruway and the Palisades Parkway in the 1950s led to a rapid migration of people from the New York City area that radically changed the rural landscape. Shopping centers and houses replaced farms. In 2009, Rockland County was a thriving suburban area with a population approaching 300,000.

With so rapid an increase in population, it was necessary to develop the infrastructure of the community services with volunteer initiative, support and direction. The burgeoning public and professional agencies looked to volunteers for cooperation and support. Women, newcomers and lifelong residents alike participated. Tess McCormack-Raso is an active participant and supporter of community development, a philanthropist and a woman who made a difference. Tess is a native of Rockland County. She has spent most of her life in the area. A veteran of the U.S. Air Force, she was a communications specialist at the Pentagon Building in Washington, D.C. She then returned to Rockland County to live and participate actively in the community. She has volunteered for the following organizations: American Heart Association, St. John's Church, Piermont Public Library, Veterans of Foreign Wars Ladies Auxiliary, Miracle Kids Program (Nyack Hospital), Designer/Holiday House (Nyack Hospital) and Hospice (Walk for Life).

She has served on the board of directors for the following institutions or organizations: Helen Hayes Hospital CAC, 1984–86; Nyack Hospital Foundation, 1986–99 (vice-chair, 1988–95); Orange and Rockland Community Grants Board, 1997–2000; Helen Hayes Performing Arts Center, 1998–2000; Nyack Hospital, 1990–2003 (assistant secretary, 1998); and United Hospice of Rockland, 1998 (board secretary, 2000–2007, and chairman of the board, 2008–present).

Tess has been variously involved in the following fundraising events for the Helen Hayes Hospital: co-chairwoman, Charity Ball, 1984, 1985 and 1986; coordinator and participant, Classic Race, 1984, 1985 and 1986; co-chairwoman, Physician's Ball, 1987–89; co-chairwoman, Travel Fundraisers, 1986–89; and chairwoman, 100 Year Celebration, 1991. (She also donated Boehm porcelain birds to Nyack Hospital in 1984.) She was responsible for a $1 million donation to Nyack Hospital in 1993. In 2006, she was chairwoman of the Night with the Stars Gala at the Helen Hays Performing Arts Center. For the United Hospice of Rockland, she was co-chairwoman, World Yacht Brunch, 1997–98; helped with Tree of Life, 1995–2008; chairwoman, Hospice Night of Laughter, 2004; and chairwoman, Hospice Gala, 2007–9.

She has to her credit a number of media events: *Fitness Over Forty: Body, Mind* and *Soul* (producer/writer/host, 1989–90); *Lifeline to the '90s* (television health talk show; producer/writer/host, 1990–94); *Health Tips with Tess* (feature reporter, TKR Cablevision, 1994–97); and *Lifeline 2001* (television health talk show). She was the society editor for the *Rockland County Times* from 2002 to 2005 and the writer of a monthly column, "Notables." She is the author of *Shopping List for Murder* and is currently writing a screenplay.

Tess has been the recipient of many awards: Woman of the Year, 1989, Rockland County Republican Committee; Woman of the Year, 1992, American Heart Association; Woman of the Year, 1996, United Hospice of Rockland; NYS Media Award, 1993–94 (for Women and Heart Disease); Sandra Dee Veterans Award, 1995 (named after the first woman killed in Desert Storm); Woman of the Year, 1999, Nyack Hospital; Women Who Have Made a Difference Award, 2002; Woman of the Year, 2003, Helen Hayes Hospital; Philanthropist of the Year, 2007; and the Medal of Honor, 2011, at the Good Samaritan Hospital Spring Ball.

While engaged in community service for twenty-five years, Tess was employed as law office administrator for the firm McCormack, Damiani, Lowe & Mellion. She is the mother of three children (Richard, Ronald and Teri); grandmother of six (Kelly, Jesse, Michael, Megan, Danielle and Zachary); and the widow of Gilbert E. McCormack, who died after a long illness. In September 2000, she married Joseph F. Raso. Tess McCormack-Raso remains a source of positive energy, support and development for the community of Rockland County.

Tess McCormack-Raso's 2012 autobiography.

Submitted by Patricia Deacon Cropsey, Rockland County Branch.

ESTER LORD MCNEIL

1811/1812–1906
PRESIDENT, FIRST BRANCH OF THE WOMAN'S CHRISTIAN TEMPERANCE UNION

The Woman's Christian Temperance Union (WCTU) began in Fredonia, New York. That first branch was established on December 22, 1873. In 1877, Ester Lord McNeil was voted its president.

Ester Lord was born in 1811 or 1812 in Carlisle, New York. She was one of ten children. When Ester was ten years old, her father died. Little is known of her life between her father's death and her marriage in 1832 to James McNeil. The newlyweds were united in their belief that alcohol was the root of many evils, and together they worked to fight against "demon alcohol."

Ester Lord McNeil moved with her husband to Fredonia, New York, five years before the women's crusade began. Two years after relocating, James passed away. This did not give McNeil any reason to shirk what she felt were her duties and responsibilities. With the death of her husband, she was responsible for thirteen children, none of them her own. Ester cared for her brother's five children (he was a missionary), as well as eight homeless children she and her husband had brought with them to Chautauqua County. Over the years, she was able to provide food, shelter and what she might have felt was most important, a Christian upbringing, for at least eighteen youngsters. She earned the nickname "Mother McNeil."

McNeil agreed with many that "the sale of intoxicating liquors is the parent of every misery" (an appeal presented to dealers of liquor in Fredonia, 1873). McNeil became a political force to be reckoned with when she accepted the office of president of the WCTU. She served the Fredonia branch for seventeen years and was also the president of the first Chautauqua County chapter, which was organized in 1882. One of WCTU's accomplishments during McNeil's "administration" was the law passed in 1884 requiring New York State schools to teach the scientific information about the effects of alcohol.

Some of her work is recognized by a plaque at the Baptist church in Fredonia, New York. A plaque also stands at the national headquarters of the temperance organization recognizing Fredonia's first chapter. McNeil died in 1906 at the age of ninety-five. After her death, friends erected a drinking fountain in her memory in Fredonia's Barker Commons in 1912.

Gardenier, Georgeanna M. *Two Decades: A History of the First Twenty Years' Work of the Woman's Christian Temperance Union of the State of New York.*

GoogleBooks. http://books.google.com/books/about/Two_decades.
html?id=N1ylrdNhbIwC.

Jamestown Post Journal. "Woman's World." March 21, 1986. Article housed at
the Barker Museum in Fredonia, New York.

Osborne, Jen, ed. "Crusaders Converge in Fredonia—Forming Woman's
Christian Temperance Union." *Chautauqua Sampler* 1, no. 8 (March 1997).

Woman's Christian Temperance Union. "Crusades." February 28, 2009.
www.wctu.org/crusades.html.

Researcher and author: Susan Pepe, Dunkirk Fredonia Branch

ANNE F. MEAD

1924–2010
ATTORNEY/JUDGE

Anne F. Mead, a former member of Islip Area branch of the American
Association of University Women, was an attorney who made a difference
as a woman and accomplished many "firsts."

Anne was a resident of Oakdale, Long Island, New York. She was a 1950
graduate of Fordham Law School and maintained a law office until 1973.
She served as Suffolk County deputy county executive, Town of Islip assistant
attorney and executive director of the Suffolk County Community Council
Inc. In 1974, she was appointed the first female district court judge, and she
became the first woman to preside over a court of record in Suffolk County.
Governor Hugh Carey appointed her to the Public Service Commission
in 1976, and she became the first woman to serve as commissioner for an
interim period in 1987.

Anne Mead received the Ruth G. Schapiro Memorial Award for her
"positive influence upon the women throughout the State of New York."
This prestigious award was established in 1992 to honor someone who has
made a noteworthy contribution to the concerns of women through pro
bono work and/or service to the bar or community organizations.

Anne was known for helping fellow female attorneys and motivating
women to strive for positions of leadership. She established a countywide
program of community health clinics that continues today. As a past president
of the Mental Health Association of Suffolk County, she was involved in
the formation of a psychiatrist rehabilitation program and established an

alternative treatment facility for women convicted of driving under the influence of drugs or alcohol.

Throughout her career as an attorney and judge, as well as in her retirement, Anne Mead continued to show her deep commitment to people in need. She was indeed a woman who made a difference.

Karson, Scott M. "Anne Mead: A Remembrance." *Suffolk Lawyer,* June 2010. www.scba.org/suffolk_lawyer/tsl0610.pdf.
National Women's Hall of Fame. "Anne F. Mead." http://www.greatwomen. org/book-of-lives-and-legacies/search-the-book/details/11/476-Mead.

Researcher and author: Marion Mahoney, Islip Area Branch

DORIS MIGA

1927–
EDUCATOR/VOLUNTEER

Doris Miga was born on February 11, 1927, and raised in New York Mills, New York. She graduated from New York Mills High School as valedictorian. She then graduated from State University of New York–Albany and was a member of Phi Beta Kappa in her junior and senior years. Her degree was in sociology. She continued her education at Syracuse University, graduating with an MA degree in social science. After graduation, Doris taught high school at West Canada Valley. She married and taught until her boys were born. Then she taught adult education at Whitesboro and New York Mills.

Doris had wanted to teach since she was three years old. Her sister, five years older, went to school first. When she came home, she talked about school. Doris then set up her own classroom at home. Her dolls became her students.

Utica College wanted someone to teach sociology for one semester and asked the members of the American Association of University Women if they knew of such a person. Doris Miga was that person. In January 1963, she started teaching. In 1997, she retired from full-time teaching; now she teaches part time. While at Utica College, she started the Foot Wetter Program for Women who had left college or had never attended.

She received many awards from Utica College. In 1980, she received the Distinguished Teaching Award, the first woman to receive this honor. In

1988, she received the Outstanding Faculty Award (as a first-time recipient). The Student Life Award was bestowed on her for the things she did for students. The Honorary Alumni Award was awarded for all the things that she did for the college. In May 2010, she was inducted into the Utica College Pioneer Hall of Fame, a sports hall of fame.

Doris mentored the players of the men's Division I basketball team. She became "Mother Miga" and attended games with her husband for forty-five years, becoming a surrogate parent. She stayed on as mentor after the college changed to Division III.

From the AAUW, she received the Triple E Award from the New York State Division of Excellence and Equity in Education. From the State University of New York–Albany, she received the Alumni Excellence in Teaching Award.

Doris was also active in the community. She served on the Utica College Board of Trustees and was a trustee at the St. Luke Memorial Hospital Center. For twenty years, she served on the Oneida Community Mansion House Board. She was also a trustee at the Lutheran Home Foundation and the Utica Senior Day Center. Doris and her husband, Walter, volunteer at the St. Luke's Gift Shop and have done so for more than thirty years. Seniors in the Mohawk Valley have an opportunity to go back to school through a program known as the Mohawk Valley Institute for Learning in Retirement. Doris teaches there about the utopian societies of the Oneida community, the Shakers and the Amish and has done so for twelve years. At the Masonic Home, she taught miniature courses on communal societies.

Doris has given hundreds of speeches to local organizations, including the New York Mills Honor Society. At the New York Mills Honor Society, she encouraged members to start a program that resulted in the creation of the Miga Mentoring Program; it still exists today. For creating this program, she received the Outstanding Alumni Award.

With AAUW, she is a fifty-year member. She was vice-president of the NYS Division for Membership and helped to form new branches. She was also former president of the Mohawk Valley Branch and a named grant recipient.

Members of the Mohawk Valley Branch are very honored to have Doris as a member and appreciate all the work she has done for the branch and the community. She has contributed greatly to the intellectual development of those with whom she comes in contact.

Miga, Doris. Telephone interviews by Joan Rajchel, November 11–19, 2010.

Researcher and author: Joan Rajchel, Mohawk Valley Branch

Franca Lippi Mills

1928–
Community Leader/Alcoholism Counselor/Author

I was born Franca Maria Ida Lippi in Florence, Italy, on October 7, 1928. The family anxiously watched my survival efforts because my two older brothers had died as infants, and my mother died when I was born. They later told me that I had been a sickly child, and that probably contributed to the fact that everybody spoiled me.

My stepmother doted on me, and I might have been a problem child if my father had not been a disciplinarian. But I took as a model the one person who treated me fairly and lovingly, as she did everything else in her life: my paternal grandmother. Nonna Maria lived life simply and by a tenet of principles that enabled her always to be there to help, but never to intrude or judge. She did the best she could and moved on. Nonna Maria believed that in life you have a duty to help. It wasn't just because you might be a good person or you might think of a heavenly reward in another life, but if God had been generous enough to give you more, you had a duty to help the ones who had less.

I was raised in a time of political chaos. As a child, I attended public school and was enlisted in the Fascist Youth and was well versed in parades and drowned in propaganda. At the tender age of fifteen, I learned a bitter political lesson that affected my views of politics for the rest of my life. In the future, I made sure that my children and grandchildren understood the importance of voting, and I would tell them about the brainwashing process of a dictatorship, the need to keep a democracy alive, but my views of politics had been jaded by the shock of so many years ago.

Nonna Maria had never taken sides. Even during World War II, she looked at the German soldiers around the holidays and felt sorry for "those poor boys so far away from home." She was hoping somebody would be kind to her grandsons who were in the military, spread all over the world. She felt just as sorry for "those poor boys" when the British army invaded her farm, and we, the younger grandchildren, rolled our eyes, unable to really understand her capacity for compassion for our enemies while the world was collapsing around us.

My voyage from a spoiled child to a survivor took five years because of a war that destroyed my way of life but never the principles to live by. I ended up marrying an American soldier and moving to New York, even though I missed my family and friends tremendously. I had been enrolled in the Magistero, which was a special school to train teachers for the elementary grades. I could have graduated at the age of eighteen, but the school closed early because there was an invading army coming up from the South. My school collapsed when the Germans blew up every available bridge in their retreat. The "Gino Capponi" had been a great mansion on the river Arno until that fatal day. I struggled a year later trying to make up courses, but I never finished. Only after many years of marriage, after my oldest daughters graduated from college and my younger son was still in high school, did I go back to school.

By that time, I was working as an alcoholism counselor at South Oaks Hospital in Amityville, and I enrolled in the ABLE (Adult Baccalaureate Learning Experience) program at Adelphi. I shocked myself when I got an A in my first English class...in English! I continued taking courses at night and graduated with my BA a few years later. But a lot of things had happened in between. When my daughters were in high school, the specter of illegal drugs had raised fears in most parents. We had thought that the sprawling manicured lawns, the friendly neighbors, the athletic activities, the new schools and the loving families had insulated us from such an invasion. It was a rude awakening to learn that drug addicts were our neighbor's children, our children's friends and possibly even our own children.

At a PTA meeting at the Farmingdale High School in 1968, I listened in total fear to the mother of a local student who had ended up in Topic House. This was a lovely, caring woman, who chose to share her story in an effort to help other parents face the reality of the situation. Some of us knew that as a community we had to do something. Three of us stood up after the meeting and agreed to meet to discuss the situation. A few more turned up; we were frightened housewives, unaware of the rules, the red tape, stepping on people's toes...but we were determined. I felt the same urgency spurred by fear, the familiar fear experienced years ago, the fear that could paralyze you or that could move you to do things bigger than yourself. Nonna Maria was never paralyzed by fear, or by self-pity, or by anger. She always moved on. And so did I.

We navigated through the twists and turns of writing a state grant, guided by the Nassau County Commission of Drugs and Alcohol in Mineola, which was encouraging local groups to open more drug prevention centers, and by Mike Tartamello, who taught health in the Farmingdale High School. Some officials petted us on the head like well-meaning housewives who were making some waves. Some listened. We now had a board of mainly women (somehow most fathers remained inactive) and a direction, and the thousand of hours we donated as volunteers fueled our efforts.

We received training from the offices in Mineola on drugs, on teenagers, on public relations and on how to decode the terms of our state grant. We had to prove we could reach the kids in our town and our first talk on drugs at the local Methodist church netted us several teenagers who became our clients and advisors and our teachers.

We opened a center with the money we collected among ourselves to pay for the first month's rent. We knew the state had approved our grant. We called it PRICE, which stood for Prevention, Referral, Information, Counseling and Education. The kids helped us set up, paint the place and set the rules. We now could have a staff and a lot of volunteers. For years, we remained involved, proud to have a center where teenagers could come and talk, or play or get counseling, hoping to have made a little dent in the insurgent problem. The center became more and more professional, and some of us moved on. They now had money to hire the proper staff.

After doing so much volunteer work, I thought that I should get a paying job. I tried to look at my expertise, and it didn't look great. I had not finished school, and whatever schooling I did have had been in Italian; the only experience I had was on drugs and alcohol. It was Mike Tartamello who suggested I take a one-year course at South Oaks Hospital on how to become an alcoholism counselor. My family encouraged me, and so I attended, did a two-month internship and was hired as an alcoholism family counselor before I even filled out the application. I had not dared to hope that much, but it was happening. The plight of the families tugged at my heart. The addicts were involved in a deadly game, but the very drugs they took warped their reality. The families watched in horror and helplessness. One of my dearest friends, Evelyn, got information on a self-help group for parents in California, and after getting the brochure, we tried to start one in New York. It was slow and tentative, but some Alanon members helped, and today, FA (Families Anonymous) has several groups in most parts of New York State. The crowning glory was when the FA headquarters in California asked me to help them translate *Today a Better Way*, a book of daily inspirational passages, into Italian, as FA has opened some groups in Italy.

Time passes, families grow and life takes a toll. I lost the man who transplanted me to this country, my gentle companion, in 1990. I am blessed with family and friends, but after I retired, there seemed to be more of a need to be involved in the community, the need to give it back. Nonna Maria's words seemed to float into my head. I was so lucky to have great kids, great-grandchildren, great neighbors and loving friends. I did some volunteer work at the library and with Meals on Wheels. I made myself available to drive my friends in need of a ride, stayed with my daughter and grandsons months at a time while my son-in-law was once in Kuwait and once in Iraq, and I became more involved in the American Association of University Women (AAUW).

My friend Terry and I became co-presidents. As a group, we were thinking of ways to make the organization more visible when we stumbled on the idea of having a project involving the community. We definitely had a lot of experience in the past involving the community.

The Book Project was born. The PTA president and the principal of the Northside Farmingdale School helped us collect children's books, new or like new, to be distributed to several worthy organizations. The first year, we collected nine hundred books, which we sorted and distributed to Head Start, the Salvation Army and so on. By the third year, we were collecting more than four thousand books.

We then thought to penetrate the middle school, and the project on "Global Warming" originated. This was a timely and community-minded subject, and when we presented it to the head of the Farmingdale School District Science Department, it was warmly received. We would give eight monetary awards for the best essays on "Global Warming."

As of today, about six hundred students and forty teachers have received thank-you letters on AAUW stationery, and sixteen elementary students and three junior high students have earned monetary awards. AAUW has been proudly mentioned on the program for the awards ceremony, and we hope we have stimulated some of the children to think about the future of their planet and also to remember our organization. And just like good stewards of our earth, we need not plunder but save our resources; in our lifetime, we need to give more than we take.

In 2011, my first book was published by Publish America just days short of my eighty-third birthday. Its title is *Strangers and Memories*, and it details the political upheaval and consequent struggle most Italians had to endure after Italy surrendered to the Allies in September 1943. Although the stories are true, the book is listed as fiction because I cannot accurately recall the names of people or of some of the places where events took place.

I have to give credit to my family and friends for coaxing me into writing some of my World War II memories. I never dreamed they would become a book. As you can see, it's never too late to start a new chapter in your life.

Franca Mills's 2012 autobiography, Farmingdale Branch.

NANCY MION

19??–
LIBRARIAN/VOLUNTEER

Nancy Mion is truly a woman who makes a difference. She has tirelessly donated her time, energy, finances and enormous talent to give assistance to women and girls in many areas.

We at the American Association of University Women (AAUW), and especially the Islip Area Branch, are very proud of her numerous accomplishments. Our organization has the mission to advance equity for women and girls through advocacy, education and research. Nancy works to promote AAUW's vision to be a powerful advocate and visible leader in equity and education through research, philanthropy and measurable change in critical areas affecting the lives of women and girls.

Nancy has been a member of the Islip Area Branch since 1975. She served as its president from 1982 to 1984 and again from 1996 to 2000 and co-president from 2009 to 2010. For many years, she has served as the Legal Advocacy Fund chair. This job involved a great deal of education and fundraising for the branch in order to help provide financial assistance for women (and men) who have been discriminated against in their teaching endeavors in higher education. Her involvement with the Islip area branch also includes holding additional offices, chairing many committees, hosting activities and performing a great many additional responsibilities for our organization.

In 2004, she was elected AAUW New York State president. Her leadership of about 5,500 members from 2004 to 2006 was outstanding. Her administration worked tirelessly on the issues of pay equity, school funding and support of Title IX, to name a few of her concerns.

Some of her other AAUW roles in New York have included being representative to New York Children's Action Network, New York Child Care Coordinating Council, Winnings Beginnings New York and New York State Pay Equity Coalition. Nancy was the New York State public policy director from 2006 to 2010, was convention director for four years and worked on the membership committee and on the Women's Work Women's Worth Task Force.

Nancy was a member of the AAUW Public Policy Committee from 2007 to 2011. As a member of this committee, she advised the AAUW Board and public policy staff on legislative actions to be pursued that would most effectively further AAUW's mission. She acted as a liaison between the board and state public policy directors encouraging grass-roots action. In addition, she worked on developing the public policy program to be presented at the AAUW conventions.

Nancy Mion has focused her attention on additional organizations in order for her efforts to truly make a difference. Since 1984, she has worked for the Suffolk County Coalition Against Domestic Violence, having served as its president, vice-president, treasurer and secretary. This organization, with a budget of more than $1 million, directly serves the women of Suffolk County by providing emergency shelter for women and children, a 24/7 manned hot line, outreach programs in schools and organizations, advocates in every precinct and an attorney on staff. It receives grants from the county and outside grants and has fundraisers in order to provide these necessary services to our Suffolk County residents.

Her activities with the Long Island Fund for Women and Girls Gender Equity Committee from 2000 to 2010 were also notable. This organization prepares a conference for about 350 ninth- to twelfth-grade girls and additional workshops for adults who work with young women of this age range. This event is held at Stony Brook University. Some topics that have been the focus of the conference have included leadership, financial planning, career planning, tolerance, opportunity, respect and twenty-first-century planning.

Nancy is a Bayport resident who prior to her retirement was employed by the Connetquot School District for thirty-seven years as a library media specialist. Besides the activities mentioned, at this time she was raising her three children and active in the Library Media Association and the Board of Cooperative Educational Services (BOCES) School Library Council.

In addition to these descriptions of her volunteer work, it is also important to note the warmth, concern and caring that she constantly exhibits to her many friends. Here, too, she can always be counted on. Her passion for the causes mentioned is evident when she speaks to individuals, as well as when she has the opportunity to address a large group.

Nancy Mion is deserving of the honor of being known as a women who makes a difference. Each of the areas mentioned have been greatly enriched by her passion, leadership, creativity, personal commitment and financial support. She is truly a source of inspiration to all who know her.

Information obtained from Nancy Mion, 2010, updated January 2013.

Researcher and author: Marion Mahoney, Islip Area Branch

MARIA SALMON MITCHELL

1818–1889
ASTRONOMER/EDUCATOR

In 1865, Maria Salmon Mitchell became professor of astronomy at Vassar College in Poughkeepsie, New York, the first person (male or female) appointed to the faculty. She was also named as director of the Vassar College Observatory. After teaching there for some time, she learned that despite her reputation and experience, her salary was less than that of many younger male professors. She insisted on a salary increase and got it.

She was friends with various suffragists, such as Elizabeth Cady Stanton. In protest against slavery, she stopped wearing clothes made of cotton.

On October 1, 1847, Maria Mitchell discovered a telescopic comet, an accomplishment for which she received a gold medal from King Frederick of Denmark. She was the first woman elected to the American Academy of Arts and Sciences, the American Association for the Advancement of Science and the American Philosophical Society. She founded and was president of the American Association for the Advancement of Women. She led one session of the Women's Congress. Maria was given an honorary degree from Columbia College, and a crater on the moon was named for her. Posthumously, a tablet with her name was put in the New York University Hall of Fame, her name was carved in a frieze at the Boston Public Library and she was inducted into the National Women's Hall of Fame. She was also the namesake of a World War II Liberty ship, the SS *Maria Mitchell*. Maria Mitchell's telescope is on display in the Smithsonian Institution National Museum of American History.

Maria was born on August 1, 1818, in Nantucket, Massachusetts. She was the third child of William and Lydia Mitchell, a Quaker family with ten children. Her parents valued education and insisted on giving her the same quality of education that boys received.

When Maria was eleven, she was a student and also a teaching assistant to her father, who built his own school. At home, her father taught her astronomy using his personal telescope. At age twelve and a half, she aided her father in calculating the exact moment of an annular eclipse.

Later, she attended Unitarian minister Cyrus Peirce's school for young ladies. She opened her own school in 1835 until she was offered a job as the first librarian of the Nantucket Atheneum, where she worked for eighteen years. She later worked at the United States Nautical Almanac Office, calculating tables of positions of Venus.

She died on June 28, 1889, at the age of seventy and was buried in Nantucket. The Maria Mitchell Observatory in Nantucket is named in her honor. She is known for a famous quote: "We have a hunger of the mind. We ask for all of the knowledge around us and the more we get, the more we desire."

She Is an Astronomer. www.sheisanastronomer.org.
Wikipedia. "Maria Mitchell." http://en.wikipedia.org/wiki/Maria_Mitchell.

Researcher and author: Mary Lou Davis, Poughkeepsie Branch

SIBYL O'REILLY MIZZI

1929–
ANTHROPOLOGIST/EDUCATOR

Sibyl was born on November 17, 1929, in New York City, the first and only child of Phyllis and Bryan O'Reilly, five years after they had arrived in the United States from Dublin, Ireland. She spent her early years in New York City and moved to Sayville, Long Island, in 1938.

She attended St. Lawrence School in Sayville and Seton Hall High School in Patchogue, and in 1947, she won a full scholarship to Manhattanville College of the Sacred Heart in New York City. In 1950, she left college and began working as a laboratory assistant at Brookhaven National Laboratory in the clinical chemistry department, where she worked with Dr. Donald D. Van Slyke (the "Father of Biochemistry") for two years. In 1952, she married Charles Mizzi and moved to upstate New York. She returned to Sayville a year later with her husband and first daughter, Patricia. Charles started teaching handicapped children on Long Island, and they had Pamel, Pia and Philip during the next ten years.

In 1960, Sibyl, along with several other women, started the Town of Islip League of Women Voters. She spent much of her spare time working for that organization and holding various positions, including president, for several years.

In 1963, she returned to her academic pursuits at Adelphi-Suffolk College and graduated with a BA degree in social science in 1966. Four years later, in 1970, she was accepted into a new PhD program at the State University of New York–Stony Brook in anthropology and began a new segment of her life. During her first semester at Stony Brook, Dr. Lawrence Slobodkin, the chair of the ecology and evolution department, received a Ford Foundation Grant called "New Horizons" and went looking for an anthropology student to work with him on his new project. Sibyl was chosen because of her experience with the League of Women Voters. The grant was to discover if it was possible to educate ordinary individuals on environmental issues and help them to become advocates for new environmental issues. Some of the issues studied included a new bridge from Long Island to Connecticut and a new planned community in Manorville, Long Island. At the same time, she chose as her anthropology project the study of women in Malta and began to do research in Malta during the summers.

The years at Stony Brook (1970–81) were packed with full-time courses and ordinary life with a husband, four children, a large house and aging parents—all needing love and attention. Sibyl remained active in the League of Women Voters for several more years and then started teaching undergraduate anthropology courses at Dowling College from 1974 to 1976. She graduated from Stony Brook University with a PhD in social anthropology in May 1981, and her dissertation, "Women of Senglea: The Changing Role of Urban Working Class Women in Malta," was published in Malta in 1982.

In 1976, she, along with her partner David M. Graham (the former executive director of the Ford Foundation Grant at Stony Brook), started a consulting firm, Pan Tech Management Corporation, in the town of Babylon and received a contract from the town to administer the new Community Development Block Grant Program. Over fifteen years, Pan Tech grew from a two-person operation to a staff of twenty-five as the funding for the town grew from $30,000 to $6 million. During those years, Pan Tech developed subsidized housing for both senior citizens and for families in the town of Babylon and administered projects such as building a new senior citizen center in Tanner Park, providing water mains in Wyandanch and developing a new community center in North Amityville.

In 1991, Sibyl and her husband retired and went to live in Malta. During her research years there, she had bought a five-hundred-year-old farmhouse, and they decided to go live in it and start a new life. Within the first six months in Malta, Sibyl and Charles had new jobs teaching at the University of Malta. Sibyl was asked to take over a brand-new effort to start an anthropology program at the University of Malta, and Charles was asked to start a new program for education of the handicapped in Malta. Sibyl stayed in Malta for seven years, and the anthropology program grew substantially. In 1995, Sibyl was invited by the Maltese government to be a consultant to the Maltese delegation to the International Conference on Women in Beijing. During these years, Sibyl brought over one grandchild every year to attend school in Malta and travel with their grandparents around the Mediterranean world.

In 1997, Sibyl and Charles returned to Sayville, New York, retired for the second time and decided to travel and see the United States after spending so much time seeing Europe and the Mediterranean. Sibyl became a member of the Islip Area Branch of the American Association of University Women and became involved in its activities. She started an anthropology seminar for AAUW that turned out to be a successful activity for all involved.

The years from 2000 to 2005 were devoted to helping her husband, Charles, in his losing battle with cancer. After her husband's death, Sibyl joined the faculty at Dowling College as an adjunct associate professor of sociology and anthropology and is currently teaching sociology at Dowling. Also in 2005, Sibyl joined New Directions, a "Community Based Research Institute," as a board member and as housing director. New Directions is currently working on developing community land trusts as an alternative way of building affordable housing on Long Island, and it is funded by a Ford Foundation Grant.

Sibyl spends much of her time with her children and grandchildren, all of whom live in Sayville—sometimes babysitting, sometimes helping and many times talking. She also travels to Malta every year, where she still has an apartment on the Mediterranean and continues her research. Some of her publications include *Islip Town Youth Board: A Feasibility Study* (in collaboration with S. Antler), Public Systems Research Inc., 1976; *An Integrated Respite Care System for Suffolk County, N.Y.* (with E. Stokes), a report of findings submitted to and published by Suffolk, New York; "Gossip: A Means of Social Control" in *Maltese Society*; and *A Sociological Inquiry*, edited by E.G. Sultana and Mireva G. Baldacchino, 1994. She is currently putting together forty years of research on Maltese women for a book to be published in Malta soon.

Information obtained from Sibyl O'Reilly Mizzi, 2011.

Researcher and author: Marlene Gilliam, Islip Area Branch

ANNA MARY ROBERTSON MOSES

1860–1961
ARTIST

Anna Mary Robertson Moses, more popularly known as Grandma Moses, was an American primitive painter. She specialized in the rural life of her childhood memories. Farm life and countryside scenes were painted with simple realism, nostalgic auras and bright colors. The exceptional way she brought life to her paintings gained her a wide following among art lovers. She became well known in spite of starting her painting career later in life. Anna Mary Robertson was born on September 7, 1860, in Greenwich, New York, the third child in a family of ten. To help meet financial needs, she was hired to help another family. Her schooling was limited, but she attended school with her employer's children. In her twenties, she married Thomas Salmon Moses, also a hired worker. They moved to Virginia, where they rented farms. With the five of their surviving ten children, they returned to New York State, where they bought a farm.

At that time, she was called Mother Moses. She enjoyed doing needlework, sewing and embroidery. Her arthritis at the age of seventy-six made it painful to push the needle through the material. In 1938, when she was in her late seventies, she took up painting, using house paint to create her first picture. Her art can be called folk art, as she was self-taught. Sometimes, her style is referred to as "primitive" art. She painted simple pictures: scenes of family, church and community, portraying the virtues of honesty and hard work. She personified these virtues. She painted many pictures of the Hoosick Valley area in all seasons. Her farm paintings depicted soap, maple syrup and apple butter manufacture, husking corn and making candles. Her "checkerboard" house that appeared in many paintings actually existed, dating back to the Revolutionary War. Two of her favorite subjects were county fairs and holidays.

In 1938, she was displaying some work in a drugstore in Hoosick Falls. A New York City art collector, Louis Caldor, saw them and liked her work. He bought several of her paintings and some art supplies for her; he also used his influence to market her work. He introduced the owner of Galerie Saint Etienne in New York City to her works. Otto Kallir arranged a one-woman show for her, calling the exhibit What a Farm Wife Painted. Grandma Moses appeared at an exhibit at Gimbel's Department Store and charmed people with her honesty and simplicity, as well as her qualities of being down-to-earth and unpretentious.

When she was younger, Anna made pictures out of yarn. Her textile pictures show how they relate to her later efforts with paint. Her textile picture of Mount Nebo has been made into fabric. She saw her art as something she enjoyed doing. It also provided extra money. By the time she was eighty, many people had heard of "Grandma Moses" and had seen her paintings. Her works were first sold for $5. Later, they were sold for between $8,000 and $10,000.

She received many awards and honors. Her painting *The Checkerboard Inn* was featured in a national advertising campaign for the lip gloss Primitive Red by Du Barry cosmetics in 1946. She was awarded the Women's National Press Club Trophy Award for her outstanding accomplishments in art in 1949. The TV show *See It Now* had her on one of its episodes. Her autobiography, *Grandma Moses: My Life's History*, was published in 1952. Governor Nelson Rockefeller proclaimed the day of her 100th birthday as Grandma Moses Day to honor the artistically gifted and talented lady. In 2006, her work *Sugaring Off* became her highest-selling work at $1.2 million. *Fourth of July*, painted to honor President Dwight Eisenhower, still hangs in the White House. She also appeared on the Edward R. Murrow TV show, showing people how to paint a picture.

Grandma Moses was honored by presidents and governors. Many books were written about her. She died at the age of 101 on December 13, 1961, at

Hoosick Falls Health Center after a fall in her home. The doctors attributed "hardening of the arteries" as the reason for her fall.

Crouse, Dorothy Robinson. An interview discussion about Grandma Moses recorded by Joan Rajchel at the James Fennimore Cooper Art Museum. In the possession of Joan Rajchel.

Researcher and author: Joan Rajchel, Mohawk Valley Branch

MARIA NAKAZAWA

19??–
COMMUNITY VOLUNTEER/HOUSE RENOVATOR

Maria's mission in life was to improve and rejuvenate her Valley Cottage neighborhood and the community in which she lived. She began more than forty years ago by volunteering to design and maintain a Japanese garden in the courtyard of Nyack Hospital. Patients, visitors and staff enjoyed it in all four seasons.

After some homes burned down in the neighborhood, perhaps due to arson, she felt compelled to take action. She decided to take the imitative and renovate one of them. Once she had finished that house, she kept going, renovating one house after another. One special project was the transformation of Mountainview Road. She removed forty years of garbage from the area swamp, filling many dumpsters with refrigerators, stoves, bicycles and rubbish that had been discarded there. She then restored the beautiful pond. Now the neighbors can fish in it. She restored the four homes that border the pond, increasing their value and the value of the surrounding neighborhood.

Forty-nine homes later, she joined the Valley Cottage Civic Association. She was a key driver of the urban renewal of the town, which was completed in 2008. She was an enthusiastic ambassador of the Focus on Urban Preservation program.

Maria Nakazawa was born in Hungary to Margit and Sander Ferenczy. In 1957, she and her brother escaped from Budapest and went to live in Toronto, Canada. In 1958, she began study at McGill University and received a degree in biology. She married Dr. Hiro Nakazawa in 1962. In 1963, they came to the United States, where she worked first at the Hospital for Joint Diseases, located at Columbia University, until their daughter, Aniko, was born in 1967. Their son, Dirk, was born in 1970. The children attended a Waldorf School, where Maria tended a garden and ran toy fairs. Later, when their daughter attended the Masters School, Maria was an active member of the Parents Association and assisted with the craft shop, which was operated to raise funds for scholarships. In the 1980s, she began serving on the Helen Hayes Theater Board of Directors and with the Girl Scouts, the Women's Shelter and the Morning Music Club. Later, she served on the boards of the Historical Society of Rockland County, Keep Rockland Beautiful, the Japanese American Medical Association, the Scholarship Committee, the Valley Cottage Library Board and the Valley Cottage Civic Association.

Her current home is the former Onderdonk House on Kings Highway in Valley Cottage. The house is about 270 years old. It was purchased from Mrs. Ward, a daughter of the MacViccker family. Maria has done extensive work on the property, including land clearing and stabilization of the cliff-like hillside next to the house and above the spring-fed pond. The pond features an island with a gazebo, all beautifully landscaped. It seems that the work is never done because Maria always has a project underway on the house or grounds. One of Maria's restorations is the former Continental Hotel at the northeast corner of Rockland Lake.

Maria Nakazawa's May 10, 2009 autobiography.
Submitted by Patricia Deacon Cropsey, Rockland County Branch.

ROSEMARY S. NESBITT

1924–2009
EDUCATOR/AUTHOR/HISTORIAN/STAGE DIRECTOR

It is rare indeed to encounter an individual with an intense appreciation for culture, a profound respect for intellect, a boundless enthusiasm for learning and a relentless pursuit of life in its fullness. Embodying these qualities, Rosemary Nesbitt also evidences an enduring faith in the goodness of people, diligence in every endeavor and an unrelenting concern for the importance of history—not least the history that is formative for life, individually and collectively. Meet Rosemary and you will find yourself changed, energized and inspired, as well as determined to redouble your effort to pursue life with all available strength and energy. You will also encounter someone who infuses the idea of leadership with new meaning, rescues the dignity of women from patriarchal domination and refreshes the concept of volunteerism for a new day.

Rosemary was born on October 12, 1924, on Columbus Day; that reference is intentional, especially if we are to be conscious of the importance of discovering that which already exists. She was raised in Baldwinsville, New York, by her parents, Matthew Alphonsus and Mary Louise Sinnett. She grew up with a sister (now deceased) and a brother, who resides in Syracuse. She gained a love for local history from her father, a love that ultimately made Oswego both home and inspiration. She sees in her parents a formative influence defining her early development, generating commitment to learning, openness to diversity, an embrace of culture, a durable work ethic and love of life.

Rosemary spoke with appreciation for her parents, citing their wisdom in securing opportunities for her to experience events of lasting significance. At the age of five, her father took her to see Franklin Delano Roosevelt when the presidential yacht visited Baldwinsville. Upon boarding the yacht, she exchanged words with the president, speaking of his granddaughter by name. The president took her on his knee, whereupon she asked him if his braces were painful. He responded to her that surely they were! She recalled the fact that she had been able to speak with the president personally and that he spoke to her with great clarity and acknowledged how grateful she was that her father would have taken her as a five-year-old, to experience such a moment.

Who among us owns such a recollection as Rosemary shares of an encounter arranged by Eunice Hilton, dean of women at Syracuse University, who selected Rosemary (while a student at SU) to have an individual encounter with Helen Keller? Rosemary carries the memories of both FDR throwing his head back in hearty laughter with her on his lap and of Ms. Keller reaching her hands toward her, feeling Rosemary's face with both hands, her fingers moving along her eyebrows, her cheekbones, the curvature of her face and then (as one knowledgeable in speaking from the heart) affirming in the memorable sonority of her voice, "Now I know what you look like!"

Rosemary, a spellbinding storyteller, inspiring stage director, distinguished teacher and esteemed local historian, was cited as excelling in whatever she did by a respected friend, Bruce Frassinelli, publisher of the *Palladium-Times*, at her June 21, 1993 retirement. To even attempt to chronicle Rosemary's accomplishments and achievements falls far short of capturing a life's journey distinguished with resplendent scenery, genuine human/cultural encounters and an indomitable will.

Rosemary earned her undergraduate and master's degrees from Syracuse University. She was one of two students to receive a master's degree while studying under Sawyer Faulk, founder of the National Theater Academy, during his twenty-five-year career at Syracuse University. While in training for her teaching career, she performed in plays in summer stock and graduate school. Her initial teaching assignments were at Wells College and Syracuse University, a period of time during which, with clear intention, she traveled to postwar Europe, taking in both the reality of war's devastation and the enduring cultural markers, museums and cathedrals—the humanity of the survivors of warfare.

Subsequently, she met and married George Nesbitt, son of the family who resided in the residence she has called home for more than forty years. In 1965, she began teaching at the State University of New York–Oswego and became more interested in stage production. Across the span of her career, Rosemary selected and mounted more than thirty productions at Oswego State, beginning with C.S. Lewis's *The Lion, the Witch and the Wardrobe* and including *Dracula*, *A Miracle on 34th Street* (brought back three times by popular demand), *A Christmas Carol*, *Romeo and Juliet*, *The Wizard of Oz*, *Tom Sawyer*, *Cinderella*, *Pinocchio*, *Alice in Wonderland* and *Arabian of the Night*, to name but a few. The last production she mounted prior to retiring was *The Taming of the Shrew*, one of Shakespeare's most famous plays.

When her teaching career began at Oswego State, three courses in theater were offered as part of the curriculum of the school's English department. Under her leadership, the theater program matured into a stand-alone department in the late 1960s even as plans were laid for Tyler Hall and Waterman Theater. The theater department as we experience it had its genesis in the leadership of Rosemary Nesbitt.

In 1971, Rosemary's husband died at the age of fifty after a brief illness. Surmounting her grief and loss and recognizing that life continues, Rosemary's parenting of their four children sought to create in them the same appreciation for culture, the strength of character and the understanding of self and world that had steeled her own experience. The summer following her husband's death, she embarked on an eleven-thousand-mile journey with the children, taking in national parks across the United States.

Mrs. Nesbitt founded the H. Lee White Marine Museum in 1983, was board president of the Port Authority, served as the Marine Museum's executive director, served as director of children's theater, led the Heritage Foundation, chaired the United Way Fund campaign for several years and led successful campaigns to refurbish St. Mary's Church. She was city historian; member of Oswego Zonta Club, the American Association of University Women and National League of Pen Women; and a consultant with Ginn & Company, school textbook publishers. She was instrumental in the erection of the monument to women and families at Fort Ontario and authored two children's books, *The Great Rope* and *Col. Meacham's Giant Cheese*. She adapted *The Great Rope* into a play for Oswego's opening bicentennial activity. More than 150 children appeared in the cast. The play received the George Washington Gold Medal, out of twenty thousand entries, from Freedom's Foundation of Valley Forge for the best college production of 1976.

Among her many honors, Rosemary won the Service to the Arts Award from the Cultural Resources Council of Syracuse and Onondaga County, given to individuals whose contributions are deemed extraordinary by the council. Other honors included the George Arens Pioneer Medal from Syracuse University. In 1973, she was among the first to receive the Chancellor's Award for Excellence in Teaching, and in 1977, her fellow professors made her a Distinguished Teaching Professor.

At the time of her retirement from Oswego State in 1995, Mr. Frassinelli noted in his editorial:

> *This extraordinary woman...came to Oswego from Baldwinsville thirty-six years ago* [and] *has been the driving force in making Oswego aware of its rich pre-1848 heritage. But perhaps her greatest legacy will be in the number of young lives she has touched in the classroom and on the stage. As a professor of Theater, she taught not only the techniques of the stage, but those of life. Characterized by single-mindedness, high ideas, impeccable moral standards, and boundless generosity, Nesbitt has always expected much from her students, colleagues and associates, but has always pushed herself, more than*

*she has pushed them. Through it all, she has kept her priorities intact.
Surrounded by her four children and* [at that time] *her granddaughter,
she said, "These are my pearls." Every community should be fortunate
enough to have a Rosemary Nesbitt among its citizens.*

In many respects, Rosemary's legacy reaches far into the future. Reflecting
fifteen years subsequent to that retirement, Rosemary spoke of the traveling
she undertook in Europe during the summers of her early years in teaching,
after the end of World War II. Traveling in England, France, Germany, Italy
and Switzerland, she came upon a Europe in the immediate aftermath of war.
By bicycle, she witnessed in many cities and countrysides the surviving culture
amid devastation. From concentration camp sites she described as incredibly
vast to the Vatican, where she marveled at Michelangelo's painting—which
appeared to her as if it were floating overhead in the Sistine Chapel—she
was conscious of the heights and depths to which human experience reaches.
She gained a sense of the indomitable human spirit. Rosemary spoke with
appreciation of the sacrifices of thousands whose willingness to give their lives
for a tomorrow they would not see and credited Baldwinsville for its continued
unique observation of Memorial Day.

She recalled a classmate from Baldwinsville, Richard Glass, who met his
death crawling over a land mine on D-Day at Normandy. He was a friend from
first grade through to his receiving a full scholarship at Syracuse University
to study medicine. There were two Jewish families in Baldwinsville. One
was the family of Joe Glass, who owned a shoe store; his wife fled Europe.
Richard was their son.

Museums, cathedrals, the Louvre in Paris, the British Museum in London
and more—they all impressed Rosemary as monuments to the human spirit,
markers of western civilization, never to be cause for arrogance, always to
serve as invitations to humility and never to be forgotten.

A brief biography of Rosemary Nesbitt's life is of necessity unfinished
and but a limited glimpse into a mind, an experience, a journey that truly
defies description. Brief as this accounting is, it would be less than complete
without noting Rosemary's reflections on "women"—*women* writ large!
Beginning with the presumed emergence of Eve from a rib of Adam in
Genesis, Rosemary has ever been astute both with respect to Biblical exegesis
and with the immeasurable costs incurred and the scorn and ignorance
perpetuated by male-dominated societies. She possessed the gift of being
able to bring the unseen to awareness. Visiting Valley Forge, Rosemary
quietly but directly inquired of the park guide, "Can you speak about the

women who were at Valley Forge?" The earnest young man was nonplussed. Rosemary offered a response, noting that General Washington had appealed to the citizens of Philadelphia for women to nurse those in the encampment, and more than one hundred responded. Rendering the invisible visible is Rosemary's gift. Not a person to lend her presence so much to organized efforts of a feminist movement, she chose an alternate route, demonstrating by her own leadership, intellect and knowledge of history the fact that people do not live by men alone. A huge cost is attached to overlooking, diminishing, underestimating, dominating or neglecting 50 percent of the population. But an even greater cost is incurred by forfeiting opportunities to learn, grow, appreciate and serve.

One could not come away from an encounter with Rosemary without recognizing that it was an encounter with a teacher, a professor, a mother, a daughter, a grandmother, a granddaughter, a historian, a dramatist, a playwright, an author, an actor, a physician, a lawyer, a priest, an American, an American cognizant of Native Americans, a jurist, a carpenter, an engineer, an architect, a builder, a pharmacist, a curator, a biologist, a traveler, an archaeologist, a theologian or a philosopher. Much like a prism refracting white light into all its composite color, Rosemary's life refracted into myriad roles. For one so thoroughly immersed in theater, her life itself was the stage on which she lived out her intentions. Her narration was spellbinding.

Listen to Rosemary's recounting of the experience of Dr. Mary Walker. You will find your heart moved at the courage and character of a woman in a world presumed to be the exclusive domain of men. Listen to Rosemary's pride and excitement over learning of her granddaughter's pending graduate study, with an undergraduate major in Arabic. The world exists to be embraced, to be learned about. It begs for leadership, intellect, character and service. Those qualities bespeak honor. They are pervasive in Rosemary's story. They illuminate her life, and through her presence and legacy, they are within reach for us as well.

Rosemary died on Sunday, August 3, 2009, in Oswego, with her family by her side.

Throughout her life and career, Rosemary Nesbitt was determined to illuminate through word and experience, on stage and in community, an enduring labor of love, lifting up the inheritance of culture and intellect and also determined to live her life with energy, enthusiasm, imagination and affection. She succeeded and so is an enduring inspiration. A monument honoring Rosemary can be found in Breitbeck Park as you approach the original ball tower from the Kingsford Starch Factory. Hers was a life larger than life—her legacy aside the river, the waters of which know no end.

Frassinelli, B. "Nesbitt's Impact Legendary." *Palladium Tmes,* June 21, 1993.
Music Educators National Conference Journal. "Educator Honored in the Gifts of Music" (1994).
Nesbitt, Rosemary. Interviewed and recorded by James Tschudy, 2009.
Palladium-Times. "Marine Museum Announces Retirement of Executive Director." February 22, 2008.

Photograph courtesy of the H. Lee White Marine Museum, Oswego, New York. Researcher and author: James C. Tschudy, Oswego Branch

PATRICIA JOY NUMANN

1941–
SURGEON/EDUCATOR

Dr. Patricia Numann's distinguished career as a surgeon at the State University of New York Health Science Center in Syracuse, New York, has received local, state, national and international attention.

Born on April 6, 1941, in the Bronx, New York, she and her family moved to the Catskill Mountains when she was five years old. Raised in the supportive atmosphere of an extended family, she was especially influenced by her parents and by her aunt, who encouraged education and perfection. After graduating from Roxbury Central School in Roxbury, New York, in 1958, she earned a BA degree from the University of Rochester in Rochester, New York, in 1962 and an MD from the SUNY Health Science Center in Syracuse in 1965. Eight of the eighty-seven students accepted were women, and six out of seventy-nine graduated. Postgraduate training as intern in mixed medicine and surgery was completed in 1966 and as resident in general surgery in 1970 at the same institution. She was granted board certification in 1966 by the National Board of Medical Examiners and in 1971 by the American Board of Surgery.

Her career began in 1970 when she became assistant professor of surgery at the SUNY Health Science Center at Syracuse, and despite obstacles as a woman, she advanced through the academic ranks to professor of surgery in 1989, a SUNY Distinguished Teaching Professor in 1994 and both a SUNY Distinguished Service Professor and the Lloyd S. Rogers Professor of Surgery in 2000. She retired as the Lloyd S. Rogers Professor of Surgery Emeritus in 2007. Administrative positions held during those years included associate dean of the College of Medicine Clinical Affairs (1989–94) and medical director of University Hospital (1999–2007). She also held professional appointments as surgeon in Syracuse hospitals: SUNY Upstate Medical Center (the first female surgeon), the Veterans Administration Hospital and Crouse Irving Memorial Hospital.

The honors she has been awarded are too numerous to list, but many deserve mention: the distinguished ranks in SUNY just listed; the *Post-Standard* Women of Achievement Award (1978); the Governor's Woman of the Year Award's Chairman of Medicine, Science and Nursing Award (1984); the American Association of University Women Syracuse Branch's Women of Accomplishment Award (1985); Friend of Trust Abroad, Cancer Treatment and Research Center, Visakhapatnam, India (1986); the National Organization for Women's Special Award of Honor (1987); the Women in Medicine Award, cosponsored by American Women's Medical Association and Onondaga County Medical Society (1991); the Distinguished Surgeon Award, Association of Women Surgeons (1991); selection for inclusion in *Best Doctors in America* (1992 and 1994); Governor Mario Cuomo's Women of Distinction to Medicine Award (1994); the New York State Women of Achievement in Science, Medicine Award (1994); selection for inclusion in *Who's Who of American Women* (1996); Governor Pataki's Women of Achievement Award (1998); inclusion in the list "America's Top Doctors: The Nation's Leading Medical Specialists" (2001); listing as *Redbook Magazine*'s "Top Doctor" (2001); the Susan G. Komen Breast Cancer Foundation Distinguished Service Award (2001); selection for inclusion in *Who's Who in American Education* (2003); inducted into the International Women in Medicine Hall of Fame in Washington, D.C., as the "First Woman Chairman of the American Board of Surgery" and as the "Founder of the Association of Women Surgeons" (2004); America's Top Surgeons Award and also listed in "Guide to America's Top Surgeons" (2004–5); listing in "Best Doctors in America" (2005); American College of Surgeons' Distinguished Service Award (2006); New York Chapter of the American College of Surgeons' Distinguished Service Award (2007); and an award from the International Society of Surgeons (bestowed in Japan in 2011).

Memberships in professional societies are numerous. A few include New York State Medical Society, American Medical Association, Association for Academic Surgery, American College of Surgeons (as a fellow), American Association for the Advancement of Science, American Women's Medical Association, Endocrine Society, American Association of Medical Colleges, Women's Medical Society of New York State, International Society of Surgeons, International Association for Endocrine Surgery, Association of Women Surgeons, American Board of Surgery, American Society of Breast Surgeons and American Surgical Association.

Various foundations benefit from her service as board member. Some include the Hospice Foundation, Everson Museum of Art, Vera House Foundation, the Carol M. Baldwin Breast Cancer Research Foundation and many others.

Her scientific and clinical interests and specializations are in the areas of thyroid and parathyroid disease and of breast disease, and she has been highly regarded as a clinical surgeon. The list of publications, grants, presentations at scholarly conferences, reports and visiting professorships show the scope of her research and contributions to her field in the United States, Europe, Latin America and Asia. A tribute to her in the Syracuse medical alumni publication estimated that Dr. Numann has treated more than twelve thousand patients. In recognition of her accomplishments, the university named its renowned breast care center for her.

The most recent honor was becoming the first woman to serve as president of the prestigious American College of Surgeons in 2011. As recently as 1975, that organization had admitted fewer than five women per year.

When asked about her most important goals and accomplishments, she replied, "Raise awareness that women make good surgeons." To put her words into action, she founded the Association of Women Surgeons. She did more than that, however, for during her entire career she has been and still is a strong role model. Another goal was to make education an academic discipline in medical school, and ten years into her career, she concentrated in surgical education and in education in medicine in general. Another goal was diversity, and as a feminist, she supported surgeons in diverse areas, and they supported her. Still another goal was to produce kind and caring surgeons. Through a bioethics program, the alumni association funded an endowed chair. She was truly a kind and caring surgeon, as attested to by the many former colleagues and patients who have remained in contact with her and formed friendships.

Dr. Numann is indeed a trailblazer, one who has been compared with Dr. Elizabeth Blackwell, the first American woman to receive a medical degree and who also had Syracuse connections. Dr. Numann, even in retirement, continues her career by holding leadership positions in medical organizations, presenting lectures and receiving awards for her pioneering work.

DeCrow, Karen. "Feminist History Is Made in Syracuse." *Post-Standard*, December 10, 2011, see A2.
Friedman, Amy. "Trailblazer." *Post-Standard*, May 12, 2011, see A15.
Numann, Patricia. Curriculum vitae, 2011.
———. Interview recorded by Marilynn J. Smiley, June 18, 2011.

Researcher and author: Marilynn J. Smiley, Oswego Branch

Catherine "Mac" O'Callaghan

1924–
Community Service/Author

She was named Catherine, but to her family and friends, she is simply "Mac" O'Callaghan. Her Irish Catholic rearing, which started on a farm in Nebraska, laid the groundwork for her common-sense approach and old-fashioned ideas. This independent woman is a mother, a grandmother and a great-grandmother. Numbers didn't matter as each was the recipient of her all-embracing love.

One cannot separate this giving, caring woman from her husband, Pearse, who shared her strong convictions to feed the homeless and care for those with **HIV/AIDS**, often taking them into their own home. This 110-year-old Victorian house would be home to a child's friend, an exchange student or an orphan, sometimes for years.

Her penchant for making do was recalled by one of her five surviving sons, Thomas, who said that his mother never cooked the same thing twice. She could make changes or use leftovers in such a way that the meal appeared invitingly different. He referred to his father as the mover and shaker, but his mother was the foot soldier, the doer.

One of her friends said that Mac is a great planner who could fulfill three functions in one week, have the house a disaster one day and the next day have one hundred people walk into a neat and tidy home. She noted that among her special qualities is the need to help anyone in trouble as she is both religious and generous. Mac's rearing of her large family never interfered with her three Tuesdays per month preparing and supervising hot meals for the homeless at Project Hospitality's Carpenter St. Shelter or feeding twenty or more people with HIV/AIDS and their children with her family in her home.

Christmas at the O'Callaghans' home meant that the clan would converge for a week. The fifty or so required sleeping bags as regular sleeping facilities were taxed to the fullest. It was a place where the voices of children filled this big barn-like house along with the chatter of stories being shared. But that was not enough, for they played Santa for about one hundred carolers from the Mud Lane Society for the Renaissance of Stapleton. There is no surprise in knowing that Mac was one of the founders and served as its secretary.

On the second floor of their home, her husband maintained a treasured library. Books are stacked from floor to ceiling, with sundry newspapers and files taking up any open space. There is one area set aside for Mac's desk, computer, typewriter and possibly four hundred or more cookbooks. With all those hungry people, she needed a source for menus whose recipes she sometimes tweaked. Here she constantly revised her hectic schedule, and here, too, she wrote the monthly newsletter for the American Association of University Women. An ongoing project is her written memoir relating family history that she has somewhat completed but hopes to complete soon. Her memoir chronicles her birth on March 3, 1924; the death of her father at age three, leaving eight children on a farm in Greeley, Nebraska; her teaching in a small rural schoolhouse; and the depression years.

Business school led to a move to Grand Island, Nebraska. At a United Service Organization dance, Mac met the U.S. Army Air Corps base's radio-radar operator and instructor. Typical of her nonconventional approach, she proposed to Pearse on the Parachute Chute Jump at Coney Island during a visit east to meet his parents. Two years after being married on September 16, 1944, following Pearse's discharge, the couple settled on Staten Island. During the span of two decades, the O'Callaghans had six sons and four daughters. Their college and doctorate degrees led to accomplishments in areas of chemistry, accounting, sales, acting and interior decorating, as well as positions as hospital hospice director, business executive and city computer official.

Not to be outdone by her children, Mac enrolled in the former Staten Island Community College in 1970 and ultimately received a bachelor's degree from the College of Staten Island. Both Mac and her daughter Catherine (Holder) were inducted into the College of Staten Island's Hall of Fame.

Mac has been employed as a legal secretary following her husband's illness and as a secretary at Curtis High School, but social activities became the bulwark of her life: Daytop Village with her husband, Pearse; the Mud Lane Society; Project Hospitality; the Staten Island Botanical Garden; Friends of Blue Heron Park; and the American Association of University Women, as well as her parish, St. Paul's Church.

Mac proudly announces that the political views and social conscience of the O'Callaghans are still in evidence with the family's involvement in local politics and social projects. Mac's total commitment belies her age as she continues to embrace her varied interests.

Is it any wonder that the *Staten Island Advance* recognized Mac as a Women of Achievement in 1987?

O'Callaghan, Catherine. *From the Prairie to the Harbor*. N.p.: self-published, 2011.

Researcher and author: Muriel Schlefstein, Staten Island Branch

BARBARA HARRIS OLDWINE

1923–
SOCIAL WORKER/BROADCASTER/EDUCATOR/ACTIVIST

The immense contributions that Barbara Harris Oldwine has made will always affect the history of the Southern Tier of New York and New York State. The list of nouns, adjectives and accolades to describe her is extensive. When descriptors such as intelligent, committed, activist, courageous, trailblazer, dynamo and inspirational are often associated with Mrs. Oldwine, it is easy not to recognize the essence of this wonderful woman. This essence fuels all of her accomplishments.

"Inspiration" should be Mrs. Oldwine's middle name. "Can't do" are two works she never utters. If anyone can arouse one's creativity, it is Barbara. She encourages all individuals she meets to identify their positive characteristics and to avert all negative thoughts. Barbara uses every opportunity to teach and empower others to share their journey and excel.

In 1923, this octogenarian was born in Binghamton, New York, and learned at an early age the value of respect for others. Barbara always viewed freedom as an inalienable human right. After graduating from North High School, she graduated from Fisk University, receiving a bachelor's degree in history.

Mrs. Oldwine's work accomplishments include being the first black case worker for the City of Binghamton (1947), being supervisor of the Medicaid Unit in the Broome County Department of Social Services, serving as teacher of Field Human Resources at Broome Community College, hosting a weekly talk show on WICZ television and being appointed by Mayor Bucci to the Community Development Committee and by Mayor Ryan to the Community Development Committee.

As an advocate for people of all ages, the rich and the poor, crossing all cultural and socioeconomic barriers, Barbara Oldwine worked tirelessly through many organizations and boards to champion many causes. She worked to improve housing for poor and middle-class families through Metro Interfaith. Her work with the Urban League Guild, Young Women's Christian Association, National Association for the Advancement for Colored People (NAACP), SOS Shelter, Broome County Cancer Society, United Way and Apalachin Alumnae Chapter—as well as being founder of Delta Sigma Theta Sorority Inc. and a member of the Vestry of Trinity Memorial Episcopal Church—provided her an avenue to work and improve the living conditions of the Southern Tier and New York State. Mrs. Oldwine has certainly led by example.

She always exuded pride in the Greater Binghamton Area, her beloved Episcopal church, her wonderful family, in being a Diamond Life Member of Delta Sigma Theta for seventy years and in being a member of the American Association of University Women for fifty-nine years. She is proud of her African American heritage and encourages everyone to know "on whose shoulders they have stood." Like the legendary phoenix, she rose from the ashes of the postslavery era, as the granddaughter of freed slaves, to a person of excellence and respect—a role model. Through all of this, she does not complain of the atrocities or obstacles she faced. She remembers the early teachings of her parents, their involvement in the civil rights movement and their founding the local chapter of the NAACP. This transitioned into her taking an active role in community service, promoting social change and becoming the advocate for people who are disadvantaged regardless of their cultural, ethnic or socioeconomic backgrounds. She never misses an opportunity to share knowledge or encourage others. It has been her life's mission to promote equality and make her community a better place to live. She has expressed this spirit throughout her life.

Mrs. Oldwine's list of accomplishments, awards bestowed on her and recognitions is extensive and reflects the impact she has had in her community and New York State. It is difficult to select to share some of her numerous accomplishments and accolades. First and foremost was her marriage to her beloved Cornelius Vernon Oldwine, followed by giving birth to her daughters, Valerie Barnes and Eilene Carter. The baton was transferred to her granddaughters and their husbands—Amira B. Barnes Williams and Troy D. Wiliams and Monica J. Barnes Lateef and Karriem O. Lateef—and to her four great-granddaughters. A few of the numerous awards she has received include the Southern Tier Division of the New York National Association of Social Workers' Public Citizen Award; the New York State Broadcaster of the Year Award; the Distinguished Citizen Award, bestowed by the State University of New York State Board of Trustees (1982); the African American of Distinction Award, given to her by the governor of New York, Mario M. Cuomo; the Binghamton Sertoma Award; the Semper Fidelis Award; the Broome County Status of Women Council Award; the Broome County Bar Association's Liberty Bell Award (1999); an award from the Southern New York Branch of the American Association of University Women (2002); and the Phoenix Award (2006).

To complete the essence of Barbara Harris Oldwine, when you talk to her, you will sense that she believes in stretching your mind and giving service beyond your comfort zone. She feels that it is one's birthright to teach someone your life skills and knowledge. By example, she has shown that age is only a number and does not define the parameters of one's ability. She relates across all generations. She values both youth and age. She could have coined the phrase, "If you first don't succeed, try, try again." Education, reading and learning have always been paramount to Mrs. Oldwine. She believes in stretching one's self beyond the boundaries of comfort.

The essence of Barbara Oldwine has been reflected through her history as the granddaughter of freed slaves and her resolve to become a beacon and guide to her community. Her fight for democracy, freedom and diversity has been her forte. She has offered a hand to those in need of support. Mrs. Oldwine has used her influence for educational equality, social justice and a democracy that will silence the voices of hate and inequality.

Archives of Delta Sigma Theta Sorority Inc., Apalachin Alumnae Chapter. Information concerning Barbara Oldwine.

Campbell, Ann. Personal interview about Barbara Oldwine by Donna Spearman, 2012.

Oldwine, Barbara. Personal interview by Ann Campbell, historian, Delta Sigma Theta Inc., March 4, 2004.

State University of New York, Binghamton Magazine. "Binghamton University Announces 2002 Public Service Awards." May 17, 2002. www.binghamton.edu/news/news-releases/news-release.html?id=751.

Researcher and author: Donna Spearman, Southern New York Branch

CHARLOTTE BLAIR PARKER

CIRCA 1858–1937
ACTRESS/PLAYWRIGHT

Charlotte (Lottie) Blair Parker—playwright, author and actress—was the daughter of George and Emily (Hitchcock) Blair and was born in the family home on Bridge Street, Oswego, New York. George Blair came to Oswego from Ireland with his family in 1832. George was a shipmaster and lake captain. Her mother (1829–1865) died when Lottie was a child. Several different dates have been given for her birth. They range from 1854 to 1858; since her mother died in 1865 (she is buried at the Rural Cemetery in Fruit Valley), that narrows the range a little. Most references use 1858.

Charlotte went to Oswego High School and graduated from the Elementary Course at the Oswego State Normal School with the July class of 1872. After graduation, she went to teach in Bay City, Michigan, in Indiana and later in New York City.

Friends stated that she had a flair for the dramatic and had taken elocution classes while attending Oswego Normal School. When teaching in New York City, she took further elocution classes and planned to become a teacher in the art of expression. Charlotte met her future husband, Henry Doel Parker, a student of drama and elocution, while in New York City. After her marriage, she studied drama under Wyzeman Marshall, a noted Shakespearean actor, in Boston. Marshall advised her to become an actress.

Charlotte and Henry acted on stage in popular dramas, playing in stock and on weekends. She performed with the stock company of the Boston Theater, playing minor rolls with considerable success. She later toured with Lawrence Barrett and Madame Janaushek, major figures of that era. She played the title role in *Hazel Kirke* and is listed as an actress in the Hollywood silent film production of *Hearts of Love*, released in November 1918.

She wrote a number of plays using the pen name "Lottie Blair Parker." In 1892, she wrote *White Roses*, a play she submitted to the *New York Herald* in a contest for best one-act play. The play received honorable mention and was purchased by Daniel Frohman. He produced it a few weeks later at the Lyceum Theatre in connection with another play. It ran the whole season. It was performed in London, where it was called *Red Roses*.

Her most popular full-length play, a melodrama entitled *Way Down East*, is said to have been written in Oswego when Mr. and Mrs. Parker spent the winter with her parents in their Bridge Street home after a financially unsuccessful dramatic tour broke up near Oswego. The Parkers tried to produce the play themselves, and it opened in the Boston Theater, where it was titled *Annie Laurie*.

The play was later revised and renamed *Way Down East* by Joseph R. Grismer, a partner of William A. Brady. Brady purchased and produced the play at the Manhattan Theatre in New York City in February 1898. It played for 152 performances, one of the longest runs of a play produced during the years between 1897 and 1906. Grismer's wife, Phoebe Davis, played the lead role in the original production and in later revivals for a total of more than four thousand performances. D.W. Griffith paid $175,000 for the screen rights in 1920. This film version starred Lillian Gish and grossed $1.4 million. Henry Fonda starred in a film version released in 1935 (by Fox) that was directed by Henry King.

Charlotte Blair Parker wrote about a dozen produced plays. The most popular were produced between 1897 and 1906 and included, in addition to *Way Down East, Under Southern Skies, Lights of Home* and *The Redemption of David Corson.*

In an interview with Earl Sparling in the *New York World-Telegram* that was printed on October 31, 1935, the headline read, "Mrs Parker Who Wrote 'Way Down East' in 1897, Likes Cocktails, Cigarets and Peach Velvet Gowns," with a subheading that read, "Now 70 or 80 Years Old, but Doesn't Care to Discuss Her Age." Charlotte Parker died at her home in Great Neck, Long Island, New York, on January 5, 1937.

Quoting Lida Penfield from a paper read for the Oswego County Historical Society in 1945, "It is pleasant to leave our account of Charlotte Blair Parker with the picture of the lady, still handsomely dressed (Peach velvet hostess gown and black satin slippers) intelligent, tolerant, with a mind of her own, distinctly up to date, still wishing success for her work, still the kind of a woman a young man would turn to notice, a person of class."

Penfield, Lida. *The Journal, 1976–1977.* Bicentennial Issue. Oswego County Historical Society, 1977.

Wikipedia. "Charlotte Blair Parker." http://en.wikipedia.org/wiki/Charlotte_Blair_Parker.

Researcher and author: Helen Butterfield Engel, Oswego Branch

LUCILLE PATTISON

1935–

LEGISLATOR/COUNTY EXECUTIVE

In 1973, Lucille Pattison was the only woman elected to serve on the Dutchess County legislature, which was composed of thirty-five members. She was the first Democrat elected to a countywide office in Dutchess County since 1906. As she stood in the back of the county courthouse in Poughkeepsie, New York, waiting to be introduced and sworn in, a gentleman said, "Well, you will be getting a lot of attention."

"It's not their attention I want," replied Ms. Pattison, "It's their respect!" As she went on to make even more political history, Lucille Pattison earned the respect *and* the attention of people throughout the country.

Born in Rochester, New York, in 1935, Ms. Pattison grew up on a fruit farm that her mother managed. Lucille, her brother and her grandfather worked long, hard hours and lived on a meager income on the farm. Although no one in her family had attended college, when Lucille was a child, the six o'clock news was on the radio every night during dinner, accompanied by lively political debates between her father and grandfather. They listened to news of World War II and the Korean War and energetically expressed strong opinions about President Roosevelt and other political figures. Since Ms. Pattison's mother was Canadian-born, the news at seven o'clock was from the CBC (Canadian Broadcasting Corporation), and that generated more talk of world events.

Lucille's exposure to world events through radio and family discussions, combined with her experience with farm labor, motivated her to be the first in her family to pursue an education beyond high school. A married couple in the neighborhood, who recognized something special in this young girl, encouraged her to attend Syracuse University. Considering her childhood dinner table conversations, it is little wonder that Lucille Pattison would go on to study history and political science at Syracuse. A bit of foreshadowing had occurred when she was a junior in high school. She was selected for a debate program called Junior Town Meeting on the Air, and as the debate team was searching for a topic, Lucille suggested discussing whether the ceiling on the national debt should be raised or remain the same. "I'm not sure most of the students knew what I was talking about," Ms. Pattison laughingly recalled.

After Syracuse University, Lucille's first job was teaching history in a Rochester high school. "I knew that teaching was never going to be my career, though. I didn't know what it was going to be, but I was never satisfied with myself as a teacher. It's too difficult to know what to leave out of the curriculum when you teach history. I thought everything was important." When a career opportunity arose for her husband in 1964, the family moved to Hyde Park, New York, where Ross began a long and distinguished career at Dutchess Community College.

In their new home, the Pattisons began a family, and Lucille became involved in political campaigns and the League of Women Voters. Ross Pattison served on the Dutchess County Democratic Committee, and in 1973, when a vacancy arose in the county legislature, they asked him to run for office. He declined the opportunity, so the committee turned to Lucille and said, "Then, what about you?" After discussing the offer with her husband and some key women in the League of Women Voters, she decided to run for the all-male, Republican-dominated legislature. As Ross pointed out, "You are doing so much of this political work anyway, you might as well get paid a little bit for it!" At that time, the Pattisons had three daughters, ages three, four and seven. With much help from her family and friends, Lucille launched her campaign and was elected to the position. But serving as a legislator was just the beginning.

Within three years, in 1976, Ms. Pattison was elected Democratic majority leader of the legislature—an incredible feat in the Republican stronghold of Dutchess County. In fact, the Democrats would not be in the majority again until 2008. "I didn't have any problems being a woman on the Legislature," Ms. Pattison stated. "It was the men who had problems with my being there. Initially, it took me about two months to earn their respect. I was involved from the outset. I think my years of participation with the League of Women Voters gave me the confidence and the experience to assert myself."

Two years later, the Dutchess County executive, a Republican, was arrested for bribery and resigned from his post in April 1978. The election was coming up in November, and it was clear that the voters were ready for a change in direction and some honest, innovative leadership. "Like Watergate," Ms. Pattison stated. "It takes something like that to get the electorate really involved." So, Lucille Pattison ran for the highest position in county government.

Because of her hard work and her refusal to acknowledge gender bias as a deterrent, Lucille made history again on November 8, 1978, when she was elected the first female Democratic County executive in the United States. Her decision to run had been based on the total support of her husband and on the friends, neighbors and constituents who not only again helped her to run a successful campaign but also helped with responsibilities at home. Ms. Pattison said, simply and sincerely, "I just could not have done it without the support of my husband." Her role model in politics was Anne Buchholz, another female politician in Poughkeepsie, a rarity in those days.

On her first day of work at the County Office Building in Poughkeepsie, women crowded around the windows and watched with pride as the first female county executive got out of her car and came in to her office. Most likely, many of those employees had experienced the sexism typical of that time period. "All of the 'firsts' I had achieved as a woman were irrelevant to me, at the time. It took me several years to realize the impact on women of what I had done. But I do remember how excited those ladies were as they stood at the windows on my first day of work."

In that first year in office, Ms. Pattison had to address the myriad problems brought about by her predecessor's corruption. So, in her typical fashion, the new county executive took charge and addressed the issues head-on. "At the end of each day, I knew I had accomplished something," Ms. Pattison said recently about her career. "I had a wonderful staff, and we worked long, hard hours, but we were surefooted. We knew what we were doing, as women often do." Although the Republicans thought that she was a "usurper" and that things would soon be "back to business as usual," Lucille Pattison continued to be reelected and ultimately served as county executive for a total of thirteen years. She opted not to run for reelection in 1991.

The list of awards and recognitions received by Lucille Pattison is extensive, and she is too modest to discuss them. To name just two, she was selected to be the 1980 Woman of the Year by the Poughkeepsie Branch of the American Association of University Women, and she proudly wears the Eleanor Roosevelt–Valkill Medal, which was awarded to her in 1994. Both of these distinguished honors were based on her advocacy for children, families and the poor while she was in office.

Throughout those years as a legislator and a county executive, Ms. Pattison and her husband raised their three children. She was determined not to bring the issues of the job home, but it was impossible to protect her girls completely. "I expected and dealt with confrontation as county executive," Ms. Pattison said, "but it was hard for my family to hear me criticized on the radio or in the press." Generally speaking, however, her daughters were unimpressed with their mother's notoriety. When asked what it was like to have such a prominent mother, they would say, "Oh, she gets up every morning, takes a shower, lays out our school clothes and gives us chores to do. She's just a working mom." And that is exactly the way Lucille wanted it to be.

Over the course of her career, Lucille Pattison met such notables as Jackie Kennedy, Nancy Reagan, Prince Phillip and the governors and politicians of New York State. But it was a woman with no college education whom she credited for modeling the management skills and determination needed to run a county. "Although she died when I was quite young, I realize now that my mother was an unusual woman. She was the first elder in the history of her Presbyterian church and a Sunday school teacher. She ran the family farm. She was a very strong person—strong-willed and very involved. As news of my various professional accomplishments reached home to Rochester, a friend said, 'Of course Lucille can do that, because of her mother!' I regret that she never lived long enough to even see me get married," Ms. Pattison reflected quietly.

Pattison, Lucille. Interview recorded by Judy Linville, January 28, 2008. *Poughkeepsie Journal.* Archives, 1973–91.

Researcher and author: Judith Linville, Poughkeepsie Branch

Ruth Stafford Peale

1906–2008
Religious Leader/Author/Editor

Loretta Ruth Stafford was born on September 10, 1906, in Fonda, Iowa. She attended what is now Wayne State University in Detroit, Michigan, and graduated from Syracuse University in Syracuse, New York. She paid for her education and her brother's by selling ribbon in a department store, among other jobs.

Her experience as the daughter of a Methodist minister persuaded her that life with a minister was "restrictive." "No way did I want to be a pastor's wife," she said. Her college roommate introduced her to Dr. Norman Vincent Peale, then a pastor in Syracuse. She said it took two years for her to make up her mind to marry him.

Ruth Stafford Peale worked with her husband to build one of the twentieth century's most influential ministries in Pawling, New York. Mrs. Peale was recognized as the driving force behind the magazine *Guideposts*, which tells "true stories of hope and inspiration" and now has a paid circulation of 2.5 million and a readership of 8 million. *Guideposts*, which also publishes other inspirational magazines, emerged from Mrs. Peale's kitchen table suggestion that her husband publish his sermons. She scrupulously edited them. "He would think up the ideas and I would find the way to put them in concrete form," she said. She became chairwoman of *Guideposts*; founder of an organization, the Peale Center, that says 600,000 prayers a year for people who request the service; and originator of the Knit for Kids program, which contributes sweaters to children in need.

Dr. Norman Vincent Peale was an immensely influential clergyman, who spread his inspirational message of "positive thinking" to millions through print, radio and television; he also offered his sermons to packed congregations at Marble Collegiate Church on Fifth Avenue in Manhattan. Mrs. Peale had the idea that energized Dr. Peale's ministry after he arrived at Marble Collegiate in 1932 and found attendance sparse; she suggested that he speak to social clubs, civic organizations and the like. Soon the pews were full.

Mrs. Peale took over much of the organizational work, first in their church and then in larger circles. She became the first woman to be president of the National Board of North American Missions of the Reformed Church in America. Dr. Peale was discouraged after his book, *The Power of Positive Thinking*, was rejected by publisher after publisher. Mrs. Peale insisted that he try one more time. Published in 1952, it has sold more than 20 million copies in forty-two languages.

Mrs. Peale also wrote several books, including *The Adventure of Being a Wife* (1971) and *Secrets of Staying in Love* (1984). She said, "I always felt I could do something if I put my mind to it and I wanted to."

She died in 2008 at the age of 101.

Martin, Douglas. "Ruth Stafford Peale, 101, Dies; Helped Ministry Flourish." *New York Times*, February 7, 2008.

Researcher and author: Mary Lou Davis, Poughkeepsie Branch

LIDA SCOVIL PENFIELD

1873–1956
EDUCATOR/HISTORIAN

In 1907, only 14 percent of Americans graduated from high school. Thinking about that gives one an idea of what a remarkable woman Lida Scovil Penfield was. She was born in Oswego, New York, in 1873. Her father, Joel B. Penfield, was a prominent and wealthy businessman (dry goods, milling and so on) who was active in civic and government organizations. He died in 1873, when she was just a few months old. That same year, her baby brother died.

Lida graduated from Boston University and also earned her PhD from that school. She joined the faculty of the State Normal and Training School (as the current State University of New York–Oswego was then called). She taught in the English department and became its chairman in 1932.

In addition to her teaching, Lida wrote a book for young people called *Stories of Old Oswego* in 1919. This small volume takes Oswego's history back to the coming of the first white men to the shores of Lake Ontario and the Oswego River. As an authority on local history, she directed a pageant covering two hundred years of the city's history that was presented at Fort Ontario. She also wrote articles for the Oswego County Historical Society about the Cooper family, for James Fenimore Cooper spent time in Oswego during the War of 1812.

Among her other activities at the college, she composed the Torchlight Ceremony, which was inaugurated in 1936. It is still an impressive ceremony and is one of the school's most important annual traditions. In her book *Oswego: Fountainhead of Teacher Education*, Dorothy Rogers described this very well. Rogers's book identified Lida Penfield as "a dainty, beautiful, cultured lady. Her real distinction was her personal influence." Her successor, Charles Wells, said, "She set a tone of culture that no one else can ever beat."

When the new college library was built in 1961, it was most appropriately named for her, as was the more recent library that was constructed in 1967. Lida Penfield represented Oswego at a meeting in Ithaca when the College Clubs made the transition into branches of the American Association of University Women, and she became the first president of the Oswego Branch.

Churchill, John. *Landmarks of Oswego County*. Syracuse, NY: D. Mason & Company, 1895.

Rogers, Dorothy. *Oswego: Fountainhead of Teacher Education*. New York: Appleton-Century-Crofts Inc., 1961.

Researcher and author: Ann Marie French, Oswego Branch

FRANCES PERKINS

1880–1965
SOCIAL WORKER/LABOR LEADER/U.S. CABINET MEMBER

Frances Perkins was the first female cabinet officer in Franklin Delano Roosevelt's administration. She served as secretary of labor from March 4, 1933, to June 30, 1945. She was remarkably suitable for this position and very effective in helping develop FDR's program of social justice. How did a woman of her social class develop into a person who understood the working man and his needs and the needs of Americans of all ages who had been devastated by the worldwide depression that began in 1929?

Frances Perkins was born in Boston, Massachusetts, on April 10, 1880, to comfortable middle-class parents who belonged to the Congregational Church. She had one sister, born in 1884. Frances was an average student at Worchester High School. She earned a bachelor's degree from Mount Holyoke College in 1902 and a master's degree in sociology from Columbia University in 1910. At Mount Holyoke, her history professor, Anna May Soule, required her students to visit the local factories and write of the working conditions there. Frances later said that this opened her mind to the idea that poverty was not merely caused by liquor or laziness, the prevailing view at the time. She supported herself by teaching and volunteered at settlement houses. She spent time at the famous Hull House in Chicago. There she began to realize that labor needed to organize to earn a decent wage so that people could take care of themselves and not need the charity of those running settlement houses. She came to live in New York City in 1909 and was hired as executive secretary of the Consumer's League. In lobbying for the league in Albany, she met Al Smith, a New York State assemblyman at the time, and Senator Robert F. Wagner.

On March 25, 1911, Frances was having tea with friends at Astor Place in Greenwich Village. Several fire trucks and emergency vehicles could be heard outside. The group went outside to see what was happening. They were just in time to see bodies falling from the upper floors of the Triangle

REMARKABLE WOMEN IN NEW YORK STATE HISTORY

Shirtwaist Company. A fire had started and quickly spread. The total dead numbered 146, and most were young immigrant women. There was only one exit. The others were locked because owners suspected that workers might steal a newly made shirtwaist or that union organizers might enter the building. There was a great public outcry over this tragedy, and investigations were demanded. Because Frances knew about factory conditions due to her work for the Consumer's League, she was asked to do investigations for the newly formed Factory Investigating Committee led by Smith and Wagner.

Her education, experiences and reading, which included Jacob Riis's 1890 book, *How the Other Half Lives* (an exposé of the terrible slum conditions in New York City), prepared her to become a vital force for labor in New York State. At that time, labor was not organized and had no rights, and workers were often exploited.

When Al Smith became governor in New York, he asked Frances to join the New York State Industrial Commission. Frances used her influence to educate men like Smith and Wagner about labor conditions by bringing Smith to a factory at the end of a twelve-hour shift to see the exhausted workers exit. She had Wagner come down a fire escape that ended twelve feet off the ground. As a lobbyist for the Consumer's League, she was successful in getting a bill passed that limited the workweek to fifty-four hours. When Franklin Delano Roosevelt was elected New York State governor, he named Frances Perkins the State Industrial commissioner. Because of the good relations she had worked to achieve with labor, business and lawmakers, she was successful in achieving a forty-eight-hour workweek for women. She pushed for laws establishing a minimum wage and unemployment insurance.

When FDR was elected president, he asked Frances to be his secretary of labor. No woman had ever held a cabinet post. Frances accepted this position only after the president-elect agreed to back her long list of social reforms, including what we know as Social Security. He also supported her goals of a shorter workweek, laws controlling child labor, setting a minimum wage and unemployment insurance. All these goals were achieved during Perkins's time as secretary of labor. Her biographer, Kirstin Downey, called Perkins the "woman behind the New Deal," and she was.

The skills she used in negotiating between businessmen and labor leaders worked well in the assured but tactful ways she dealt with Roosevelt's all-male cabinet, Congressmen, lobbyists, citizens and the president. Her experience, knowledge and personal qualities were major factors in helping settle strikes and heading off strikes in industries that produced needed war materials—first for lend-lease and then goods for the war itself.

Perkins's personal life was difficult. She married Paul Caldwell Wilson in 1913. They had a baby who died and then a daughter, Susanna. They were financially comfortable and lived on Paul's family inheritance. Paul, however, lost their fortune in speculative investments. Frances realized that she would have to support her family when Paul developed manic-depressive symptoms and spent years on and off in mental institutions. As an adult, their daughter also was apparently mentally ill.

Frances continued to work for the government in Harry Truman's administration, serving on the United States Civil Service Commission from 1945 to 1952. In that year, her husband died, and Frances went to Cornell University as a teacher and lecturer in the New York State School of Industrial and Labor Relations. She continued there until her death in 1965 at age eighty-five.

Though Frances Perkins came from an upper middle-class background, had an excellent education and was a successful social worker, she developed an early empathy with the working class. She saw and understood the dreadful places where they had to live and work. She made great contributions to the major portion of the population in the United States by helping to achieve social security, unemployment insurance, minimum wages, limited workweek hours and codes for secure working places. She also believed in universal healthcare and would have been happy to see that becoming available to all our citizens.

Downey, Kirstin. Lecture at Hyde Park, New York, FDR's home, presidential library and archives, June 20, 2009.
———. *The Woman Behind the New Deal: The Life of Frances Perkins, FDR's Secretary of Labor and His Moral Conscience*. New York: Random House, 2009.
Passachoff, Naomi. *Frances Perkins: Champion of the New Deal*. New York: Oxford University Press, 1999.
Perkins, Frances. *The Roosevelt I Knew*. New York: Penguin Group, 1946.
Wikipedia. "Frances Perkins." http://en.wikipedia.org/wiki/Frances_Perkins.

Photograph from the Library of Congress.
Researcher and author: Marjorie Regan, Kingston Branch

DARLENE L. PFEIFFER

19??–
ENTREPRENEUR/PHILANTHROPIST

Darlene Pfeiffer is a very successful businesswoman in Kingston, New York. As the chief executive officer and holder of two franchises with Kentucky Fried Chicken (KFC) for forty-five years, Darlene has had an outstanding business career both locally and nationally. She is also very active in civic affairs and philanthropic causes. Darlene is especially noted for her great support of scholarships for deserving young people.

She has the highest respect for Colonel Harland Sanders and the Colonel's way, which the KFC franchises recognized as a formula for success. They became accustomed to doing for themselves and doing for others in their system. They banded together to share ideas and help each franchise to be successful. Eventually, they merged into an international organization.

Darlene recognized early that there was a need for KFC franchises to combine their negotiating power in order to remain independent and prosperous. She was the first woman to serve as president of the Association of Kentucky Fried Chicken Franchises (AKFCF). Serving two terms as president, she represented what has become one of the most influential groups of restaurateurs in the United States. During that time, PepsiCo bought KFC and decided to impose a new contract on its franchisees. PepsiCo wanted to eliminate "territorial protection" for the franchisees set by the KFC franchises' contracts. It planned to set up KFC in service stations, in the frozen food case at the corner supermarket or anywhere people gathered. Their new contracts would also eliminate good-faith negotiations for new KFC locations and the rule that KFC products could be sold only in KFC restaurants. During the negotiations, the AKFCF realized that the contract it already had would not be renewed even though it had been assured that it would be. There were letters and documents that gave them the right to renew the contract. Under the leadership of Darlene Pfeiffer, the AKFCF decided to sue and raised millions of dollars in anticipated legal fees. It was a long struggle. During those years of litigation, Darlene was elected again as president and is the only individual to be asked to serve twice. In the end, PepsiCo decided to settle. The AKFCF won its suit.

In the September 2000 edition of the magazine *QSR*, Darlene was asked how she managed to run such efficient and successful franchises even though she spends much time on the road working for the AKFCF. She answered, "I try to empower people to succeed, to help them grow. I give them knowledge, background and education and then turn them loose to let them prove themselves to themselves. Recognition of people when they do well is very important. We have a great bonus program. But everyone who works for me is someone I think of as family, especially my management team."

Darlene is a ten-year member of the KFC National Advertising Council, holding the office of president for three years. She has served on the KFC Advisory Council for four years, has been a board member of the Kentucky Fried Chicken Purchasing Co-op and was a founder of a magazine for KFC franchises.

Darlene believes in giving back to her community. She is a past president of Kingston Kiwanis. She has been the chair for the KFC Dare Program, a former member of the board of directors for the Benedictine Hospital Health Foundation and a former president of the Kingston YMCA Board of Directors.

In 2005, she established the Kentucky Fried Chicken Scholarship presented by Darlene Pfeiffer with the Ulster Community College Foundation Inc., which she supports with personal contributions. Five $1,000 scholarships are awarded annually to Ulster Community College students who plan on careers in business, nursing or other health-related areas and who demonstrate an entrepreneurial spirit. In addition, Darlene helped to establish the national Colonel's Scholars Program, which awards fifty $20,000 scholarships annually to qualified high school seniors to be used toward four years of tuition at a state-sponsored school. Due to Darlene's fundraising efforts at a KFC Convention, $1 million was raised, and the Colonel's Scholars Program was able to award scholarships to students in the locales where the franchises had contributed. Students from Ulster and Dutchess Counties received two $20,000 scholarships in 2008. Two Ulster Community College students were awarded $20,000 scholarships in 2009. More than 250 students throughout the United States have been sponsored by the Colonel's Scholars Program.

Recently, Darlene gave a very generous gift to Ulster Community College. Her gift changed the scholarship fund into an endowment. Furthermore, the Ulster Community College Foundation is included in her estate plans with a legacy gift that will be added to the endowment. In the fall of 2011, the Darlene L. Pfeiffer Center for Entrepreneurial Studies opened at Ulster County Community College. Darlene feels strongly that small businesses play very important roles in the community. In order to encourage and help other people to create and maintain successful businesses, Darlene started this program, which will include courses and resources for those who plan to start their own business. It is her hope that it will motivate others to follow her example.

Darlene was born in Ohio and attended Capital University in Columbus. She graduated summa cum laude from the State University of New York–New Paltz. She has a son who is a flight attendant and a daughter who works in human resources. Her favorite hobby is traveling, and she has visited many places around the world. She also enjoys reading. Darlene is an advocate for the young women of today. She remembered when she had to leave her position as a flight attendant when she got married. She remembered when the bank refused to loan her money because she was a married woman. She wants to help the young women of today achieve their goals. She has made outstanding contributions to our society.

Pfeiffer, Darlene L. Interview recorded by Patricia Stedge, 2010.

Researcher and author: Patricia Stedge, Kingston Branch

Barbara Pickhardt

19??–
Educator/Conductor/Composer

Barbara Pickhardt is a dedicated musician who has enriched and enhanced the musical life of the Hudson Valley. As a teacher, conductor, composer and arranger, she has helped to develop outstanding musicians and musical groups. She is also a very accomplished pianist and harpsichordist. Barbara has taught all levels of public school music and served several years as piano teacher and head of the choral department at Ulster Community College.

She was born and grew up in Duluth, Minnesota. Barbara remembered accompanying her kindergarten class on the piano for songs she played by ear. Always encouraged by her mother, she started formal lessons on the piano at the age of seven. In speaking of music as a very important part of her life, Barbara said, "When I was a child, it was a play activity. My friends would come to my house, we'd gather around the piano, and we would sing." In high school, she composed music for the school band, participated in all musical activities, accompanied musicals and created and led a vocal ensemble of students who gave up their lunch hour to practice with her in order to maintain an active performance schedule.

Barbara went on to earn a bachelor's degree in music from the University of Minnesota, where she received the Sigma Alpha Iota (SAI) Performance Award in piano. As an undergraduate, she was made the conductor of the university's Nurses Chorus, a position given to a promising conductor in the music department.

In 1969, she came to the Hudson Valley and soon became a part of the area's musical scene, first as a singer in the choral ensemble Ars Choralis (then called Mid-Hudson Madrigal Society) and then as its conductor. She was the pianist with the Diemer Piano Trio, led by renowned cellist Eleanor Diemer, the founding pianist/harpsichordist of the Woodstock Chamber Players and the harpsichordist/pianist and supporting choral conductor with the Woodstock Chamber Orchestra. Barbara was also the assistant music director/pianist of Overlook Lyric Opera and worked with composer Robert Starer as pianist and stage director for his new operas, which were performed in the Hudson Valley and in New York City.

In 1995, she founded the Hudson Valley Youth Chorale, a chorus that thrived under her leadership, and for thirteen years, she served a diverse population of children, offering them opportunities to develop musical skills and perform for the New York State legislature and the United Nations, as well as at area universities, colleges and community events. Having a strong foundation, the chorale continues today, giving young singers a great opportunity to develop musically. Under the Youth Chorale's Bridges Program—intended to explore understanding and respect for differences among people through music—Barbara took the chorale abroad to perform for orphans, in churches and in schools where the youth chorale singers attended classes and interacted with children of different cultures. According to Barbara, "We tour because it's the perfect way to break down cultural barriers—to bring people together." While on tour in Vienna, Barbara was privileged to have the opportunity to lead the combined Hudson Valley Youth Chorale and the Vienna Boys Choir in a reading of Oscar Peterson's "Hymn to Freedom."

Barbara Pickhardt's belief in the importance of bringing music into the lives of children was further carried out in the community when, as a member of Ars Choralis, she wrote and organized concerts for the chorus to take into public schools. As the coordinator of the Prelude Concerts at Maverick Concert Hall, she always made a point of including children among the esteemed artists performing on the program. She also coordinated the Saturday Children's Concerts as part of the Maverick Concert Series; along with her daughter, cellist Erica Pickhardt, she also developed a program contrasting seventeenth-century and contemporary instruments that they performed in schools throughout the county under the auspices of Maverick Music for Children.

In the early 1990s, Barbara decided to do graduate work. She graduated from the Westminster Choir College in Princeton, New Jersey, with a master's degree in music and received the Ruth and Raymond Young Award in composition. At the same time, she continued all her musical activities, including directing Ars Choralis, performing and teaching.

Barbara may be best known for her decades of leadership with the choral ensemble Ars Choralis. Under her direction, and supported at the piano by daughter Kristen Tuttman, the chorus has given outstanding concerts of traditional choral repertoire and out-of-the-ordinary programs. Noteworthy among her concerts are those that have reached across racial and religious divides, such as *Honoring the Dream*, a concert that brought together two diverse communities to honor the life and work of Dr. Martin Luther King Jr. In the *Times-Herald* review, Eddie Bell wrote, "The concert was an emphatic statement against racism...It was the antithesis of racism."

Messengers of Peace, a concert in response to the common yearning for peace among people, was first performed in Kingston, New York, on the eve of the millennium and was repeated in Woodstock, New York; Budapest, Hungary; and Vienna, Austria, in 2001 and again as an offering of solace and hope after the 9/11 disaster and the 2003 tsunami.

The Long Road Home concert honored the people of the Mississippi Delta after Hurricane Katrina and celebrated the rich contribution they have made to our American musical heritage.

Music in Desperate Times: Remembering the Women's Orchestra of Birkenau, a choral concert set during the Holocaust, tells the story of how music saved the lives of female musicians who were forced to play for the Nazis at the Auschwitz/Birkenau concentration camps during World War II. It was first performed in Kingston, New York, in 2006 and repeated by popular demand the following year. In 2009, Ars Choralis was invited to give this program at the Cathedral of St. John the Divine in New York City and also in Germany at the Heilig Kreuz Passion Church in Berlin. The chorus was the first musical group invited to perform at the Ravensbrueck/Ukermark concentration camps in Furstenberg, where survivors held their sixtieth annual Liberation Day ceremonies on April 18 and 19, 2009. Members of the chorus remember these concerts as very emotional. Barbara's feeling that music is an international language that brings people together was justified by the response the concerts received.

Barbara, commissioned to write for the Woodstock Cycle, furthered the need to keep the stories of the people who suffered and died in the Holocaust alive by teaming with lyricist Johanna Hall to write the opera *Hope*, based on the apocryphal story of the power of faith and hope demonstrated among people hiding from the Nazis during World War II. With Johanna, Barbara also wrote and produced the opera *Miracle in Bethlehem*, which premiered in 2004.

Ars Choralis has produced a very fine CD, *We Dream a World*. Barbara chose music that beautifully exemplifies this theme. It conveys the longing for peace, for a world where all human beings are free and respected, for love and compassion, for faith and hope and for freedom. It is fervent, dynamic and exciting. The chorus, soloists and instrumentalists combine to create a truly excellent musical presentation.

Barbara's prodigious musical talent and versatility have contributed much to the musical life of the Hudson Valley, extending to the international community as well. She is a great leader. People have confidence in her musical ability, her excellent programming, her ability and willingness to work with others and her motivation to continue to look for new opportunities to bring music to life. She said, "I delight in the creative process, the way an idea takes root and reveals itself, finding its way to the concert stage."

When she came to New York with her husband, Mel, Barbara said that her move to the Hudson Valley felt like "coming home." She added, "Whether it was the natural beauty of the region, the rich artistic atmosphere, or the people; my life has been defined by the cultural climate of this valley."

Pickhardt, Barbara. Interview recorded by Patricia Stedge, 2011.

Researcher and author: Patricia Stedge, Kingston Branch

BELVA PLAIN

1915–2010
AUTHOR

Belva Plain was a novelist and New York City native. She was the author of more than twenty bestselling novels, even though she started writing after her children were grown and she was a grandmother. Belva's writing covered a span of several decades. Her epic novels of family and forgiveness were written in longhand on a yellow pad. Although her books were well received by her many fans, the reviews from critics were not very enthusiastic.

Her first novel, *Evergreen*, published in 1978, was on the *New York Times* bestseller list for forty weeks. It was later developed into a popular television series.

In 1939, Belva graduated from Barnard College in New York City with a degree in history. As a teenager, she wrote poetry, and she later wrote short stories for many magazines.

Belva died in October 2010 at the age of ninety-five. Her recently completed sequel to *Evergreen* is named *Heartland* and was published after her death.

Dixler, Elsa. "Belva Plain, Novelist of Jewish American Life, Dies at 95." Obituary. *New York Times*, October 18, 2010. www.nytimes.com/2010/10/18/books/18plain.html.

Random House. "Belva Plain." Author bio, 2012. www.randomhouse.com/features/belvaplain.

Ryan, Joe. "Belva Plain, Acclaimed New Jersey Author, Dies at 95." *Star-Ledger*, 2012.

Researcher and author: Marion Mahoney, Islip Area Branch

LILIAN POPP

19??–
EDUCATOR/WRITER

A retired school principal, English teacher and guidance counselor, Lilian Popp is a five-foot-tall dynamo who has never been cowed by controversy.

She has proven to be a leader of dedication who has been courageous, incorruptible and upbeat, and her leadership has continued to affect the lives of Staten Islanders.

In November 1992, as a member of the school board, she was the only board member at a packed meeting of more than one thousand Islanders to vote against having the board scrap lessons on sexism and gay and lesbian families. Three police officers had to usher her away from an angry crowd. When one woman shouted, "You'll have to answer to God," Mrs. Popp responded, "I hope she's good to me." Her "defense of principle in the face of unwarranted and unreasonable attack at the school board hearings held earlier that year is an excellent example of her courage and dedication," wrote Samuel D. Finkelstein of West Brighton (an area in Staten Island), a man who was one of many who nominated Mrs. Popp as a Woman of Achievement.

On her native Staten Island, she has often sided with dissenters. Mrs. Popp rallied against secession, marched against the home port and supported Children of the Rainbow curriculum. During her thirteen-year tenure on the school board, she was the voice of opposition. When the board met behind closed doors in violation of the state's Open Meetings Law, Mrs. Popp protested, spurring a successful lawsuit against the board.

She continued to have faith in education, stating, "You never give up on a kid. You have to keep fighting and working until an injustice is reversed," and she added, "We have to give kids skills and knowledge and help them to establish values and become good citizens." Her activism and education go hand in hand. She feels that one always has to fight for human rights. It is necessary to "help the indigent and raise people up. Education does that."

Born Lilian Mustaki, she is the daughter of a wealthy Greek businessman and a mother who could trace her ancestry to seventeenth-century settlers on Staten Island. One of the streets, Cary Avenue, is named after her mother's family, who owned a farm in West Brighton. Mrs. Popp asserted that her mother taught her to stand up for principles and that she should never feel superior or inferior to anyone else. Her aunt, Elmire Gwinnell, started the Mother's Club, which blossomed into the Staten Island Federation of Parent-Teacher Associations.

Mrs. Popp's husband, the late Robert Popp, retired in 1976 as managing editor of the *Staten Island Advance*. He had previously been fighting in the war as an army lieutenant.

She has compiled five anthologies of literature and edited three books. Her first public work appeared as a letter to the editor in the *Advance* at the height of World War II. In the 1945 letter, Mrs. Popp took the minority view, protesting discrimination against the "Negro nurse." Her letter emphasized, "Isn't it more important that our sons and husbands who are fighting to the death this monstrous threat to liberty be ministered to on the battlefield where medical help is urgently needed, than whether the hands that tend them be pink or brown."

Mrs. Popp has spent most of her life in schools. She earned a bachelor's degree from the former Notre Dame College in Staten Island and has two master's degrees, one in English from Columbia University and another in guidance from Hunter College.

Her career in McKee High School in Staten Island spanned twenty-five years, as an English teacher, a guidance counselor and an assistant principal. In 1971, Mrs. Popp took a job as principal of William Howard Taft High School in the Bronx. Responding to crime against the elderly, she launched a student-run escort service. Hundreds of students accompanied seniors to grocery stores and doctors' offices. Though she rose through the ranks of the school system that encouraged pregnant teenagers to drop out, she launched an early teen pregnancy program at Taft. "I was begging girls to stay in school," she said. As a principal, she never stopped teaching. A twenty-five-year professor of guidance at Wagner College, she graded most Staten Island supervisors, including Christy Cugini, the district schools' chief.

In 1982, two years after she retired from Taft, Mrs. Popp started a child abuse prevention program in which Delta Kappa Gamma volunteers counseled children.

Once a month, she leads a book discussion group at Snug Harbor Cultural Center, Livingston, Staten Island. She is also the leader of a news discussion group for the Staten Island Chapter of the Brandeis University National Women's Committee. The members meet monthly at the local Jewish Community Center and focus on important current news events. The past president of the New York City Association of Teachers of English, Mrs. Popp belongs to the American Association of University Women and the Staten Island Human Rights Community Council. She also is president of the Women's Coalition of Staten Island, which is composed of major women's organizations in the borough that are currently active and involved in political and social action. Mrs. Popp continues to fill the role of a major contributing participant. She has been honored with service and leadership awards from organizations such as Staten Island's Business and Professional Women and the World of Women.

D'Angelo, Laura. "Woman of Achievement." *Staten Island Advance*, October 24, 1984.

Information obtained from Lilian Popp via personal contact with the author, 2008.

Researcher and author: Barbara Levitt, Staten Island Branch

MEHITABLE WING PRENDERGAST

1738–1812
PIONEER/ADVENTURER

Mehitable Wing Prendergast's historic horseback ride has been likened to Paul Revere's by more than one historian. Had she not taken that ride in 1766, very probably Jamestown would not be Jamestown; it would be known by a different name and have a different history. The history of Chautauqua County, New York, also would have been different. Mehitable (the spelling varies), of Scottish heritage, was born on March 20, 1738, in Dutchess County, New York. In 1755, she married William Prendergast, an Irish immigrant born on February 2, 1727. They settled in Dutchess County, where they became the parents of seven sons and six daughters, all but one of whom survived to adulthood. The family had limited financial means and were unable to purchase land to farm. They leased a small plot of land owned by the English lord Philip Philipse, paying as rent a portion of their crops and cattle, as well as their time and labor.

Many other immigrants were also tenant farmers for Philipse and other lords. William was angered when he learned that the amount he paid to Philipse to rent his few acres was the exact sum Philipse paid to the British Crown for his vast estate. Nothing was done to relieve their burden despite numerous protests, and violence ultimately erupted. William was a born leader; thus it was he who organized the farmers into an army of two thousand. Inevitably, more violence erupted, now between the king's Twenty-eighth Regiment of the Grenadiers and the tenant farmers. They marched on New York City to visit the governor, Sir Henry Moore, who listened sympathetically. Moore was not successful in appeasing the landlords, who demanded that the English soldiers disband the renegade army and capture their leaders.

William had escaped but surrendered at Mehitable's urging. He knew that he would be tried for high treason against the King of England and likely be sentenced to death by hanging. Justice being what it was in that time, William was not allowed counsel of an attorney. Mehitable stepped into that role, presenting a strong and logical case on his behalf. The prosecution requested that she be removed because her charm and beauty were disrupting the jury. It was to no avail, as the jury consisted of landlords only. On August 14, William was convicted of treason and sentenced to be hanged on September 28, 1766. There was no time to waste.

Mehitable perhaps already had her plan in place, anticipating the verdict. She mounted her horse and headed south to plead with Governor Sir Henry Moore, more than seventy miles away. She was granted an audience with him, where she pleaded for a stay of execution and a pardon from the king. The stay was granted "until His Majesty, King George's III pleasure should be known." The governor even allowed Mehitable to draw up the petition to the king. Once accomplished, she journeyed back by horseback to William, his friends and the landlords with the news. A dramatization of Mehitable's ride was the subject of a *Cavalcade of America* broadcast in the 1940s, a copy of which can be found in the Fenton Historical Center's Archives in Jamestown.

The pardon from King George III arrived six months later; William was a free man. Ten years later, in 1776, as future Americans fought for freedom from the English, William, Mehitable and their family remained loyal to the king. Forty years later, in 1806, Mehitable, William, nine of their children and their families arrived in Chautauqua County. The elder Prendergasts were by this time advanced in years. However, they undertook and survived the arduous journey across New York and settled on a farm in the hills south of Mayville in the town of Chautauqua, overlooking Chautauqua Lake. William died on February 14, 1811, and Mehitable on September 4, 1812; they are buried on their farm at a small family cemetery still known as the Prendergast Cemetery.

Their fifth child, James, purchased one thousand acres of land in 1806 at the south end of Chautauqua Lake, where he later built his home and a sawmill. Known initially as the Rapids, the tiny settlement's name was changed to Jamestown in 1815. Two of James's brothers also settled at the Rapids and operated the first store in 1813 as a branch of their Mayville store. What if Mehitable had not attempted that ride and had not been successful with the governor? How would the history of Chautauqua County read?

Thompson, B. Dolores. "Mehitable Wing Prendergast." *Jamestown Post Journal*, March 1985.

Vimmerstedt, Jennie. "Mehitable Wing Prendergast." *Jamestown Post Journal*, March 20, 1956.

Researcher and author: B. Dolores Thompson, Jamestown Branch

HELEN QUIRINI

1920–2010
LABOR LEADER/COMMUNITY ACTIVIST

At age twenty-one, Helen Quirini became a factory worker at the General Electric (GE) plant in Schenectady, New York, in 1941. She took the job as a means to earn money for college, but with the advent of World War II, she felt that it was her patriotic duty to continue there until the war was over. She stayed for thirty-nine years.

By the end of the war, she had achieved leadership in the International Union of Electrical Workers. One can imagine the challenge of being a woman working in a factory during those years, but Helen persevered and went on to become shop steward, executive board member, recording secretary and treasurer.

Helen was an activist not only for organized labor but in her community as well. A lifelong Schenectady resident, she cared deeply about social justice and human rights. She worked with a wide variety of human service organizations to advocate for the less fortunate, especially working women and senior citizens and on issues such as healthcare, violence against women, day care and racial discrimination.

It was in retirement that Helen was most prominent in the public eye. She was tireless in her efforts to win better benefits for GE retirees. She regularly showed up at GE stockholder meetings to speak up for cost of living adjustments and health benefits. For fourteen years, she was president of the GE Retirees Council, coordinating nationwide picketing and rallies to bring attention to the economic needs of retirees. She organized rallies at the GE gate and was even the subject of a play, *Helen and Jack*, written by GE stockholder Gail George. Her efforts achieved some measure of success, but Helen showed no signs of slowing down.

She wrote extensively about her life. Twenty-seven cubic feet of her papers reside in the archives of the State University of New York–Albany Library. Included among her memoirs are records of her union work and her community activities, as well as her vast correspondence.

Albany Times Union. Helen Quirini obituary. Albany, New York, November 11, 2010.

Coalition for Retirement Security.

Helen Quirini Papers–University at Albany Libraries. http://library.albany.edu/speccoll/findaids/apap102.htm.

Pension Rights Center. "Helen Quirini." www.pensionrights.org/action/activists/helen-quirini.

Quirini, Helen. *Helen Quirini and GE: A Personal Memoir.* www.albany.edu/history/histmedia/Hq.html.

Researcher and author: Julie Burgess, Schenectady Branch

VIRGINIA L. RADLEY

1927–1998
EDUCATOR/COLLEGE PRESIDENT/SCHOLAR

Virginia L. Radley made headlines on March 22, 1978, when she became the first woman in the history of the State University of New York (SUNY) to become a college president. This occurred when she was appointed the eighth president of SUNY-Oswego in its 126-year history.

Radley was born in 1927 in Marion, New York (Wayne County), the youngest of five children (and the only girl) to parents Howard Radley, a businessman, and Lula Ferris Radley, a teacher. Her mother (originally from Savannah, New York) stressed the importance of learning to her five children. She shared her love for reading with them and taught them the art of being articulate. Lula Radley made great sacrifices to send her children to college.

Virginia had a typical small-town upbringing, with rather atypical parents who set standards and expectations and lovingly expected the children to live up to them. The family attended the First Baptist Church in Marion.

Mentors in her early life were two high school teachers. One taught English and physical education, and the other taught English, Latin and French.

Majoring in English, she earned four college degrees: a BA from Russell Sage College in 1949, an MA from the University of Rochester in 1952, an MS from Syracuse University in 1957 and a PhD from Syracuse University in 1958.

Her earliest job was teaching English at Emily Howland Central School in Aurora, New York (1949–51), but from that time on, she was involved in higher education. The first position was as instructor of English at Chatham Hall, a women's college in Chatham, Virginia, from 1952 to 1955. Second was assistant dean of students and assistant professor of English at Goucher College in Maryland from 1957 to 1959. Third was several positions (professor of English, chair of the English department and associate dean of the college) at her undergraduate alma mater, Russell Sage, from 1959 to 1969. Fourth was dean of the college and professor of English at Nazareth College in Rochester, New York, from 1969 to 1973. Her fifth position in higher education was as provost for undergraduate education at the central administration office of SUNY in Albany from 1973 to 1974. Her sixth was at SUNY-Oswego, where she served as executive vice-president/provost and professor of English from 1974 to 1976, acting president from 1976 to 1978 and president from 1978 to 1988. During her career, she also served as visiting professor at other institutions. She retired from the SUNY system in 1992 but became a scholar in residence at Russell Sage College and maintained strong ties to the SUNY-Oswego's campus.

Her major field of concentration was nineteenth-century English literature, especially Victorian English poetry, and she authored two books (*Elizabeth Barrett Browning* in 1972 and *Samuel Taylor Coleridge* in 1966), as well as numerous articles. There were also many presentations at conferences.

She loved teaching and taught English classes (composition, British literature, the Romantic era, great Victorians and so on) throughout her distinguished career, even when her chief responsibility was as an administrator. In her own words, she said, "Teaching is what it's all about. A president who isn't a teacher isn't going to do very well. As president, you're teaching all the time: at receptions at your house, helping students with their vitae and letters of application, and giving them pointers on how to present themselves." Students referred to her teaching as incredible, passionate and very influential.

At Oswego, there were many accomplishments during her years as president. Dr. Radley started the honors college, advocated languages in the curriculum, created a general education division, reorganized the curriculum, promoted enrollment of members of social minorities, oversaw a marked increase in the number of women in faculty and staff positions, started the Sheldon Associates to encourage alumni contributions, established the Student Advisement Center, rewarded excellence, promoted research and grant applications and tightened academic standards, making Oswego more competitive. The university was listed in important college guides. Incoming student test scores rose during her tenure, even though this was a period when there was an overall decline in the state and nation. "Excellence" was her battle cry, and she was known for her commitment to quality throughout her career.

Dr. Radley was a tireless advocate for women and was acclaimed for her advancement of women in education and in the workforce. At the state level, she was cited for her support of women by the New York Senate and New York Assembly and at the local level through her support of the Women's Caucus (faculty) and Women's Center (students) on campus. She was particularly sensitive to the needs of female students—their safety, their academics and their need for strong role models. From 1975 to 1985, the percentage of all women employed at the SUNY-Oswego rose from 34.4 percent to 45.0 percent, increasing by well over one-third for faculty and more than doubling at the executive level. There was an increase of tenured positions held by women; in 1975, only 13 percent of the faculty were female, and in 1987, this figure increased to 20 percent. Improvements were made in affirmative action policies, and Virginia regarded herself as a role model. A believer in networking, she kept an eye out for talented women and helped them advance.

There were, however, some controversies during her administration. It was a period of severe state budget cuts and resulting job losses. Her manner was sometimes regarded as formal, authoritarian, elitist and highhanded. Some people were afraid to cross her because she was very strong-willed, yet she was also known for her strong sense of humor and compassion for others. It must be acknowledged that it was difficult to be the first female president of a male-oriented institution. Alice Chandler, former president of SUNY–New Paltz, said, "I think she was a true pioneer…simply being the first woman president in the system … was a real breakthrough. (You could fit all the woman presidents in the country in a very small room.) [It is important to realize the] impact the first ten or twenty woman presidents had."

A compelling speaker, Dr. Radley gave presentations at a number of conferences on women's advocacy, issues in higher education and nineteenth-century English literature. One speech on women was for a convocation of SUNY women held in Buffalo in November 1986. Chancellor Clifton Wharton had designated 1986 as a year for evaluating the progress of SUNY women in the years of the "International Women's Decade" from 1975 to 1985. The theme of the conference was "SUNY Women: Past Triumphs, Present Needs, Future Goals." At this convention, Dr. Radley urged the 360 women attending to strap on those breast plates and move ahead, patterning her words after those of a militant female protagonist in an Edmund Spenser tale. She also participated in a daylong forum on state policy and independent higher education in 1988 and spoke at the Middle Atlantic Summer Institute at Bryn Mawr in 1975. Her support of the American Association of University Women was admirable, for she willingly gave presentations at district and local meetings.

Her honors are too numerous to mention individually, but a sampling include an honorary doctorate from her alma mater, Russell Sage College, in 1981; the Trailblazer in Education Award from the Central New York Chapter of the National Organization for Women in 1982; the Pathfinder Award for her outstanding contribution to the advancement of women in administration from the New York State Association for Women in Administration in 1981; and listings in *The World's Who's Who of Women*, *Directory of American Scholars* and the *International Who's Who in Education*. She has also served on boards of accreditation (Middle States Commission), colleges (Goucher and Marymount Manhattan) and several national educational councils.

She liked to know people and entertained faculty, students and guests generously at Shady Shores, the president's residence. One year, she gave forty-three different receptions, dinners, luncheons and breakfasts, a record of which she was very proud.

Virginia Radley died on December 20, 1998, at age seventy-one. Her life and career can be summarized in comments about her presidency made earlier in 1998 by her three vice-presidents: "A commitment to delivering high quality service to students while keeping a close eye on the expenditure of public funds" (Dr. Ralph Spencer, former executive vice-president and provost); "An emphasis on the centrality of liberal education, an almost relentless outspokenness on the need for high academic standards and effective teaching" (Dr. Donald R. Mathieu, executive vice-president and provost); and "Commitment to the total development of the college student, to molding responsible citizens…Setting high expectations of what kind of student behavior would be tolerated, restoring traditional ceremonialism through such events as the annual Honors Convocation, and graciously entertaining student leaders in her home" (James Wassenaar, vice-president for student services).

News releases, articles, speeches, curriculum vitae, memos, interviews, correspondence, bulletins and obituaries found in the Office of Public Affairs and in Special Collections of Penfield Library at the State University of New York–Oswego.

New York Times National. "Virginia L. Radley, 71, A SUNY President." Obituary, December 24, 1998.

Palladium-Times. "Former Oswego President Remembered." Obituary, December 22, 1998.

Peterson, Gloria. "Yes, Virginia, a Woman Can be President." *Rochester Review* (Winter 1978).

Syracuse Post-Standard. "Woman Educator Made History with SUNY Oswego Post." March 13, 1993.

Update. "Yearning in Desire to Follow Knowledge: The Radley Era at Oswego." Special Issue. Published by the Office of Public Affairs for the Oswego State University Community, July 1998.

Researcher and author: Marilynn J. Smiley, Oswego Branch

GRACE S. RICHMOND

1866–1959
WRITER/NOVELIST

Grace Louise Smith Richmond was born on March 31, 1866, in Pawtucket, Rhode Island, the daughter of a Baptist clergyman. Living in New York State during her high school years, she attended Syracuse High School and had private tutors for college courses. Her father moved her family to Fredonia, New York, in 1885 when he became the pastor of the First Baptist Church.

In 1887, at the age of twenty-one, she married Dr. Nelson Richmond. She was married in the home she and her husband would share in Fredonia and where her four children were born. After her death, her funeral services were also held in this house.

Two years after marrying Dr. Richmond, she began her writing career. Her first short stories were published in various women's magazines, including the *Women's Home Companion*, *Ladies' Home Journal* and *Everybody's Magazine*. Richmond wrote twenty-seven novels between 1905 and 1936. Her first novel, *The Indifference of Juliet*, was published in 1887.

Among her most popular books were the "Red Pepper Burns" series, the first of which was published in 1910. Some people felt that she drew her inspiration for Red Pepper from her husband. She was noted for her strong-willed yet compassionate characters, and Red Burns was no exception. His red hair and quick temper earned him his nickname, but this kind, charming country doctor endeared himself to his readers. Because of the success of *Red Pepper Burns*, Richmond followed with *Mrs. Red Pepper* (1913), *Red Pepper's Patients* (1917) and *Red of the Redfields* (1924).

Besides her "Red Pepper Burns" books, some of her other popular titles included *On Christmas Day in the Morning*, *Under the Country Sky* and *Bachelor Bounty*. Richmond wrote about romance, mystery and a deep love for home, all of which appealed to her readers. In 1923 alone, she realized $28,000 in royalties from her books and magazine stories.

In 1924, she was awarded an honorary doctorate from Colby College in Waterville, Maine. She maintained memberships in the League of American Pen Women, the Authors League of America, the Authors Guild Inc. and the Society of Authors, Composers and Playwrights.

Grace Richmond died on November 28, 1959. At the time of her death, she was still living on East Main Street in Fredonia with her daughter, Jean. She is buried at Fredonia's Forest Hill Cemetery.

Dunkirk (NY) Evening Observer. "Mrs. Grace S. Richmond Dies; Author, Long III, Was 93." Obituary, [November 27, 1959].

Fantastic Fiction. "Grace S. Richmond." www.fantasticfiction.co.uk/r/grace-s-richmond.

Merriman, C.D. "Grace S. Richmond." Literature Network. www.online-literature.com/grace-richmond.

Richmond, Grace S. "My House Means Home to Me." *Dunkirk Observer.* Reprinted on June 17, 1973. Originally published in December 1928.

Researcher and author: Susan Pepe, Dunkirk Fredonia Branch

BARBARA S. RIVETTE

19??–
RESEARCHER/AUTHOR/EDITOR

Barbara S. Rivette is a researcher, author and editor concentrating on environmental and historical topics. She also handles archive and records management projects for local towns, villages and counties.

Active in environmental organizations, she has been chairman of the Onondaga County Environmental Health Council since 2002, a member of the Outreach Committee of the Onondaga Lake Partnership and a member of the Town of Manlius Environmental Council since its founding in 1973. She also serves as president of the Fayetteville Cemetery Association.

Barbara has written numerous local history books, as well as the histories of printing and weekly newspapers in New York State. She also has written twenty-five sections for the *Encyclopedia of New York State*, including the "Onondaga County" section.

As a life member of the Onondaga Historical Association (OHA) and a member of its board of directors for more than thirty years, she received the OHA Medal, the organization's highest honor, in 2004 for the "study, preservation, and interpretation of Onondaga County history for more than thirty years."

She is historian for the town of Manlius, the village of Manlius and the village of Fayetteville, and in 1973, she photographed and documented Onondaga County's first National Register Historic District in the village of Manlius. In 2007, she received the Local Government Historian Award for Excellence from the Association of Public Historians of New York State.

Barbara has done research in the Library of Congress, the National Archives, the New York State Archives and in libraries and courthouses throughout New York State. She followed accounts of early Onondaga County residents who moved westward, tracking them and their careers by examining sources in libraries and courthouses in Pennsylvania, Ohio, Indiana, Illinois and California.

Her career as a newspaper reporter, photographer and editor spanned fifty years, and for fifteen years, she served as the executive editor of seven weekly newspapers in Onondaga and Madison Counties. In 1989, she was president of the 350-member New York Press Association.

Barbara is a 1948 honors graduate from the School of Journalism at Syracuse University with a dual major in journalism and public administration and a minor in history. Her mother and her mother's twin sister were half of the first graduating class of Syracuse University's Department of Journalism in 1923.

Publications researched and written by Barbara S. Rivette include *Solvay* (2011) and *Oakwood: A Special Place* (2009) for the sesquicentennial of Oakwood Cemetery, Syracuse, New York. For the *Encyclopedia of New York State* (2005), she wrote the following sections: "Onondaga County" plus towns/villages of "Baldwinsville," "Camillus," "Clay," "DeWitt," "East Syracuse," "Elbridge," "Fairmont," "Geddes," "Jordan," "Lysander," "Marcellus," "Mattydale," "Minoa," "Onondaga," "Salina," "Van Buren" and "Westvale." Segments were also written on "Ice Harvesting," "Genesee Road/Great Western Turnpikes," "James Geddes" and "Weekly Newspapers."

She also wrote the following: *Matilda Joslyn Gage: Fayetteville's First Woman Voter* (1969 and 1985, with additional material in 2005), *Promise and Performance, 1954–2004* for the Rosamond Gifford Charitable Corporation, *The First 50 Years of the Fayetteville-Manlius School District* (2001), *125 Years of the Onondaga County Bar Association* (2000), the *Our Glorious Workplace* series for the Onondaga Historical Association, *Onondaga Savings Bank* (1997), *Niagara Mohawk* (1998), *Onondaga County Court House* (1999), *Syracuse Newspapers* (2000), *New York Central Train Station* (2002), *Crucible Steel* (2003), *The Roots of Our Future: 200 Years of Weekly Newspapers in New York State* (1997), *This Is a Beautiful Country of Land* for the Onondaga County Bicentennial (1994), *Young Men Built This County* for the Onondaga County Bicentennial (1994), *Our Town at 200* (1994), *Glimpses of Fayetteville* (1994), *Grover Cleveland: Fayetteville's Hometown Boy* (1987), *Today's Environment, Tomorrow's Hopes* (1981), *Manlius: Onondaga County's First Village* (1976) and *Historic Sites of Fayetteville and Manlius* (1974).

The following were edited and designed by Barbara: Arkie Albanese's *To Manlius, With Love* (2002); Elinore Horning's *The Man Who Changed the Face of Syracuse* (1988) and Betsy Knapp's *Rocks, Fields and Beauty Forever* (1989).

Barbara S. Rivette's 2012 autobiography.

Submitted by Barbara Brown, Syracuse Branch.

ADELAIDE ALSOP ROBINEAU

1865–1929
CERAMIST/EDITOR/EDUCATOR

Adelaide Alsop Robineau was an influential ceramist, known for her innovations in making very thin porcelain and *grand feu* glazes, as well as editing magazines and teaching. Her career spanned many artistic movements, ranging from classicism, naturalism and folk traditions to the arts and crafts movement and art deco and later to a more abstract style. It also included early work as a china painter and an interest in ceramics, as well as her international recognition in that field.

She was born Adelaide Beers Alsop on April 18, 1865, in Middletown, Connecticut, the daughter of Charles R. Alsop and Elizabeth Gould Beers Alsop. Although there were nine children, only four lived to adulthood. Her father, who had failed to graduate from Yale, had a talent for invention and a love of adventure but little business sense. As a result, the family moved several times from east to west and back.

In 1883, Adelaide enrolled at St. Mary's Hall, an Episcopalian girls' boarding school at Faribault, Minnesota, near Minneapolis, and she graduated in 1884 at age nineteen. In 1885, the family moved to Syracuse, New York, and Adelaide, then twenty-one, lived by herself and listed her name in the city directory as an artist; she was decorating china, as many women did at that time. Her father took the family west again in 1887, and in 1892 Adelaide returned to Faribault and taught classes in art and physical education at her alma mater, St. Mary's Hall.

Although self taught as a painter, in the summer of 1895 she studied watercolor and painting with the well-known American impressionist William Merritt Chase at his school in Shinnecock Hill, Long Island. The next fall, she set up a studio in Manhattan and supported herself by decorating china and teaching. In the meantime, her mother and father separated in 1896, and her mother and two sisters moved to Syracuse, New York.

While in Manhattan, she met Samuel Edouard Robineau, an acquaintance from Minnesota. Born in France, he was a businessman who had made money in wheat farming near Fargo, North Dakota, but who was interested in historic ceramics and collecting. They married on March 9, 1898, and two months later, they started a magazine, *Keramic Studio*, which she would edit for thirty years. In the early years, she addressed a variety of subjects related to china painting and stressed the importance of design standards.

The magazine reached out to artists (particularly women) in rural areas, small towns and large cities.

Realizing that she did not enjoy china painting, Adelaide took classes in pottery with Charles Volkmar in 1901 and classes at Alfred University in 1902. She was in her thirties, but she soon believed that she had truly found her calling. Inspired by the writings of Taxile Doat, a prominent French ceramist, she used the technique of *grand feu* (high fire) in which she would paint the porcelain before glazing it at a high temperature.

In 1901, the Robineaus moved to Syracuse to consolidate the editorial and managerial offices of *Keramic Studio*. Two nationally circulated magazines (*Keramic Studio* and *The Craftsman*, published by Gustav Stickley) made Syracuse a nerve center for the arts and crafts movement in America.

About that time, Adelaide began to experiment with making porcelain and learned to use the potter's wheel in 1903. After a fire nearly erupted from the basement kiln in their rented house, they purchased land in 1903 from the estate of William Roberts in an undeveloped part of Syracuse and built a pottery with three kilns in the basement. In 1904, they built a home beside it called Four Winds, designed by the architect Katherine C. Budd, whom Adelaide had met while studying with William Merritt Chase. The grounds featured extensive gardens and pools. There were three children in the family: Maurice (born in 1900 or 1901), Priscilla (born in 1902) and Elisabeth (born in 1906).

By 1905, Adelaide's reputation was expanding. Tiffany & Company became an agent for her porcelain, and she exhibited at the Society of Ceramic Arts in New York City. A trademark of her decorating technique was conventionalized motifs carved or excised in low relief in pottery after it was dry. In 1910, she was invited to teach at the Art Academy of the American Women's League in St. Louis, Missouri, and there she created the *Scarab Vase*, one of her most intricate and impressive pieces.

During the summers from 1912 to 1914, the Robineaus held a six-week arts and crafts school for seventy students at Four Winds. Their dream of expanding this project with an arts and crafts colony was shattered by the beginning of World War I. By 1913, she had developed her distinctive "high fire bronze," which was a thin black-brown glaze that did not obscure the carving on her porcelain.

Despite the challenge of managing three children and a busy household, she continued to create pottery and win awards in Chicago, San Francisco, Boston and Detroit, and she was elected a member of the Société Nationale des Beaux-Arts in Paris. In 1916, the Syracuse

Museum of Fine Arts purchased more than thirty of her porcelains. One year later, she was awarded an honorary Doctor of Science degree in ceramics from Syracuse University and began teaching there as an assistant professor in the Course in Design. By 1921, she had moved her pottery studio there. For nearly a decade, she inspired college students, many of whom later pursued successful careers.

Her last exhibit was held in 1928 and was organized by the American Federation of Arts; it was held first at the Metropolitan Museum of Art and then moved to major public institutions in the East and Midwest. She died on February 18, 1929, while preparing work for a London exhibit.

Her husband wrote, "Hers was a beautiful and useful life: a full life as artist, writer, teacher, and mother—and that is the all important thing."

Many of her works are exhibited in the Everson Museum in Syracuse, as well as in museums throughout the country and world. The undeveloped area of Syracuse where the Robineaus built Four Winds in 1904 is now called Strathmore. Her influence is very much alive through the Ceramic Nationals, a competition that was started in 1932 by the Syracuse Museum of Fine Arts (now the Everson Museum of Art) to honor her spirit and her work. It is right to remember her influence as an educator through her writings and teachings, as well as the inspiration of her development as an artist from a china painter to an internationally acclaimed ceramist.

Conole, Patricia Corbett. "Strathmore Homes Tour." *Post-Standard*, June 13, 2010.

Lundborg, Pam. "Home & Garden Tours." *Post-Standard*, June 5, 2010.

Piche, Thomas, Jr., and Julia A. Monti, eds. *Only an Artist: Adelaide Alsop Robineau, American Studio Potter.* Syracuse, NY: Everson Museum of Art, 2006.

Thomas, Jo. "Celebrating the Legacy and Contributions of Adelaide Alsop Robineau, a Former Strathmore Resident on the 100th Anniversary of the Scarab Vase." *The Apotheosis of an Artist: A Brief History of Adelaide Alsop Robineau & Her Scarab Vase.* Syracuse, NY: Strathmore by the Park Historic Homes Tour Committee, a Committee of the Onondaga Park Association, 2010.

Researcher and author: Marilynn J. Smiley, Oswego Branch

DOROTHY ROGERS

1914–1986
EDUCATOR/PSYCHOLOGIST/AUTHOR/ACTIVIST

During her seventy-one years, Dorothy Rogers fulfilled many roles: distinguished educator, licensed psychologist, author, traveler, feminist and activist.

Born on May 31, 1914, in Ashburn, Georgia, she was class valedictorian when she graduated from high school at age fifteen. She received her bachelor's and master's degrees in English from the University of Georgia and then studied educational psychology on a fellowship at Duke University, receiving her doctorate in 1947.

Dr. Rogers taught in public schools in Georgia and Alabama for ten years before coming to the State University of New York–Oswego in 1946, where she taught until 1985 and became almost a legend. As a master teacher, she was highly respected by her colleagues and extremely popular with her students. Sections of her classes filled early, and it was not unusual for her to teach two hundred students per semester, and even then with a waiting list. She really tried to know her students, and at one time she took a picture of each one on her Polaroid camera the first day of classes so she could identify and remember them.

Besides teaching, Dr. Rogers served as interim chair of the psychology department and took an active role in faculty government through various offices and activities in the Faculty Assembly. A strong advocate for the women on the faculty, she was a founder of the Women's Caucus at Oswego and co-chaired the first such caucus at the state level for the State University of New York system. In 1978, she was promoted to the rank of distinguished service professor.

As an author, she wrote more than twenty-five books, many of which are psychology textbooks, on almost all phases of life. The volume *Adolescents and Youth*, published by Prentice Hall, went through five editions, and her book *The Adult Years* went through three editions. At the time of her death, three of her books were top sellers among psychology texts throughout the country.

Her first book, however, was *Jeopardy and a Jeep*, a popular travelogue published in the United States in 1957 and in Great Britain in 1962. In it, she described her adventures exploring Africa in the 1950s, before the modern tourist industry made the "dark continent" easily accessible to average Americans, particularly women. She traveled through about one hundred countries on six continents, often in primitive and remote regions. She circled Australia by car twice, sailed on a boat of South American emigrants bound for New Zealand and was once suspected of being a spy in the Soviet Union. These trips are described in a book, *Highways Across the Horizon*, published in 1961.

For the centennial of the college, she wrote its history, entitled *Oswego: Fountainhead of Teacher Education*. To commemorate the 125th anniversary of the college, she wrote a sequel, *SUNY College at Oswego: Its Second Century Unfolds*, before her death, and it was published posthumously in 1988. Several other manuscripts were left behind, some of them being light verse.

Dr. Rogers was much in demand as a speaker and consultant throughout the Northeast. The recipient of many honors and distinctions, she was recognized as a Woman of Distinction (one of fifty-eight) by Governor Mario Cuomo at the 1984 New York State Fair in Syracuse.

A strong advocate of women's rights, Dr. Rogers was a protégé of Alice Paul, an author of the Equal Rights Amendment and founder of the National Women's Party. Dorothy served on the council of the National Women's Party for thirty years before being elected as its first vice-president in 1983, and she served as the party's liaison for the Women's Vote Project in New York State.

She loved life and lived it to its fullest. This is evident in a newspaper article of 1982, for which she said, "The Rogers family is consumed and dominated by anything intellectual. Life is constantly a challenge. I feel like there is a limited amount of time, and you've got to pack everything into your lifetime—pack it in, pack it in."

News releases, Faculty Data Form of 1972, nomination packet for Empire State Woman of the Year in 1984, catalogue of her publications and undated articles located in the Office of Public Affairs and the Special Collections of Penfield Library at the State University of New York–Oswego.

Oswegonian. College student newspaper, various articles.

Palladium-Times. Obituary, January 1986.

———. Various articles.

Post-Standard. Obituary, January 1986.

———. Various articles, 1946–86.

Photograph courtesy of the State University of New York–Oswego, Penfield Library Archives. Researcher and author: Marilynn J. Smiley, Oswego Branch

Jeanne Fields Rogers

19??–
Artist/Educator

Jeanne Fields Rogers has been a member of the American Association of University Women since 1962. During that time, she has held appointed offices under several presidents. She held the office of implementation chair during "Societies' Reflection of the Arts," lending her art expertise to the two-year study topic. She later held the office of legislative chairwoman and ran a successful operation bringing books to the Suffolk County Prison in Riverhead, enhancing the education of inmates. Lastly, she was also Fine Arts Study Group leader for several years, guiding members in fine arts and crafts activities. She remained an active member, hosting at her home numerous Summer Socials and serving four years as hostess for the kickoff Progressive Dinner, which was always a successful fundraiser.

In the fall of 2009, Jeanne was elected president of the National League of American Pen Women (NLAPW), Suffolk County Branch. This prestigious organization, which dates back to 1897, encourages creative works of art utilizing professional standards in visual, literary and musical arts.

During a recent NLAPW art exhibit at the Bay Area Friends of the Fine Arts (BAFFA) Gallery, she presented an NLAPW state-funded check for a youth outreach program in keeping with the goals of NLAPW. In August, Jeanne was selected to join the Stony Brook Art Museum's open juried show, Works on Paper, and the Fire Island Lighthouse Show, where she annually donates proceeds from sales of her watercolors to the Fire Island Preservation of the National Seashore. She also contributed artwork to the Caumsett State Park during the annual fundraising galas. On October 25, Jeanne received an award from the East Islip Arts Council's juried show held at Bayard Cutting Arboretum for her large acrylic painting *Grand Canyon*.

Jeanne Fields Rogers, who grew up in Islip, New York, now resides and has her home studio in East Islip. She received her Bachelor of Fine Arts degree from Alfred University and her Master of Science degree in art education from the State University of New York–New Paltz. Postgraduate studies included those from C.W. Post and the Parsons School of Design.

Her professional training in watercolor included workshops under the direction of noted members of the American Watercolor Society. Though watercolor remains a favorite, she successfully works in oils, acrylic, pastels (especially for portraits), collage, mixed media and graphic design. Though landscapes, seascapes, florals and still lifes predominate in her subject matter, she continues to accept commissions to paint or render in pen and ink, as well as personal house portraits, which she finds enjoyable as well.

Besides working as a freelance artist, she has taught art at all levels in both public and private schools, was a consultant and adjunct professor at Dowling College and taught staff development courses in painting to teachers for the Teacher's Center of the Islips. Her award-winning works have been shown in local galleries, libraries, benefits, invitationals and juried shows and can be found in private collections, as well as permanent collections.

Jeanne's abstract acrylic painting *Color Explosion* was selected for the premiere edition of the magazine *Suffolk Woman Watch*. She belongs to the following art associations: National League of American Pen Women (a visual, literary and music arts organization); South Bay Art Association of Bellport, Long Island; Wet Paints Studio Group of Sayville, Long Island; East End Arts Council of Riverhead, Long Island; and Brookhaven Arts and Humanities Council of Farmingville, Long Island.

Information obtained from Jeanne Rogers, 2010.
Wet Paints Studio Group. Biography and sampling of paintings. www. wetpaintsgroup.homestead.com.

Researcher and author: Marlene Gilliam, Islip Area Branch

ELEANOR ROOSEVELT

1884–1962
FIRST LADY/DIPLOMAT/AUTHOR

Eleanor Roosevelt played many roles in her life: wife, mother, grandmother, teacher, First Lady, political activist, community volunteer, diplomat, public speaker and journalist.

Mrs. Roosevelt reached beyond her social class to champion the rights of women, children, minorities, workers and the poor. From her earliest work in the New York City settlement house movement in the 1920s to her chairmanship of President Kennedy's Commission on the Status of Women in the 1960s, she was a tireless fighter for those whose voices were weak.

Except for her years in Washington, D.C., as the wife of Assistant Secretary of the Navy and then President Franklin Delano Roosevelt, as well as time spent at her boarding school in England, Mrs. Roosevelt lived in New York. The Hudson Valley "played a major role in molding the character of a woman whose life is legend...The Hudson Valley was where Eleanor Roosevelt grew up, married and retired."

She was born in New York City, but after her mother's untimely death and her father's alcoholism, she came to Dutchess County to live with her Grandmother Hall in Tivoli. After she married her cousin Franklin, the young couple kept homes in Manhattan and at his mother's home in Hyde Park. They also lived in Albany for the years he was governor.

After Franklin Roosevelt's death in 1945, Mrs. Roosevelt moved into an apartment at Val-Kill in Hyde Park, a few miles away from the Roosevelt home, which had been turned into a national park. She always felt that Val-Kill was the only home of her own. Her apartments in New York were owned and furnished by her mother-in-law.

She would often be seen by neighbors riding her horse, walking or driving around Hyde Park. At Val-Kill, she entertained people her mother-in-law would have looked down on: labor union leaders, juvenile delinquents, female politicians, foreign diplomats and students from the United States and abroad.

She used her daily column "My Day," many articles in magazines and public speeches to convey her thoughts, ideas and observations. In 1928, she wrote an article in *Redbook* magazine, "Women Must Learn to Play the Game as Men Do," as a response to what she saw as women's passivity and ineffectiveness in the political arena. In whatever position she held, she encouraged the appointment of women to high offices, insisted that only female reporters cover her in the White House and pushed women to run for elective office.

Although Mrs. Roosevelt never attended college, a fact she regretted all her life, she learned from all of her experiences and from the people around her. She taught at a variety of schools: the Todhunter School in New York City, Barnard College, Brandeis University and at labor schools for female workers. She was a much sought-after commencement speaker and lecturer at colleges and schools all over the country, but she had a special place for those in the Hudson Valley. She believed in the importance of explaining ideas so that ordinary people could participate in discovering them and then use the political process to forward their goals.

The organizations that most shaped Mrs. Roosevelt, and the ones to which she devoted many of her efforts, included the League of Women Voters, the Women's Trade Union League, the Democratic Party (especially the women's divisions), the United Nations, the American Association for the United Nations and the National Association for the Advancement of Colored People.

One of her proudest accomplishments was the ratification of the United Nations' Declaration of Human Rights in 1948.

Cook, Blanche Wiesen. *Eleanor Roosevelt.* Volume 1, *1884–1933.* New York: Viking Press, 2005.

Ghee, Joyce, and Joan Spence. *Images of America: Eleanor Roosevelt, a Hudson Valley Remembrance.* Charleston, SC: Arcadia Press, 2005.

Gurewitsch, A. David, MD. *Eleanor Roosevelt, Her Day.* New York: Interchange Foundation, 1973.

Photograph courtesy of Franklin D. Roosevelt Presidential Library, Hyde Park, New York, taken in March 1949 in Calgary, Canada.
Researcher and author: Eleanor Charwat, Poughkeepsie Branch

BEULAH COUNTS RUDOLPH

1911?–1973
LIBRARIAN/EDUCATOR

Born in about 1911, Beulah Counts grew up in Missouri. She received her BA degree from Park College, Parkville, Missouri, in 1932; her BS degree from the Graduate School of Library Science at the University of Southern California in 1944; and her Master of Library Science degree from the University of Illinois in 1950. She also completed additional graduate studies at Columbia University in New York City.

She married Jay Rudolph, a retired member of the State University of New York–Oswego faculty in October 1954, and although her major contributions concerned children's literature and working with children, she had no children of her own. Professor Jay Rudolph died in 1959.

When she came to Oswego in 1937, Beulah Counts was secretary to the then president of the Oswego Normal School, Ralph Swetman. In 1944, she was appointed as Campus School librarian, and in 1963, she became part of the SUNY–Oswego English department as a teacher of children's literature. She retired from SUNY in 1968.

During her twenty years as librarian at the Campus School, she saw what was an unorganized collection of some two thousand volumes expand to a meticulous library of more than ten thousand volumes. She is quoted in one article as saying that "books can help to fill a child's need for security, love and aesthetic enjoyment. Appreciation, however, has to be cultivated." She indicated that children are entitled to this heritage of our culture.

Mrs. Rudolph was recognized as a leader in the development of school libraries and was in demand as consultant, speaker and adviser on library problems to school librarians and teachers of the central New York area. Her thesis at the University of Illinois was a study made of the facilities and programs of all campus school libraries of the teachers' colleges in New York. She published several articles in various journals regarding her library expertise.

Widely traveled, both in the United States and abroad, Mrs. Rudolph made it her mission to collect children's figurines and other memorabilia connected with particular children's books wherever she went. Upon her death, she bequeathed her entire collection to the University of Minnesota's famous Kerlan Collection of children's literature. Dr. Irvin Kerlan was a medical doctor who worked for the Food and Drug Administration and was an avid collector of children's books, as well as an author himself. It is impressive that Beulah Rudolph's collection is with some of several others that are in a special collection named after him.

Not just a believer in children, she was also a believer in the rights of women. At one point, she helped to put together an exhibit on the women's rights movement displayed in Penfield Library at SUNY-Oswego. She was an active member of the Oswego Branch of the American Association of University Women, serving at one time or another in almost every office, including president. She was particularly helpful in organizing book sales to benefit the Educational Foundation and was honored in 1968 by the Oswego Branch with a named grant in her honor.

Some of the other organizations that benefited from her active membership were Pi Kappa Delta, Beta Phi Mu (the national library science honorary fraternity), Phi Kappa Phi and the Campus School Librarians of New York State Faculties Association, of which she was chairman. In addition, she was a member of West Baptist Church in Oswego (always busy at one of the church functions), the Art Guild, the Heritage Foundation and the American Cancer Society.

Beulah Rudolph died in an accident on the New York State Thruway in October 1973. An article in the *Palladium-Times*, the Oswego newspaper, shortly after her death talks about her gifts, her energy, her sense of humor and her love and concern for others, both for children (including the son of the person writing) and the elderly. The article noted that "Missouri was her home, Oswego was her life for around forty years." The same article concluded by saying, "She was Beulah Counts Rudolph, a unique individual. Her maiden name was especially appropriate—she counted. We'll not see the likes of her again. Oswego is the lesser for her passing. It is the greater for her having been here."

Oswegonian. Various articles. State University of New York–Oswego campus newspaper.
Palladium-Times. Obituary, October 1973.
———. Various articles, 1937–73.
Personal anecdotes from friends.

Photograph courtesy of the State University of New York–Oswego, Penfield Library Archives.
Researcher and author: Juanita Tschudy, Oswego Branch

MARIBEL SANSONE

19??–
COMMUNITY LEADER

Maribel Sansone has been described as a quiet, low-key, dependable Staten Islander who speaks from the heart. Maribel, whose background is Italian and Puerto Rican, grew up in Park Slope, Brooklyn, New York. She said that she was taught by her family to look out for other people who were not as fortunate as she and her family.

She is a retired employee of the Human Resources Division of the New York City Department of Health. Maribel is busier than ever as, among other things, board president of the recently formed Community Health Center of Richmond and an executive board member of Project Hospitality.

Maribel is the founding member and on the board of the El Centra de Hospitalidad. The building housing this organization was converted through Maribel's creative abilities into a welcoming building for the newly arrived immigrants and is Staten Island's first immigrant resource center. Maribel is also the board president of the New York Institute on Disability Inc., an organization dedicated to improving the lives of people with disabilities.

She is a member of the Coalition of Staten Island Women's Organizations and an executive board member of the Friends of the College of Staten Island, as well as the president of Friends of Porzio's Pond Environmental Group on the South Shore of Staten Island. Maribel was appointed recently by the borough president as a member of Community Board no. 3.

Sansone, Maribel. Interview recorded by Ann M. Clinton, March 23, 2012.

Researcher and author: Ann M. Clinton, Staten Island Branch

EVA SAULITIS

1963–

POET/ESSAYIST/BIOLOGIST/TEACHER

Eva Saulitis was born in 1963 in the Bronx, New York, the daughter of Latvian immigrants. When she was four years old, Eva and her family moved to Chautauqua County to live in Silver Creek, New York. In 1981, Saulitis graduated from Silver Creek High School.

Pursuing her interest in science, Saulitis attended the Environmental Science and Forestry School in Syracuse, part of the State University of New York, where she earned a

Bachelor of Science degree in fisheries biology. She went on to earn two master's degrees from the University of Alaska, Fairbanks. Her interest in aquatic life led to a Master of Science in marine biology, and her love of writing led to a Master of Fine Arts in creative writing.

A passion for both biology and creative writing has led to a career that makes it impossible to separate the two. She is able to build a relationship between science and her art. One reviewer (Nancy Lord, author of *Beluga Days: Tracking the Endangered White Whale*) wrote that "she embraces both rigorous inquiry and spirited passion in her quest to understand, broadly, the natural world that surrounds and connects us."

In 1987, Saulitis began volunteering at the North Gulf Oceanic Society (NTGOS) in Homer Alaska, an agency with which she still works. It was through the nonprofit NTGOS that she began her research on killer whales, much of it focused in Prince William Sound, Alaska. For her more than twenty years of research, she has received international recognition.

Alaska—the land, the water, the animals and the people with whom she has developed such intense relationships—inspires much of Saulitis's writing. She has published poems and essays in magazines, journals and anthologies. She has received fellowships from the Alaska State Council on the Arts, the Island Institute and the Rasmuson Foundation and was awarded a residency at Ventspils House, a center for writing and translation in Latvia.

In 2008, Eva published *Leaving Resurrection*. The collection of essays received strong, positive reviews by both people who know the Alaska that Eva Saulitis writes of and by those who now wish they did.

Saulitis puts as much passion into her teaching as she does her research and writing. Her teaching statement on the University of Alaska's webpage notes, "I am a passionate teacher. My teaching practice involves close attention to the work of individual students and the promotion of voracious reading across genres."

Eva Saulitis teaches on a part-time basis. In the fall, she teaches undergraduates at the Kachemak Bay campus of the University of Alaska in Homer. She also teaches in the University of Alaska's low-residency Masters of Fine Arts program, mentoring students most of the year (through e-mail) and meeting with them in the summer for a residency. She is also involved in the Arts in the Schools program. Biological research starts in the spring, when writing is a priority. During the summer months, Saulitis can be found in the field, on the boat, studying whales.

Lord, Nancy. Review of *Leaving Resurrection*. "Eva Saulitis." News from Red Hen Press, March 2008. http://redhen.org/authors/eva-saulitis.

Saulitis, Eva. Interview by e-mail, recorded by Susan Pepe, March 14, 2009.

———. *Leaving Resurrection: Chronicles of a Whale Scientist*. Fairbanks, AK: Boreal Books, 2008.

University of Alaska–Anchorage. "Eva Saulitis—Teaching Statement," March 14, 2008. www.uaa.alaska.edu.

Photograph by Niles Dening. Taken at the Anderson Lee Library, Silver Creek, New York. February 11, 2008.

Researcher and author: Susan Pepe, Dunkirk Fredonia Branch

BARBARA EPLEY SHUCK

1936–

VOLUNTEER

Barbara Epley Shuck was born on November 28, 1936, in Nebraska. She graduated from Hastings College in Hastings, Nebraska, in 1957 and from the University of Nebraska in 1961. She graduated from Hastings at the age of twenty after having taught grade-school music in Superior, Nebraska, for one year. She then married Elmer Shuck, who was studying for a physics degree at the University of Nebraska. She planned to teach in Lincoln, Nebraska, but being pregnant, she wasn't allowed to teach. Lincoln didn't allow pregnant teachers, even if married. She found a job as a secretary to the mechanical engineering department at the University of Nebraska–Lincoln. There she qualified for a journalism scholarship. She worked on the *Lincoln Daily Journal* newspaper as a general assignment reporter/photographer and was a member of two journalism honorary societies as she received her advanced degree. She was also named Woman Journalist of the Year by one journalism honorary. Her last degree earned was her PHTS (Putting Husband Through School).

Her husband was offered a job at General Electric in Utica, New York, where she contributed her journalism/teaching skills to the community, as well as became the mother of two more boys, born in Utica. Her first son was born in Lincoln, Nebraska.

She has edited newsletters for the Dunham Manor Association (where she lives), the League of Women Voters and, currently, the local branch of the American Association of University Women. She served on the board of the Young Women's Christian Association (YWCA) for six years and was in charge of public relations. Barbara worked part time in a paid position for many more years. During that time, she helped to establish the Hall House for battered women and children and the Rape Crisis Center. She was honored by the United Way in the 1970s as one of five women in the community who excelled at helping others. She was president of the local Church Women United and then state president, and today she serves on the national board as Northeast regional coordinator. She was moderator of Presbyterian Women in her local church and presbytery and served on the synod (all the Northeast) board for six years. She was also moderator of the synod of the Northeast Presbyterian Church during the time a mission relationship was cemented with Madagascar's prominent Protestant church. One of the major projects was getting books for the seminary library and motorcycles, which eliminated the need for walking, for the pastors. Many of them had several churches.

In her local church, she worked with others to start the inner-city mission, which began as a resource center and is now a food pantry and clothes closet open during the week. She served as mission chair for twelve years in her church and at the presbytery level another twelve years. She chaired three community Thanksgiving dinners where more than one thousand people are served annually. She is currently a lay preacher in the Presbyterian church, filling in when pastors are on vacation, sick and so on. She has done this for twenty years.

Barbara served as president of the Mohawk Valley Branch of AAUW, president of the Parents Club, president of the Western College group, Cub Scout den mother and den mother coach. Another community office held by Barbara was vice-president of the League of Women Voters. She currently serves on its nominating committee. In 2009, the Mohawk Valley Branch of AAUW contributed to the Educational Foundation in her name. Through the years, she has taught Sunday school, Vacation Bible School, some adult education church classes and a few grandchildren.

We are grateful for all that Barbara Shuck has done for the community, including the Mohawk Valley Branch. She has truly provided an opportunity to supply the spiritual, material and intellectual needs of others.

Shuck, Barbara. Interview by e-mail, recorded by Joan Rajchel, November 19, 2010.

Researcher and author: Joan Rajchel, Mohawk Valley Branch

BEVERLY SILLS

1929–2007
OPERA SINGER/IMPRESARIO

Beverly Sills was born Belle Miriam Silverman on May 25, 1929, in Brooklyn, New York, the youngest of three children, to Shirley Bahn, a musician, and Morris Silverman, an insurance broker, both Jewish immigrants. Her mother was from Odessa, Russia, and her father from Bucharest, Romania. She was nicknamed Bubbles by her mother's doctor, for she came out of the womb with a bubble of saliva on her mouth, and the nickname stuck.

At the age of three, she won a "Miss Beautiful Baby" contest in which she sang "The Wedding of Jack and Jill." By age four, she was performing professionally on the Saturday morning radio program *Rainbow House*. At age seven, she began serious singing lessons with Estelle Liebling, an esteemed teacher of distinguished operatic artists, who was her only teacher for thirty-four years, as well as a friend for life. Liebling encouraged her to audition for Columbia Broadcasting System (CBS) Radio's *Major Bowes' Amateur Hour*, and on October 26, 1939 at the age of ten, Sills was the winner of that week's program. Bowes then asked her to perform on his *Capitol Family Hour*, a weekly variety show, and she appeared frequently. By this time, she had adopted her stage name, Beverly Sills. She attended Erasmus Hall High School in Brooklyn and Manhattan's Professional Children's School.

In 1945, Sills made her professional stage debut with a Gilbert and Sullivan touring company produced by Jacob J. Shubert. It played in twelve states and Canadian cities and offered seven different Gilbert and Sullivan operettas. She credited this tour for helping develop her comic timing.

Her operatic stage debut was made in 1947 as Frasquita in Bizet's *Carmen* with the Philadelphia Civic Grand Opera Company. During 1951–52, she toured North America with the Charles Wagner Opera Company, and on September 15, 1953, she made her debut with the San Francisco Opera. Returning to New York, she sang in any opera role offered to her in commercials and on television.

In 1955, she joined the New York City Opera and became the company's diva. Her first appearance was on October 29 of that year as Rosalinde in Johann Strauss II's *Die Fledermaus*. She continued singing opera on tours and in recitals throughout the United States.

Sills married Peter Greenough, wealthy newspaper journalist with the *Plain Dealer*, in 1956 and moved to Cleveland, Ohio. The couple had two children, Meredith ("Muffy") in 1959 and Peter Jr. ("Bucky") in 1961. Since Muffy was born deaf and Peter was born autistic and epileptic, Beverly restricted, but did not halt, her performing schedule to care for their children.

Her reputation expanded in 1958 with her performance in the title role in the New York City Opera's premiere of *The Ballad of Baby Doe* by Douglas Moore. In 1960, the family moved to Milton, Massachusetts, and Peter worked for the *Boston Globe*. Beverly sang many roles with the Opera Company of Boston, directed by Sarah Caldwell, as well as with the New York City Opera and other opera houses. When Peter retired, they moved to New York City.

The turning point in her career was the 1966 New York City Opera's revision of Handel's then virtually unknown opera seria, *Giulio Cesare*. Her sensational success in the florid role (which she recorded) made her an international opera star and led to a series of bel canto opera revivals at the New York City Opera, including Donizetti's trio of operas about Tudor queens: *Maria Stuarda* (1972), *Anna Bolena* (1973) and Elizabeth in *Roberto Devereux* (1970). Sills regarded this latter opera as her finest accomplishment and as the most taxing of the bel canto repertoire. Appearances in major European and South American opera houses quickly followed. She sang works by Donizetti, Rossini, Massenet, Offenbach, Verdi, Handel, Mozart and other major opera composers.

She learned more than one hundred operatic roles and sang fifty or sixty of them in every major opera house in the world, except the Metropolitan Opera House in New York City. Rudolf Bing, director of the Metropolitan from 1950 to 1972, never invited her to sing there. Some possible motives were that he preferred engaging only Italian stars, believed that Americans could not sell tickets or refused to engage the prima donna of a rival opera company. His successor, Goeran Gentele, changed that. Sills's Metropolitan Opera debut as Pamina in a new production of Rossini's *The Siege of Corinth* took place on April 7, 1975, just twenty years after her debut at the New York City Opera. At the Metropolitan Opera House, she was welcomed like a long-lost child with an eighteen-minute ovation. Sills continued to perform for both the New York City Opera (her own opera house) and the Metropolitan, as well as other opera houses throughout the world, until her retirement at age fifty.

Sills had a profound effect on opera. Besides her successes as a singer, she popularized opera through talk show appearances and helped dispel the traditional image of the temperamental opera diva. She also devoted herself to various arts causes and charities, especially those to fight birth defects, such as the March of Dimes, which she promoted in 1972. *Newsweek* magazine featured her in a cover story after her debut at La Scala in Milan in 1971 and described her as "America's Queen of Opera." Presidents Nixon, Ford, Carter and Reagan invited her to sing at the White House. There were many honors and awards, including honorary doctorates from Temple University, New York University, New England Conservatory of Music, Harvard University and the California Institute of the Arts, as well as Grammy and Emmy Awards and other music-related awards from the Kennedy Center, the National Endowment for the Arts, the Metropolitan Opera and others.

After retirement as a singer, she became director of the New York City Opera from 1979 to 1989, ensuring its financial stability (through extensive fundraising), continuing its artistic reputation (through quality productions) and differentiating its mission from that of the Metropolitan (through premiering operas by contemporary composers and those from America). This was an entire career change, and she was successful, despite initial criticism from others in the opera world that "here was a woman doing a man's job, and she obviously was going to fall on her face." Sills then became chair of the Lincoln Center Board from 1994 to 2002 and chair of the Metropolitan Opera from 2002 to 2005, resigning due to the illness of her husband, who died in September 2006 at the age of eighty-nine. She gave only a few interviews after that. She died on June 28, 2007, at age seventy-eight of lung cancer.

Throughout her life, she delighted opera audiences with her lyrical coloratura voice, though she also sang a number of heavier dramatic coloratura roles later in her career, and she impressed colleagues with her administrative skill. Opera lovers continue to enjoy her singing through the extensive selections on her recordings.

Mender, Mona. *Extraordinary Women in Support of Music*. Lanham, MD: Scarecrow Press Inc., 1997.
New York Times. "Sills, Beverly." Obituary. July 3, 2007.
Pederson, Rena. *What's Next? Women Redefining Their Dreams in the Prime of Life*. New York: Perigee Books, 2001.
Sills, Beverly. *Bubbles: A Self Portrait*. New York: Bobbs-Merrill, 1976.
Sills, Beverly, and Lawrense Linderrnan. *Beverly: An Autobiography.* Toronto: Bantam Books, 1987.

Researcher and author: Marilynn J. Smiley, Oswego Branch

HELEN BUCKLEY SIMKIEWICZ

1918–2001
EDUCATOR/AUTHOR

Born on June 6, 1918, in Syracuse, New York, Helen Buckley grew up in Syracuse, attended public schools in Syracuse and received Bachelor of Science and Master of Science degrees from Syracuse University following graduation from Syracuse Normal School. She pursued her degrees while teaching in the elementary schools. She received her Doctor of Education degree from Teachers College, Columbia University, in New York City. In January 1970, at the age of fifty-one, she married Francis Simkiewicz and became an instant mother to Niesha, ten years old at the time. Niesha Simkiewicz Anderson described Helen as a "firm, loving and extraordinary" mother.

She was an educator for fifty years, and for twenty-seven of those years, she taught in the State University of New York–Oswego in the Campus School (nursery, kindergarten and first grade), in the education department and then in the English department to teach children's literature courses and writing. In 1978, she began teaching courses in writing books for children. She and Rosemary Nesbitt were contemporaries and were asked many times to give dual presentations at various conferences and meetings. Helen also taught as an adjunct professor at University College, Syracuse University, from 1979 to 1989 and was voted teacher of the year in 1981. She gave many solo talks to teachers, children, librarians and parents over the years, including appearing on TV in Syracuse at least once to talk about her first book.

Helen is probably best known for her prolific writing of books for young readers. She wrote at least fifteen books from 1959 until her death in 2001, including *Grandfather and I, Grandmother and I, Where Did Josie Go?* and *The Little Pig in the Cupboard*. *Grandfather, Grandmother* and *Little Pig* have all been published in Japanese, and she had some of her other books published in German. *Little Pig* was based on and dedicated to her friend, Richard Shineman, who retired from the chemistry department at SUNY-Oswego. A complete listing of her books is given at the end of this chapter.

In 1990, Helen was honored by the *Syracuse Post-Standard* newspaper as one of eleven women who improved the community's quality of life in the Women of Achievement program. The recipients of the honor were chosen by an independent jury on the basis of "contribution and dedication." Helen was given the Arts and Letters Award.

Dr. Buckley Simkiewicz was a member of the Society of Children's Books Writers and is mentioned in *Contemporary Authors, 1969–74*. When she retired, she and her husband wintered in Bradenton, Florida, but still came to Ramona Beach in Pulaski, New York, to spend their summers. She died at age eighty-three on July 27, 2001.

BOOKS AUTHORED BY HELEN BUCKLEY SIMKIEWICZ

Grandfather and I, Grandmother and I, My Sister and I, The Little Boy and the Birthdays, Where Did Josie Go?, Some Cheese for Charles, Josie's Buttercup, Josie and the Snow, The Little Pig in the Cupboard, The Wonderful Little Boy, Too Many Crackers, Michael Is Brave, Someday with My Father (dedicated to her husband, Frank, and daughter, Niesha), *Take Care of Things Edward Said* (illustrated by Katherine Coville, a student and friend of Dr. Buckley and wife of author Bruce Coville) and *Moonlight Kite.* Also note that the "Josie" books and *Some Cheese for Charles* were illustrated by one of Eliot Ness's wives, E. Ness.

Information obtained from Niesha Simkiewicz Anderson (stepdaughter) by Juanita Tschudy, 2009.

Oswegonian. March 2, 1960; May 17, 1968; December 10, 1965.

Perspective. March 1975. SUNY publication.

Post-Standard. February 9, 1990.

SUNY-Oswego Alumni (Fall 2001).

Photograph courtesy of the State University of New York–Oswego, Penfield Library Archives.

Researcher and author: Juanita Tschudy, Oswego Branch

MOLLIE SNEDEN

17??–1810
FERRYWOMAN OF SNEDENS LANDING

Snedens Landing is located on the Hudson River in the quiet, bucolic hamlet of Palisades, New York. Here Mollie Sneden, a strong and robust widow, operated a ferry to the Westchester shore for almost fifty years until shortly before her death.

During the century and a half of river traffic, Snedens Landing played an important role in the development of the commerce and history of our country, particularly during the Revolutionary War. In the 1800s, it was not a serene place but rather was a commercial link to New York City to the south and the river towns to the north. There was a constant stream of boats docking at the landing to take on or unload cargo. Among them was the ferryboat that transported people and wagons to the Westchester shore at Dobbs Ferry.

Many stories have been told of the rich and famous people at that time who were transported by this lively ferrywoman. In the fall of 1775, Martha Washington was traveling from Virginia to join her husband in Massachusetts. Because there was already talk of war with the British, Mrs.

Washington crossed the Hudson River at Snedens Landing, which was considered a more secure locale from which to cross.

There is little information detailing Mollie's youth, but it is believed that she was the daughter of John and Abigail Dobbs. She was baptized on August 2, 1709, in Tarrytown, New York. Mollie married Robert Sneden Jr. in about 1730, and they had nine children during their marriage.

In July 1752, Robert Sneden purchased land on the opposite side of the Hudson River that included a ferry site. He died shortly thereafter, and Mollie took over the operation of the ferry. In order to attract more travelers, she got a license to operate a tavern at the landing so travelers could rest and refresh themselves with food and drink. Snedens Landing operated a busy and profitable business until the Revolutionary War. The majority of her children and their families were Tories, British sympathizers. Only one son had the same political views as his mother, and they were staunch Loyalists.

American soldiers built a blockhouse for five hundred soldiers above the ferry landing so they could watch the movement of the British fleet, which lay off Sneden's dock. General Washington wanted to prevent the British from sailing up the river to West Point.

On July 29, 1776, the family members were asked to sign a "Declaration of Allegiance to the Cause of Liberty," but they refused. Subsequently, the Committee for Safety decided that because of the family's loyalty to the British, the Sneden family could no longer operate their ferry on the Hudson River.

Mollie's children fled to Nova Scotia, and it is believed that they never returned to Rockland County. After the war, Mollie and her son John once again began to ferry people across the Hudson.

Mollie Sneden died on January 31, 1810, at the age of 101 years. Her tombstone can still be viewed at the Palisades Cemetery.

Bedell, Cornelia F., comp. *Now and Then and Long Ago in Rockland County.* New York: Arno Press, 1968.

Gilman, Winthrop S., comp. *The Story of the Ferry, Palisades, Rockland County.* New York, May 30, 1903.

Nicholas Gesner's Diary. New York, May 30, 1903.

Savell, Isabelle K. *The Tonetti Years at Snedens Landing.* New York: Historical Society of Rockland County, 1977.

Researcher and author: Elisabeth Palombella Vallone, Rockland County Branch

NANCY E. SPAULDING

1938–
EDUCATOR

Nancy E. Spaulding was born in Cortland, New York, in 1938 and attended local schools. In 1960, she graduated from Syracuse University with a Bachelor of Science degree in geology. Then Nancy moved to Elmira and taught Earth science at the Elmira Free Academy from 1961 to 1997. In 1966, she graduated from Elmira College with a Master of Science degree in education and continued her education at the University of Rochester with a Master of Arts degree, specializing in Earth science education.

In addition to her teaching job, she has held other career-related positions. Since 1988, she has served as Earth science mentor at the Global Science and Technology (GST) Board of Cooperative Educational Services (BOCES) Teacher's Center, and since 1970, she has been an Earth science regents exam writer and reviewer for the New York State Education Department. She has also been a textbook author, writing *Earth Science* with Samuel Namowitz, starting with the 1985 edition.

Nancy belongs to many organizations, including American Association of University Women, Elmira-Corning Branch (president 1990–92, 1996–99); Delta Kappa Gamma, Alpha Rho Chapter; Daughters of the American Revolution, Chemung Chapter; Retired Teachers Association of Elmira and Area; Science Teachers Association of New York State; New York State Science Education Leadership Association; National Science Teachers Association; National Association of Geoscience Teachers; and the National Association of Earth Science Teachers.

In 2007, she was presented with the prestigious Service Award by the Science Teachers Association of New York State, Southern Zone.

Spaulding, Nancy E. Interview recorded by Elizabeth Reiter, 2009.

Researcher and author: Elizabeth Reiten, Elmira-Corning Branch

ELIZABETH CADY STANTON

1815–1902
SUFFRAGIST

Elizabeth Cady Stanton has long been known as a driving force in gaining the right to vote for women. Although she died before seeing the passage of the Nineteenth Amendment, she devoted her life to the fight for women's equality.

Born on November 12, 1815, she was one of five daughters born to Judge Daniel Cady and Margaret Livingston. They also were parents to four boys, three dying in infancy and another at the age of twenty. Judge Cady, now without a son, didn't hesitate to tell Elizabeth, "I wish you were a boy." Even though another son was born later in life, he also died in infancy.

Elizabeth was educated at Johnstown Academy and the Emma Willard's Troy Female Seminary. She attempted to attend Union College along with other male classmates, but she was denied acceptance because of her gender.

In 1839, Elizabeth met Henry Brewster Stanton, whom she married on May 1, 1840, in Johnstown, New York. It was a marriage unpleasing to her father, as Henry, being an abolitionist and orator, was considered not to have a trade or profession. Henry was offered an opportunity to study law with his new father-in-law upon his return from England, where Henry and Elizabeth had traveled to attend the first world Anti-Slavery Convention in 1840. There Elizabeth was denied a seat, and the seeds were planted for pursuing a women's rights convention. Meeting Lucretia Mott and other women was just what Elizabeth needed to give her the push to fight for equal rights for women.

The women's rights convention held in Seneca Falls, New York, in 1848, was the impetus for the women's rights movement. Elizabeth wrote the Declaration of Sentiments, and it is said that this was the beginning of the struggle to gain equal rights for women. Elizabeth then joined forces with Lucretia Mott, Susan B. Anthony, Martha Coffin Wright, Jane Hunt, Mary Ann McClintock and others to actively seek equality for women. Women were eventually given rights to own property, rights to wages and equal guardianship of their children. In 1878, Elizabeth drafted a federal suffrage amendment that was used in the final ratified amendment in 1920.

Elizabeth Cady Stanton authored many books and worked closely with Susan B. Anthony. Together, they founded the National Woman Suffrage Association. They continued throughout their lives to stay focused and pursue the fight for women.

Although Elizabeth Cady Stanton died without seeing the total fruits of her labors, she continues to this day to be honored for her work. She was one of the first women to be inducted in the Women's Hall of Fame in Seneca Falls, New York. The home in which she lived in Seneca Falls is now part of the Women's Rights National Historic Park. In Johnstown, New York, she is remembered throughout the city. A New York historical marker stands where the Cady Home was once located. In a city park, there is a marker dedicating this city as the birthplace of the woman who was instrumental in crusading for women's rights.

It is only recently that the home in which Elizabeth Cady Stanton and Susan B. Anthony worked on the third volume of the book *The History of Woman Suffrage* was purchased, and it will become the home for a museum, honoring the history that was made there for women. This was made possible through the newly formed Elizabeth Cady Stanton Hometown Foundation, which is currently working to get legislation passed to establish a Women's Rights History Trail, which would establish a trail to properties and sites associated with women's rights for promoting education and awareness.

The first female mayor of Johnstown, Sarah Slingerland, was sworn into office in January 2006, using a Bible signed by Elizabeth Cady Stanton. The Amsterdam-Johnstown-Gloversville Branch of the American Association of University Women has honored Elizabeth Cady Stanton by naming the consortium, recently formed at the local community college (Fulton Montgomery Community College), the Elizabeth Cady Stanton Women's Consortium. The New York State legislature has designated November 12, Elizabeth's birthday, as Elizabeth Cady Stanton Day to honor her.

Honoring Women's History Month. *Women of Distinction.* Sponsored by the New York State Senate, March 2003. Available in the New York State Library Digital Collection. http://128.121.13.244:8080/awweb.

Ward, Jeffrey C., and Ken Burns. *Not for Ourselves Alone: The Story of Elizabeth Cady Stanton and Susan B. Anthony.* New York: Alfred A. Knopf, 1999.

Photograph used with permission of Coline Jenkins.
Researcher and author: Virginia (Ginni) Mazur, Amsterdam-Johnstown-Gloversville Branch

WENDY CORSI STAUB

1964–
AUTHOR

Wendy Corsi Staub is a native of Dunkirk, New York, and a graduate of the State University of New York–Fredonia, where she delivered the 2008 commencement address, was a featured speaker at the 2011 convocation and serves on a special advisory committee to the dean of arts and sciences. She is an internationally recognized author probably best known for her suspense, romance and young adult novels.

An avid reader as a child, she was inspired by the writing of Laura Ingalls Wilder, and she devoured her *Little House* books. She decided in third grade that she, too, wanted to become an author. At the age of eight, Corsi Staub was determined to become a published author and became single-minded in her efforts to see her dream fulfilled.

Her love of books led her to seek a job working in a local bookstore while in high school. She continued to work at independent bookstores through college. Having access to so many authors' works, having the occasional opportunity to meet visiting authors and seeing the retail side of the book business were steps taken toward fulfilling her dream of becoming an author.

In 1986, after graduating from college, Corsi Staub moved to New York City to become a writer. Before she started moving up the bestseller charts, however, she found work that was able to further prepare her for the business end of publishing books. She worked as a book editor for a publishing company in Manhattan and also as an account coordinator for a major advertising agency. Her other job, of course, involved writing constantly.

Six years after moving to New York, at the age of twenty-seven, the author sold her first novel, the supernatural young adult thriller *Summer Lightening*. This first novel earned her the Romance Writers of America (RWA) Rita Award (romance publishing's Oscar) for the Best Young Adult Novel. This was just the first of many awards Ms. Corsi Staub has won during her relatively short but prolific career.

The author has published more than seventy books. Besides writing under her name, she also uses the pseudonyms Wendy Markham, Wendy Morgan and Wendy Brody. She has also ghost-written and co-written several novels, including a mystery series with former mayor of New York City Ed Koch.

During the course of her career, Corsi Staub has written novels of suspense and horror, historical fiction, contemporary romance novels and biographies, as well as television and movie tie-ins. Her "Lily Dale" series for young adults was optioned and is in development with Freemantle Entertainment as a television series. She loves that writing allows her to be a stay-at-home mom, but she approaches writing, as much as she loves it, as her job. She sets a writing schedule for herself that has her up well before daybreak and often continues into the evening. When she is working toward a deadline, it is a seven-days-a-week job. She has said that for her, it is better to put "dribble" on a page than nothing at all. One can always go back, edit and rewrite; the important thing is to keep writing, keep the ideas flowing and keep producing until the book she wants emerges.

The author lives with her husband and two sons in suburban New York City. The first title in her first suspense trilogy for Harper Collins Publishers achieved a starred review in *Publisher's Weekly* and received a Mary Higgins Clark Award nomination at the 2011 Mystery Writers of America Edgar Awards. Other awards include the Romantic Times 2008 Career Achievement in Suspense and the 2007 Romance Writers of America–New York City Chapter (RWA-NYC) Golden Apple for Lifetime Achievement. She was recognized as one of Westchester County, New York's "Millennial Authors" in 2000, and four of her novels have been honored with the WLA.

Her Wendy Markham novel *Slightly Single* was selected as one of Waldenbooks' 100 Best Fiction Titles of 2002. Her thriller *The Last to Know* was nominated for a Romantic Times (RT) Book Club Reviewers' Choice Award. Five of her novels—*Bride Needs Groom*; *Don't Scream*; *Hello, It's Me*; *The Last to Know*; and *Mike, Mike, and Me*—were each awarded one month's top pick review by that magazine.

Her work has been translated into more than a dozen languages worldwide. A number of her titles have been selected as Mystery Guild, Literary Guild, Doubleday Book Club, Large Print Book Club and Rhapsody Book Club picks.

The loss of both her mother and mother-in-law to breast cancer turned Corsi Staub into an advocate for breast cancer awareness. She uses any opportunity available to spread the word, including her official webpage, community site, Facebook and Twitter.

Corsi Staub, Wendy. Interview by e-mail, recorded by Susan Pepe, October 17, 2011.

Fresh Fiction. "Wendy Corsi Staub." http://freshfiction.com/author.php?id=7407.

Maberry, Jonathan. Interview of Wendy Corsi Staub. International Thriller Writers, March 1, 2009.

Pepe, Susan. Rick Donovan interview, September, 2007.

Wendy Corsi Staub Community. www.wendycorsistaubcommunity.com.

Wendy Corsi Staub—Official Website. www.wendycorsistaub.com/index.html.

Researcher and author: Susan Pepe, Dunkirk Fredonia Branch

IDA CRAWFORD STEWART

1922–

CORPORATE EXECUTIVE/ART EDUCATOR/AUTHOR

Mrs. Stewart is truly one in a million. She is an art educator by training, worked as a corporate executive for Fortune 500 companies and has been an internationally recognized speaker whose unique blend of wit, wisdom and warmth has entertained and enlightened audiences from New York to Tokyo and from San Francisco to London for more than fifty years. Ida is the epitome of working hard, living fully and caring deeply. She exemplifies service and leadership, and that's why she continues to receive recognition and to earn honors from institutions of higher learning, professional groups and communities around the globe.

Born on December 13, 1922, in Clinton, South Carolina, she was the third of four children of James Roy Crawford and Fannie Mae Wade Crawford. She received her Bachelor of Arts degree in 1943 from Winthrop College, now Winthrop University in Rock Hill, South Carolina, and is one of its notable alumni. She also received a Master of Arts degree in health education from the University of Maryland. Mrs. Crawford worked as an educator in the South Carolina Public School System and at the University of Maryland. She coauthored *Camp Counseling*, a textbook for counselors now in its fourth edition (and still the authoritative text on the subject).

She married her beloved Robert Murray Stewart at Riverside Church in New York City, where they met. The famous organ player Virgil Fox, who played the organ at their wedding, was a good friend of her husband, who himself was a great pianist and organist. Robert was the corporate secretary for the California Texaco Oil Company for years. The couple lived in North Tarrytown, New York, and in York and Aiken, South Carolina, where they raised trotter and pacer horses. Her husband passed away in 1981.

After finishing graduate school, Mrs. Stewart worked as educational director for Bristol Myers in New York City. She developed the company's highly successful school hygiene program and introduced new visual approaches for teaching children, which she then expanded to the company's adult education activities.

In 1961, she joined the Estee Lauder Company and was soon named Mrs. Lauder's personal assistant and corporate vice-president, working closely with Mrs. Lauder to develop the fledgling company. During these years, she was involved in all aspects of the cosmetic giant, including product development, quality control, marketing, public relations and training. As Mrs. Lauder's representative, she introduced new products and opened Lauder markets in Europe, Asia and Australia.

After retiring from the Lauder Company in 1982, she conducted seminars on profit-building techniques and sales approaches and was a much sought-after keynote speaker and workshop leader. She always delivered her message with enthusiasm and energy, igniting audiences, including such diverse groups as the National American Equipment Dealers Association, sales and marketing executives, the Hugh O'Brien Youth Leadership organization (HOBY), countless beauticians' groups and students and faculty at colleges and universities, including Kent State, Mississippi University for Women and Winthrop University, her alma mater.

Mrs. Stewart's lifelong commitment to learning and service brought her many awards, including an honorary doctor of humane letters from the University of South Carolina, a Woman of Achievement Award from the South Carolina Commission on Women and Winthrop University's Mary Mildred Sullivan Award, its highest alumni award.

An eclectic and copious reader, Mrs. Stewart's commitment to education is reflected in the scholarships and trusts that she has established at numerous colleges and universities, including an endowed chair in the Sociology of Maturity at the University of South Carolina–Aiken, where she established the Center for Lifelong Learning.

Her many accomplishments, both professionally and personally, have brought her recognition and inclusion in numerous biographical publications, including the *World Who's Who of Women*, *World Wide Business* and *The Directory of Distinguished Americans*.

The University of Miami School of Medicine and the American Cancer Society have benefited from her fundraising abilities. More personally, she traveled to Mexico City and Nicaragua to participate in a Habitat for Humanity building project. In New York City, she volunteers at a number of social services projects in Central Park and the St. Peters Church Soup Kitchen, among many more.

Mrs. Stewart is a member of the International Speakers Association, the Fashion Group, the Sales and Marketing Executive Club, the National Association of Female Executives and the Older Women's League. She has served on many advisory boards, including the American College for Applied Arts, Atlanta, Georgia; the Columbia College Founders Society, Columbia, South Carolina; and the Roger and Jerry Silverman School of Fashion Merchandising, Kent State University, Ohio.

She has been an active member of the American Association of University Women's New York City Branch, since 1965. Mrs. Stewart exemplifies AAUW's mission in the manner that she has lived her life and as an advocate and activist for women's causes. She invites new members, nurtures current ones and promotes mission-based programs. Mrs. Stewart is the force behind the beautification of the branch house's patio, an oasis for guests to enjoy during the warmer days in New York City. She also produced a video of this feature of the branch house.

She takes painting, writing and water aerobics classes daily. One of her current projects is a video of a city pigeon that she nurtured back to health and that lived with her for four years. She is doing all of this while remaining actively involved in several other philanthropic causes.

Today, after more than six decades of remarkable professional and personal accomplishments, her insatiable need to work, produce and serve is stronger than ever. Mrs. Stewart, the trailblazer, the educator and the philanthropist, continues her commitment to improving the lives of others—as she says, to "give back all the great things I have enjoyed."

She is an inspiration, and it is always an honor to work with and learn from this superwoman.

Information obtained from Ida Crawford Stewart, including written research and résumés by Rosalie Spaniel, a close friend of Ida's, 2010.

Photograph provided by Rosalie Spaniel.
Researcher and author: Dayra Bernal-Lederer, member at large

PAULINE GEORGE STITT

1909–1996
PHYSICIAN/MEDICAL ADMINISTRATOR/EDUCATOR

Pauline George Stitt knew at the age of seven that she wanted to become a doctor. The journey to the prestigious halls of the United States' government health institutions, to the University of California and Harvard schools of public health, to the teaching posts in Boston and Hawaii and to the World Health Organization in the Far East was littered with obstacles that would have defeated anyone else.

Pauline was born on May 28, 1909, in the village of Frewsburg, New York, six miles south of Jamestown, into a family of modest means and limited education. While reading *Little Women* at age seven, she decided that if Nan could become a doctor, then she, too, as a female, could become a doctor.

As a child, devastating illness only strengthened this resolve. Stricken a short time after her decision with severe measles and then pneumonia, she received care that inspired her for a lifetime. Two years later, the household was stricken with polio, and both Pauline and her brother, William, were left with paralysis. They were treated in Boston by the same doctors who were rehabilitating soldiers wounded in World War I. This experience taught her that "disasters happen but that you pick up, get fixed up the best you can and go on." At age ten, she had acquired a philosophy of life few persons ever achieve.

The care of William was left to Pauline, whose mother was unable to cope with the situation. William died, and for years, Pauline felt that she could have saved him if she had known better how to care for him. Her resolve to become a doctor was strengthened even more.

Pauline's father was adamantly opposed to her decision to attend college. His idea of a proper career for her was that of a "towel girl" in restrooms. With support from the rest of her family, her teachers and her high school principal, she embarked on a lifelong career of studying, learning and teaching. She entered medical school in September 1929 with scholarship assistance from the Jamestown Branch of the American Association of University Women. She supported herself during these years by doing domestic work.

Residual effects of her childhood bout of polio precluded a private practice in her chosen field of pediatrics. In addition, her practice came to an abrupt halt in 1940 with the onset of tuberculosis, common in the medical field at this time in history. As she recuperated, it became clear that she could not resume private practice. She turned her talents and energy to administration, teaching, researching and consulting in the field of maternal and pediatric public health. She held posts with the United States Children's Bureau; the U.S. Public Health Service; the U.S. Department of Health, Education and Welfare; and the 1970 White House Conference of Children and Youth. She taught at the University of California's School of Public Health, the Harvard School of Public Health, Boston University Medical School and the University of Hawaii, from which she retired as professor emeritus.

Pauline was selected as a World Health Organization fellow in the late 1970s, researching maternal and child health issues in Thailand, Hong Kong, the Philippines, Japan, Taiwan and Korea. She never saw statistics as numerical data or abstractions. Having worked for many years in the medical field, she saw these figures as real human lives. She claimed that maternal and child health work is always an uphill battle because "despite pious protestations to the contrary, public officials see children as little people with little problems, and women's problems are equally invisible."

Throughout all these years, Pauline was subject to personal health problems stemming from the childhood polio and its lingering effects. She remained undaunted, taking the setbacks in stride. Her only concession to her physical health was her decision to live in Hawaii, with its more felicitous climate. She devoted her long life to improving medical care for women and children. She died on September 11, 1996, in Hawaii. The citizens of Frewsburg, New York, placed a historical marker on the site of her childhood home in May 1999.

Bumbalo, Dr. Thomas. Letter to B. Dolores Thompson, 1994. Private collection.

Honolulu Star Bulletin. April 18, 1980.

―――. May 22, 1975.

In Her Own Words. A collection of oral histories of female physicians, 1977. New Haven, CT: Yale University Press, 1982. Private library.

Interviews with her personal friends by B. Dolores Thompson, 1994.

Marquis Who's Who. New Providence, NY, 1994.

Stitt, Pauline Gregory. Personal letter to B. Dolores Thompson, 1994.

Thompson, B. Dolores. *Jamestown Post-Journal,* March 1994.

Researcher and author: B. Dolores Thompson, Jamestown Branch

BERTHA STONEMAN

1866–1943
BOTANIST/EDUCATOR/COLLEGE ADMINISTRATOR

Bertha Stoneman is revered by South African women of education as the founder of the South African Association of University Women (SAAUW) and a pioneer for higher education for women of South Africa. Bertha was born on August 18, 1866, in Lakewood, New York (a Jamestown suburb), a daughter of Bryan and niece of Kate Stoneman, the first woman admitted to the New York State Bar. She graduated from Jamestown High School in 1885, when secondary education for women was still uncommon. She continued her education at Cornell University, an undertaking that took nine years since she had to earn her way by teaching school. Ultimately, she earned a Bachelor of Pedagogy and Doctor of Science (DSc) in botany. The Stoneman family had always championed equal education for males and females.

In 1897, one year after completing her Doctor of Science degree, she was invited to join the staff of the Huguenot College in Wellington, South Africa. She accepted, as there were no positive prospects in the United States; she was put in charge of the botany department of the newly formed college for women. By 1905, she had built a large botany laboratory and herbarium and was deeply involved in botanical research. In 1906, at the request of the Cape Education Department, she published

Plants and Their Ways in South Africa, the first book on South African plants. It became an immediate success and the standard text on plants throughout the country. Additionally, she taught zoology, psychology and logic and chaired the Department of Philosophy.

In 1921, Bertha was appointed the third president of the college, a post she held until her retirement twelve years later. During this time, she was instrumental in forming the SAAUW, which was incorporated on May 30, 1923. She held the position of president for its first five years. She was a lifelong member of the African Association for the Advancement of Science and served on the University of South Africa Council from its founding until her retirement in 1933.

Bertha was also a talented poet, beginning at Cornell and eventually publishing a book of poetry, some of it on the whimsical side and some set to music. She also translated poetry from Afrikaans to English. She was keenly interested in sports and donated generously for athletic facilities. Her scholarships for indigent students helped many with university expenses. Bertha was a gifted teacher, endowed with the ability to inspire her students to achieve to the best of their ability even while having great rapport with them. She was their friend and teacher, taking them with her on field expeditions, walking and picnicking. Her home in Bainskloof, called Stonemansion, was available on weekends when she was not in residence, and many students spent holidays there. Many students became lifelong friends; one of them, Lily Daws, "cared for her as a daughter cares for a mother" during her final years of illness. Many of her students attained prominent positions throughout South Africa in government, medical fields and educational institutions.

Bertha died on April 30, 1943, at her home in Bainskloof, Cape Province. Her funeral was held at the Dutch Reformed Church and conducted by ministers of several denominations. Her ashes remained in South Africa until the end of World War II, when they were returned to the Stoneman family plot at the Bentley Cemetery in Lakewood. In Bertha's honor, the SAAUW administers the Bertha Stoneman Fellowship for Botanical Research, which can be granted for master's or PhD work and is a fitting tribute to an exceptional woman.

Carlson, Norman P. Stoneman family records. Private collection.
Fenton History Center records. Fenton History Center Library, Jamestown, New York.

International Federation of University Women (IFUW) records. Private collection.

Thompson, B. Dolores. "Bertha Stoneman." *Jamestown Post Journal*, March 1987.

Whitmore, Joan S., national president of South African Association of University Women. Records, 1987. Private collection.

Researcher and author: B. Dolores Thompson, Jamestown Branch

KATHERINE "KATE" STONEMAN

1841–1925
ATTORNEY/EDUCATOR/ACTIVIST

Katherine Stoneman changed the course of history for women in New York State in 1886. Women were, by law, denied the right to practice law until Kate challenged the law and won her case in an amazing show of support and strength by the women of the Albany area.

Kate, our latter-day "Portia," was born in April 1841 on the Stoneman farm in Lakewood, New York (a Jamestown suburb), into a very liberal-minded family who did not thwart her educational ambitions. She was first a student at Albany State Normal School and then a teacher there, beginning on August 18, 1866. During her forty-year career, she taught geography, drawing and penmanship. These were very common, standard subjects for women to teach (and learn), as the more difficult subjects were considered "too rigorous for a woman's delicate constitution." Indeed, there were many proponents who supported the theory that a university education would so sap a woman's strength as to render her sterile.

While teaching at the normal school, Kate began to pursue her ambition to become a lawyer. Among the few books available to her as a youth was a huge, musty law book that she read and reread numerous times, partly out of interest and partly because there was little else to read. The seed had been planted. She "read law" during the summer months, at night and over weekends for three years in the office of W.W. Frothingham. After becoming executrix of a relative's estate, she decided to take the bar exam, passing both the oral and written exams creditably.

However, she was refused admission to the bar by three Supreme Court judges because she was a woman. The justices gave their reasons: "no precedent," "no necessity" and the laws in place denied women the right. Undaunted, Kate went to work. It was late May 1886, and the legislature and Supreme Court would be adjourning at any time. Kate marshaled suffrage supporters and educators to her cause. According to Kate, a bill passed in both houses of the legislature with hardly a dissenting vote. The same afternoon, she visited the governor and the secretary of state, both of them signing the bill. Three days later, as the Supreme Court was about to adjourn, Kate appeared before the justices with the signed bill and was duly admitted to the bar.

Both the New York State legislature and Supreme Court passed the amendment in May 1886. In 1898, twelve years after passing the bar exams and being admitted to the bar, Kate became the first woman to graduate from Albany Law School. She apparently enjoyed a limited practice during the later years of her life.

In her eighty-four years of life, Kate was a strong advocate and dedicated volunteer in the suffrage movement; she has been described as the "prime mover" and "the core and center of a suffrage agitation." She also supported the cause of temperance. In 1919, another of the causes for which she worked tirelessly came to fruition. She had championed the establishment of a world peace organization, and the birth of the League of Nations fulfilled yet another of the ideals to which she devoted many years of her life.

Kate died on May 19, 1925, in Albany and is buried at Albany Rural Cemetery. Her accomplishments have been recognized by the New York State Bar Association, the Women's Bar Association of the State of New York and the New York State Division for Women.

Albany Law School records. Albany, New York.

Chapter 425 of the Laws of 1886. Official NYS journals, James Pendergast Library, Jamestown, New York.

New York State Supreme Court Reports HUN 40. Official NYS journals, James Pendergast Library, Jamestown, New York.

Office of the late Jess Present, New York State Senate.

State University of New York–Albany. Historical records.

Stoneman, Kate. Interview in the *Knickerbocker Press*, February 9, 1919.

Thompson, B. Dolores. "Katherine Stoneman." *Jamestown Post-Journal*, March 1983.

Researcher and author: B. Dolores Thompson, Jamestown Branch

ROSE HILLER TALMAN

1891–1993
MISSIONARY/COMMUNITY SERVICE

Born in Alexander, New York, on November 8, 1891, Rose Hiller graduated from Elmira College in 1914 with a Bachelor of Arts degree in mathematics, German and Latin. She taught for two years before marrying Lyman Talman in June 1916.

Shortly after their marriage, Rose and Lyman were called to China to work in the mission services of the Dutch Reformed Church. They spent thirteen years stationed in Amoy, which is located on the China coast about halfway between Hong Kong and Shanghai. During their years in China, the Talmans devoted much of their time to mastering the Amoy dialect of the Chinese language. They also taught English in a boys' school, and Rose tutored local girls in English and mathematics.

In 1929, Rose and their two young daughters were ordered back to the United States for health reasons. Lyman remained a little longer, until 1930, when the Communists began infiltrating throughout north China, and all foreigners were evacuated.

After leaving China, Lyman received a call from the Reformed Church in Hyde Park, New York. The Talmans worked in Hyde Park during World War II and Franklin Roosevelt's presidency. Prominent visitors to their area during that time included the king and queen of England and Prime Minister Winston Churchill. A highlight of those years was the Sunday when President and Mrs. Roosevelt, Princess Julianna of the Netherlands and MacKenzie King, the prime mister of Canada, attended Reverend Talman's Sunday worship.

After their ten years in Hyde Park, the Talmans changed membership from the Dutch Reformed to the Presbyterian Church. Lyman accepted calls to three Presbyterian churches in New York (Stillwater, Ontario Center and Rock Stream) before retiring to Penn Yan, New York, in 1957.

Reverend Talman died the year after his retirement, but Rose continued to be active in the church for many decades. She served in various positions in the Presbytery, including president of United Presbyterian Women of the Penn Yan Church. In 1976, Rose was recognized as one of New York State's Valiant Women by Church Women United.

She was also active in the American Association of University Women, the Elmira College Club, the Keuka Park Conservation Society and the Auxiliary of Soldiers and Sailors Hospital.

In 1985, Rose moved to White Springs Manor in Geneva, New York, where she lived until her death on January 5, 1993.

Information obtained from the Yates County Branch of the American Association of University Women Archives.

Researcher and author: Ellen Hegarty, Yates County Branch

LOLA J. WOODMANSEE TEARS

1928–2008
MAYOR/SUPERVISOR/LEGISLATOR

Lola J. Woodmansee Tears was born in Starrucca, Pennsylvania, on June 2, 1928, to Nelson and Minerva Woodmansee. She graduated from Corning Free Academy in Corning, New York, and Rochester Business Institute.

Lola was married to Raymond E. Tears, who predeceased her; upon her death, on September 14, 2008, survivors included a daughter, a granddaughter, two great-grandchildren and two stepdaughters.

Over the years, she was employed in varied positions: in the dental practice of Hugh Keenan in Corning, at Westinghouse Corporation in Bath and as an executive secretary at Corning Glass Works. Lola retired in 1984 and then became involved in municipal government. She was the mayor of Savona, New York; supervisor of the town of Bath; and a Steuben County legislator for eight years, from January 1994 to December 2001.

She drew high praise from her fellow legislators, and they passed a resolution honoring her soon after her death that stated, "Lola was a dedicated public servant who was always generous to her community with her time, talents and support." Following are two tributes from her peers. Phillip Roche, chairman of the Steuben County legislature, stated, "She was great to work with, she was one of those people who understood government, just understood the process of how to get things done." Steuben County attorney Fred Ahrens stated on September 2, 2008, "She was a true manager and a dedicated public servant. What sticks in my mind was more of her management style; no need for hysteria; she was cool under fire; thoughtful, just a terrific person."

In addition to her government service, Lola was involved in many human service organizations, such as the Steuben County Affirmative Action Committee, the Health Services Board, the Regional Human Services Committee and the Inter-County Association of Western New York. She was particularly interested in service to the elderly and the less fortunate, donating extensive service to the Steuben County Office for the Aging and Pro-Action. Linda Tetor, director of Office for Aging, recalled Project Care, which utilizes area volunteers to provide services to senior citizens. "She took her role very seriously," Tetor said, "and she would always speak up for the good of senior citizens. You could not find a more passionate advocate."

Lola was honored for her work in Pro-Action and the Office for the Aging with a room named for her in the Steuben-Yates Pro-Action Building. Lola was an enthusiastic member of the Women's Republican Club, Bath Business and Professional Women's Club, Bath Rotary and Quota Club.

Lola enjoyed traveling extensively with her husband both here and abroad. She found much pleasure in her family and vast network of friends. Lola was a remarkable, prominent woman who made a significant difference in our community.

Corning Leader. Various resources.
Price, Rob. *Courier-Advocate*, September 2008.

Researcher and author: Bonnie Weber, Bath Branch

LINDA TETOR

1943–
VOLUNTEER

There are few seniors in Steuben County who do not know the name Linda Tetor, director of the County Office for the Aging.

In 1943, when Linda Tetor was born in Bath, New York, volunteer organizations utilizing senior citizens were not common in our communities.

Volunteerism, however, was beginning to be important largely due to the wartime needs (then World War II), but it was not extended to helping with the problems of the elderly. Linda said that she has always been fond of older people, and as a child, she spent a great deal of time with her maternal grandfather and grandmother, who also lived in Bath.

Following college, marriage and a family, Linda became part-time director of the newly forming Retired Senior Volunteer Programs (RSVP) in 1974 under the Department of Social Services. In 1975, this became full time for her. Linda was skillful in recruiting volunteers and matching them to tasks they found meaningful. Seniors were encouraged to volunteer and were given jobs that utilized their skills and gave them the opportunity to meet new people and continue to feel needed.

The many problems of the elderly also became apparent as contact with this population was greater and as the number of elderly increased. In 1984, the State Area Agency on Aging was turned over to the county, and Linda became the first director. She was at the forefront in the county urging the state and local governments to recognize the needs of the elderly population.

Her organizational skills made it possible to create an agency (the Office for Aging) that is well run and staffed with employees who were dedicated to their positions. RSVP became a project under the Office for Aging and has continued to grow. Many services designed to keep the elderly safe and cared for in their own homes (if this is where they wish to be) are being operated by the staff and volunteers. Most recently, an endowment fund has been created to provide private money for necessary programs as the elderly population continues to grow older, the number of people becoming seniors increases and government funds are not sufficient.

Linda always gives credit to others for the work they have done. She never fails to recognize those who are working for the elderly. Without her leadership, guidance and energy, this rural area of the state would doubtless be lacking in many necessary programs.

Tetor, Linda. Interview recorded by Barbara Welles, 2008.

Researcher and author: Barbara B. Welles, Bath Branch

MARGARITA DUNCAN TOMKO

1928–
EDUCATOR/COMMUNITY LEADER/POET

Margarita Duncan Tomko was born on June 8, 1928, in Chuquicamata, Chile, to her Puerto Rican mother, Margarita Ramirez de Ossandon, and her Chilean father, Juan Ramon Ossandon. Her father worked as an accountant for the Anaconda Copper Mining Company after his graduation in the United States from Pace University. The family returned to the United States in 1928. Her older brother, Elton, was three years old, and Margarita was a year old. Margarita celebrated her first birthday crossing the equator aboard the SS *Aconcagua*.

When the family returned to New York City, they lived in an apartment in Manhattan. After a few years, they moved to Brooklyn and lived in the second-floor apartment of a two-family home in the Flatbush section of the borough. When the youngest child, Gilbert, was born five years after Margarita's birth, the family moved to a home in the same neighborhood. It became home to the Ossandon family for a lifetime.

Margarita was educated in the New York City public schools, Brooklyn's Public School 208 on Avenue D, close to Margarita's home, graduating from eighth grade in June 1942 during World War II and Samuel J. Tilden High School in June 1946. In her high school yearbook, she listed her goal to be a Spanish and English teacher. She completed her undergraduate studies at Hunter College in New York City, majoring in Spanish and completing a special minor in education, graduating with a Bachelor of Arts degree in January 1950.

She married Earl Kenneth Duncan of Louisville, Kentucky, in February 1950. They lived in Louisville, Kentucky, and Fort Wayne, Indiana, when they were first married. Eventually, they decided to relocate and moved back to Brooklyn. Her husband began working at Sperry Gyroscope in New Hyde Park. Margarita worked for the New York Telephone Company in Brooklyn until she left to await the birth of her firstborn son. She still wanted to pursue her dream of becoming a teacher. When she was expecting her firstborn, she passed the New York City Teaching Licensing Exam for teachers.

After her son Gary was born in 1952, she worked as a substitute teacher in New York City public schools. She was a substitute teacher at William J. Gaynor Junior High School teaching physically and emotionally disturbed children in the sixth and seventh grades in the beginning of the 1953 school year. She was asked to work as a permanent substitute for the remainder of the school year when the teacher she was subbing for decided to retire. In 1953, Margarita and her husband were able to buy a home thanks to the GI Bill. They moved to Farmingdale, New York. Margarita continued teaching in the city until 1955, when her second son, Richard, was born. After his birth, Margarita worked as a substitute teacher in the Farmingdale Public School System.

She did not have a New York State Permanent Teaching Certificate, needed to teach in the state. She passed the written state exam for a provisional teaching certificate and was required to complete thirty credits of graduate work within five years to earn a permanent certificate "for service in a public secondary school as a teacher of Spanish and English." The State Education Department granted her a permanent teaching certificate effective September 1, 1962. After her daughter, Diane, was born in April 1958, Margarita began her thirty-two-year teaching career in Farmingdale in September 1959. She was hired to teach Spanish at Main Street School in Farmingdale in the new Foreign Language in the Elementary School (FLES) program that she helped develop. The Farmingdale Public School District received the New York State James E. Allen Award for its outstanding foreign language program, spanning from the elementary schools through high school. Margarita completed her three-year probationary period and was granted tenure as a Spanish teacher in the Farmingdale Public School System.

Nina Policastro, one of Margarita's Main Street students in the FLES program, described her as "dynamic and energetic. She taught the language on an elementary child's level and made it fun to learn. With games and interesting activities, she made the language come alive." Her influence on Mrs. Policastro was such that the pupil has now become a teacher. Mrs. Policastro has been a teacher for more than thirty years and teaches Spanish and French at Farmingdale High School, where, she says, she still uses some of Margarita's teaching methods.

Margarita transferred to Howitt Junior High School in 1963. During her years at Howitt, she was the teacher liaison to the Weldon E. Howitt Parent Teachers Association and received the Jenkins PTA award. In the latter part of her career, she was transferred to the English department, thus fulfilling her goal of wanting to be both a Spanish and English teacher. She was also given the opportunity to work with the gifted students in the Horizons program. Horizon students completed independent studies and participated in the Olympics of the Mind competition.

When she was an English teacher, she had a special end-of-the-year writing exercise for her seventh-grade students. Her students wrote a letter to themselves. Margarita told them that she would not read the letters but rather would mail them to the students just before they graduated from high school. They addressed an envelope to themselves with the correct postage. Margarita placed the letters in a large envelope with their expected year of graduation on the envelope. She mailed the letters out as promised the year the students graduated. After she retired, she continued mailing out the letters until the last class she taught graduated. Both students and parents have enjoyed this last writing assignment. During her years at Howitt, she was also an active union volunteer and was elected by her peers to be their union representative on the Farmingdale Federation of Teachers Board of Trustees. She was also the faculty adviser to the Honor Society. On April 30, 1971, her husband, Kenneth, passed away. They had celebrated their twenty-first wedding anniversary that year.

In 1975, she visited Lois, her best friend and college classmate, in Phoenix, Arizona. During her visit, Lois and her husband, Dick, introduced her to their good friend David Peter Tomko. Little did they realize they were matchmakers. Dave and Margarita were married on October 10, 1975. They celebrated their twenty-fifth wedding anniversary in 2000, but tragically, Dave suffered an aneurysm and passed away on December 11, 2001. Margarita believes that he was always the "wind beneath her wings."

Margarita has been a member of the American Association of University Women's Farmingdale Branch since the 1970s. She personifies the mission of the AAUW to promote equity for all women and girls, lifelong education and positive societal change. She retired in 1991 after a thirty-five-year teaching career. In 1997, she received the New York State United Teachers' Friend of Education Award in recognition of her service to the "Children and Teachers of our Public Schools" and for her efforts during the contract discussions not only as president of the Farmingdale Federation of Teachers/ Retiree Chapter but also as a forty-four-year resident of Farmingdale.

In May 2006 the New York State United Teachers (NYSUT) Board of Directors selected Margarita, a fifty-three-year resident of Farmingdale and retired teacher, as a recipient of the NYSUT 2006 Retiree of the Year in recognition of her leadership in union activities, advocacy for union issues and the personification of the principles of the American labor movement. NYSUT represents more than 500,000 teachers statewide.

The American Federation of Teachers (AFT) held its biannual convention in Boston in July 2006. As part of the celebration of the 150th anniversary of women's rights in the United States, the AFT Women's Right's Committee presented the Living the Legacy Award on July 23, 2006. It is presented to AFT women members who have provided leadership and demonstrated interest in issues of women's rights; maintained decades of involvement in local, state and national AFT affiliates; worked in the trade union movements; acted as mentors, coaches and role models for other women; and have been recognized as a community leader. Margarita—president of the Farmingdale Federation of Teachers/Retiree Chapter (FFT/RC) and first vice-president of NYSUT Retiree Council 17—was one of the eight women who received Gold Recognition for "forty years of exceptional leadership and union advocacy in support of women's rights."

When NYSUT included retirees in its organization in 1991, she helped establish the local retiree chapter. She was elected president. The FFT/RC has among other activities actively protected retiree health benefits; been a top fundraiser in the NYSUT Making Strides Against Breast Cancer Walk held in October; and established five $500 awards, given annually to Farmingdale High School graduating seniors. One of these awards is given in Margarita's honor.

She also volunteers her time to other organizations and causes. NYSUT recognized her efforts in 1997 with its Community Service Award for her work as a lead teacher of the ESL classes offered by the Outreach Ministries of the Farmingdale United Methodist Church for eleven years. As a church member, she coordinates the annual Christian Rural Overseas Program WALK of Church World Service, raising funds used locally and around the world to help those living in poverty with a help up rather than a handout. After she retired, she volunteered in the church New to You Thrift Shoppe for ten years. On December 22, 1996, she was one of the first recipients of the Order of the Christmas Secret, presented by the Farmingdale United Methodist Church. The recipient of this honor "has kept the faith by keeping the Christmas Secret...The Secret of Living is Giving." She has been a church member for more than fifty years.

In addition to all her volunteer activities, Margarita pursues many personal interests. Her poetry has been published in local literary publications. In 2010, she self-published her first poetry collection, *The Girl in the Blue Taffeta Dress*. She was a featured reader of a Performance Poets Association event in November 2010 in the Barnes & Noble bookstore in Huntington, Long Island. She is an award-winning quilter and a winner of multiple swimming medals. She participates in the swimming events of the Long Island Senior Games held every June at Suffolk Community College for those fifty and older.

Margarita is an eighty-two-year-old mother of three baby boomers, grandmother of three grandsons and great-grandmother of two great-grandsons. She is the widow of Earl Kenneth Duncan and David Peter Tomko.

Margarita Duncan Tomko's 2011 autobiography, Farmingdale Branch.

MARY LAWRENCE TONETTI

1868–1945
SCULPTOR/COMMUNITY DEVELOPER

Mary Lawrence Tonetti was born in 1868 in New York City to a prominent, wealthy family. She is best known as the creative developer of Snedens Landing, a quiet, private area nestled between Rockland County and New York City in the hamlet called the Palisades, along the shores of the Hudson River. When she was two years old, Mary's father acquired a farm at Sneden on which he built his estate, an imposing mansion known as Cliffside. Mary spent most of her childhood growing up there and in New York City. She was a robust child with an independent streak. She enjoyed the outdoors and the company of dogs, horses, stable boys and fishermen rather than the more feminine pursuits of dance and charm school. She also showed an interest in art, mainly sculpture. At the age of fourteen, Mary made a sculpture of her dog, Dandy, an early piece of her work that survives. Her independent nature was manifested in her early teens when she bought a mule and a wagon with her first earnings. In that way, she felt she could come and go as she pleased.

It is widely believed that the potential of an individual is realized with the help and encouragement of others. There were several people in Mary's life who helped her to excel in art and sculpture. First, her parents recognized and nurtured her talent. Second, her aunt, Annie Underhill, was very influential in supporting her interest in sculpture. It was her aunt who accompanied Mary on a Grand Tour of Europe in 1886–87. There, in Paris, Mary studied drawing and sculpture at the Julien Academy. She was an excellent student. Aunt Annie continued to be an important part of Mary's life, living at Snedens Landing with the Lawrence and Tonetti family until her death at the age of 102.

The third influence in Mary's career was sculptor Augustus Saint-Gaudens. Mary first studied with him at the age of seven when he taught art to a group of youngsters at Snedens. He became her teacher again when, at the age of nineteen, she went to Europe to study sculpture and chose him as her instructor. Mary became his most admired student, eventually taking over his classes in New York City at the Art Students League. With Saint-Gaudens' help, Mary invaded a male-dominated preserve: the world of sculpture.

There was one incident that made Mary aware that women were not automatically accepted as sculptors. In 1893, when Saint-Gaudens found himself too busy, he assigned Mary to create a specially commissioned statue of Columbus that was to be the keynote figure at the World Columbian exhibition in Chicago. At the age of twenty-five, Mary was responsible for its creation. Some people questioned whether a woman—any woman—should be the sculptor of the fair's most important statue. There was an undercurrent of resistance to her project. Some people wished to minimize Mary's role in creating the statue, saying that it was entirely Saint-Gaudens' idea. However, the *Chicago Post* on June 18, 1893, while attributing the statue to him, conceded that it was "sometimes called the Lawrence statue." In reality, the figure of Columbus was a collaboration between the two of them. Saint-Gaudens was quoted as saying that Mary "modeled it and executed it and to her goes all the credit for the virility and breath of the treatment which it revealed."

Mary's contribution in creating the Columbus statue and the recognition given to her by her mentor motivated her to return to Europe and continue to study sculpture. However, after a time, Mary discovered that the competitive and abrasive side of the art world was one she neither liked nor wished to emulate. In her book *The Tonetti Years at Snedens Landing*, Isabelle Savell wrote that as a result of this discovery, Mary never again undertook a major public work of art. Her focus was no less intense, but she now limited her artwork to portrait busts, high reliefs, bas reliefs and memorial sculptures. During the 1880s and 1890s, Mary continued to study and work in Paris.

In Paris, Mary met François Tonetti. At their introduction, he vowed that someday he would marry her. In 1897, François arranged a commission and came to New York to work…and also to marry her. Saint-Gaudens wrote a letter of introduction, and Mary agreed to make part of her studio available to him. In 1900, they married at Grace Church in New York City. They set up housekeeping at Snedens Landing in what was called the Ding Dong House because of the bell that hung over the front gate. A separate building on the property served as their studio. The couple had six children. Although both Mary and François were gifted sculptors and loved art, it was François who remained a sculptor and became well known. Mary chose to channel her creative energy into developing Snedens Landing. In so doing, she "rendered a contribution far larger than her own life for she created at Snedens an atmosphere which enabled and encouraged other artists to do their work."

Mary enjoyed renovating buildings. As a teenager, she redesigned her first studio, a small summer house. She had the north side torn out to make a larger window, cut away trees for maximum light, had a large stone fireplace built and hung lanterns throughout the interior. Mary began acquiring properties, and with great energy, she rebuilt and decorated the houses and gardens so that she might rent them to her artist friends. It is difficult to say how many homes there were at any given time, but in 1936, when Mary made Snedens her year-round home, she owned sixteen dwellings.

The houses were planned for beauty, not efficiency. Although Mary's ideas seemed to come spontaneously, they were really the result of "tireless concentrated thought and dreaming." Each dwelling was special. Stables and barns became charming homes, each planned with either a special river view, an arbor or a terrace. Here, Mary hoped that artists, authors and creative people could live surrounded by inspiration without worries about payment and maintenance. For this reason, Mary rented the places, furnished, at such low rates that she actually lost money on them.

Mary also used her money to support a ferry service for crossing the Hudson River from the train station at Dobbs Ferry so that friends could visit. Even after most residents at Snedens had cars, she kept the ferry running. Mary sought to keep Snedens Landing a private place so that friends could live quietly and work. She used her talents to create a community for gifted artists. Some of the people whom Mary attracted to the area were legendary: Noël Coward, Laurence Olivier, Ethel Barrymore and John Houseman.

Mary Lawrence Tonetti was a strong, vital force. She was a liberated woman before women's liberation became a strong political issue. She died at Snedens Landing in 1945 at the age of seventy-seven. What her daughter, Ann, wrote about Mary describes the essence of her life and work: "She brought the world of artists to the river, sloughed off her Victorian concepts, and freed the landscape. She was a 'hippie' of the Victorian era, but more. She was dedicated to beauty, its essence flowed through her. She maintained her own identity and purpose, and she had an incredible eye and vision." Mary helped shape Rockland's landscape. She is one of the women who made an indelible imprint on Rockland County.

Savell, Isabelle K. *The Tonetti Years at Snedens Landing.* New York: Historical Society of Rockland County, 1977.

Researchers and authors: Marjorie M. Hallett and Myrna Silberman, Rockland County Branch

MARGARET TOWNER
1925–
MINISTER/PHOTOGRAPHER

Reverend Margaret E. Towner was the first woman to be ordained in the Presbyterian Church in the United States. The ordination occurred on October 24, 1956, in Syracuse, New York.

She was born in Columbia, Missouri. A woman of many talents and interests, she studied voice and freshman English at Northwestern University in Evanston, Illinois; typing; business math; and English at Gregg Business College in Chicago. She earned her Bachelor of Arts degree at Carleton College in Northfield, Minnesota. She was a medical photographer for the Mayo Clinic in Rochester, Minnesota. After going to Syracuse, New York, where her parents had moved, she became a staff photographer for Syracuse University. Because she was involved with many churches in the area, she was encouraged to go into the ministry.

Margaret earned her Master of Divinity degree at Union Theological Seminary in New York City in 1954. She was ordained at the First

Presbyterian Church at 620 West Genesee Street in Syracuse, New York, where she celebrated the fiftieth anniversary of her ordination on October 15, 2006. She preached and was received at a reception in her honor.

Progress has been slow in all churches for women. The presbytery did not recognize women as deacons until 1906 and as elders until 1930. "There were bumps in the road," she said. "Acceptance of women in the ministry has been slow…Even today, there is opposition to the ordinance of women." Early in her career, she was excluded from officiating at communion services.

She has served in six presbyteries and was vice-moderator of the 193rd General Assembly of the Presbyterian Church United States of America. Margaret has also served on a national committee on Language about God, which addressed many issues, including gender-inclusive language.

She now resides in Sarasota, Florida.

Gadoua, Renee K. "Margaret E. Towner." *Post-Standard*, October 16, 2006.
Life. "A First Lady Minister in Robes of a New Role." GoogleBooks. http://books.google.com/books?id=vkEEAAAAMBAJ&pg=PA151&source=gbs_toc_r&cad=2#v=onepage&q&f=false.
Presbyterian Outlook. "Women Ministers (1955–1966) and Margaret Towner." Editorial. www.pres-outlook.com/reports-a-resources3/presbyterian-heritage-articles3/1104.html.

Researcher and author: M. Edwina Norton, Syracuse Branch

SOJOURNER TRUTH

1797–1883
ABOLITIONIST/SUFFRAGIST/SPIRITUALIST

Sojourner Truth had four major roles in life: mother, abolitionist, suffragist and spiritualist. She was born a slave in 1797 on the Johanes Hardenbergh estate in Ulster County, New York. She was the second of thirteen children born to Elizabeth and James Bomefree and started life as Isabella Bomefree. Before John Dumont, she had three masters; then she was sold to Dumont of New Paltz, New York. She was his slave for eighteen years. She had five children. Her first language was Dutch, but she later learned English. She could not read or write, so she studied the Bible and other great books by rote. She remained a social, political and religious activist all her life.

Isabella Bomefree was promised her freedom by John Dumont, her last owner. At the last minute, he changed his mind, and so she escaped in 1826 with her youngest child. She went to live with Isaac Van Wagenen, who bought her freedom. She adopted his name and continued to be very proactive in securing her rights. When her son was sold illegally, she brought suit against the perpetrators and won. Later, when she was accused of being a part of a murder plot, she sued for slander and successfully won the suit in 1829.

Isabella had always been actively involved in religion. As a child, she claimed to have heard voices and seen visions. In 1827, Isabella had a "Pauline" experience in which she reported that she felt "the breath of God." This had such a profound effect on her that she changed her name to Sojourner Truth. Later, in 1829, when she moved to New York City, she joined the African Methodist Episcopal Zion Church. She worked as a housekeeper for Elijah Pierson, who belonged to the Perfectionist sect. Even though her relationship with these religious extremists was short-lived, she continued her zealous commitment to studying the Bible, developing her oratory skills and reforming the role of blacks and women in American society. In 1843, Sojourner Truth became ill and was treated by David Ruggles, a black abolitionist. In addition to him, she met many other abolitionists. This ushered in a new phase of her life.

In 1846, at age forty-nine, Sojourner Truth became fully entrenched as a suffragist and abolitionist. In order to pay her expense as she traveled to propagate her beliefs, she published *The Narrative of Sojourner Truth* in 1850, written by Olive Gilbert. In 1851, she bought a house in Northampton, Massachusetts. She continued to travel extensively, giving antislavery speeches and championing the rights of women combined with fearless, charismatic preaching of the Bible. Her famous "Ain't I a Woman" speech was delivered in 1851 at the second annual Ohio Women's Rights Convention in Akron.

During the Civil War, Sojourner Truth recruited for Michigan's Black Regiment, counseled freedwomen and set up employment opportunities for freed people. She initiated the desegregation of the streetcars in Washington, D.C., and had an audience with Abraham Lincoln. In 1864, she moved to Michigan and settled in Battle Creek. She died in 1883, attended by the physician John Harvey Kellogg.

Lerner, Gerda. "Sojourner Truth: A Life, a Symbol." *The Nation* 264, no. 2 (January 13, 1997): 2,594.

Macmillan Profiles: Humanitarians and Reformers. "Truth, Sojourner (c. 1797–1883)." New York: Macmillan Reference, 1999.

Photograph from the Library of Congress.
Researcher and author: Jacqueline Goffe-McNish, Poughkeepsie Branch

PATRICIA KOO TSIEN

1918–
INTERNATIONAL RELATIONS AND WOMEN'S RIGHTS ADVOCATE

Patricia Koo Tsien served in the United Nations Secretariat from 1947 to 1979. From 1971 until her retirement, she was chief of the Africa Division, Department of Political Affairs, Trusteeship and Decolonization.

During her years of service at the United Nations Secretariat, she was active in staff and women's rights issues and served as elected or appointed member of several administrative bodies, including the Appointment and Promotion Board, the Joint Appeals Board, the Compensation Board and the Joint Staff Pension Board. In 1971, together with several other female colleagues, she founded the Ad Hoc Group on Equal Rights for Women, which soon became recognized by the administration as the formal body representing women's interests in the Secretariat. The Ad Hoc Group was instrumental in bringing about the revision of the staff rules and regulations to provide for equal treatment of men and women throughout the international civil service system of the United Nations. This equal treatment included permission for a spouse to visit his/her home country once a year. In her last year at the United Nations, Patricia was able to take her husband with her on her home visit to China.

Since 1979, Mrs. Tsien has served with the Association of Former International Civil Servants and for three years was the president of this organization, which had more than two thousand members. For some ten

years, she devoted much of her time doing research for the translation into Chinese of the *Wellington Koo Oral History* under the aegis of the Institute of Modern History. On her trip to China in 1994, the institute celebrated the publication of the thirteenth and last volume of the *Koo Memoirs* in Chinese.

Mrs. Tsien received her Bachelor of Science honors degree in physics and mathematics from London University. Her husband, Tsien Kia Chi, also a physicist, died in 1993. She has one daughter, one son, a granddaughter and a grandson.

Her father was V.K. Wellington Koo. In 1912, he received his Doctor of Philosophy degree in international law and diplomacy from Columbia University. Koo returned to China in 1912. Shortly thereafter, he married Pao-yu "May" Tang, and in 1915, Koo was made China's minister to the United States and Cuba. In 1918, Patricia Koo was born, and her mother died of influenza. Patricia's father became a member of the Chinese delegation to the Paris Peace Conference, later briefly acting premier, interim president and foreign minister. Then he was ambassador to France and the Court of St. James. He was a founding member of the United Nations, became an ambassador to the United States and was a judge in the International Court of Justice in the Hague. Koo is the first and only Chinese head of state known to use a Western name publicly.

Information obtained from Patricia Koo Tsien, 2010.

Researcher and author: Julie Harrison Kleszczewski, New York City Branch

HARRIET TUBMAN

1820–1913
ABOLITIONIST

Harriet Tubman (a National Women's Hall of Fame inductee) was an American black woman who helped hundreds of slaves escape to freedom. She became the most famous leader of the Underground Railroad, which helped slaves fleeing to the free states and to Canada. She was known as the Moses of her people.

Tubman was born a slave on a Maryland plantation. At age twenty-four, she married John Tubman, a free black. She escaped to freedom in 1849, leaving behind her husband, parents and sisters. She vowed to return and help other slaves to freedom.

In 1850, the United States Congress passed the Fugitive Slave Act, making it a crime to assist runaway slaves. She was not deterred and traveled back eighteen times to free about three hundred slaves. She outwitted many slave catchers despite the fact that a $40,000 award was offered for her capture.

In 1857, she led her family to freedom and settled on a farm in Auburn, New York. Tubman became active in the women's rights movement in New England and New York. During the Civil War in the 1860s, she served as a scout, nurse and spy and helped free another seven hundred slaves. After the war, Tubman returned to her farm and began caring for orphans and elderly people. It became known as the Tubman Home for Indigent Aged Negroes. She died at the age of ninety-three and is buried in Auburn, New York.

For the past several years, the National Park Service has planned Tubman Parks for both Auburn, New York, and Maryland. So far, Congress has vetoed any monies for that purpose. Maryland has recently found another source of money, so that state will be starting soon to build its park. Auburn will still be on the waiting list for the present.

Groom, Debra. "Tubman Drawing US Notice." *Post-Standard*, June 2009.

Honoring Women's History Month. *Women of Distinction*. Sponsored by the New York State Senate, March 2003. Available electronically in the New York State Library Digital Collection. http://128.121.13.244:8080/awweb.

Mark, Weiner. "Mark Weiner's Washington Notebook." *Post-Standard*, 2008.

Post-Standard. "Elusive Tubman Park." Editorial, August 31, 2011.

Women in History. "Harriet Tubman Biography." Lakewood Public Library. www.lkwdpl.org/wihohio/tubm-har.htm.

World Book Encyclopedia 19 (1975): 391–92.

——— 20 (1975): 12a.

Photograph from the Library of Congress.
Researcher and author: Arlene Bolton, Syracuse Branch

MARTHA VAN RENSSELAER

1864–1932
EDUCATOR/HOME ECONOMIST

Martha Van Rensselaer was a pioneer in the field of home economics. In recognition of her efforts, Cornell University erected a building bearing her name to house the College of Human Ecology that was dedicated on February 15, 1934.

Martha was born on June 21, 1864, in Randolph, Cattaraugus County, New York. Following graduation from the Chamberlain Institute in 1884, she held a variety of teaching positions. She then was elected a school commissioner, a six-year post that required a great deal of travel by horseback with overnight stays in local farmhouses. She lost her 1900 reelection bid, though, a bitter disappointment. However, it opened the door to her thirty-two-year association with Cornell University, ended only by her death in 1932. During her travels, Martha was struck by the plight of the farm wives. Liberty Hyde Bailey, dean of the Agricultural College at Cornell, agreed. He wanted to publish bulletins for the farmers' wives, and Martha had many ideas gleaned from her travels. Mainly, she wanted to know what the women wanted. A questionnaire was sent to the wives of farmers, who subscribed to the farmer's reading courses. Based on the responses, Martha began to send out five bulletins per year to twenty to thirty thousand women. She also organized the Cornell Study Club, resulting in more than three hundred clubs of about twenty-five women each. She traveled to all of these, assessing their viability and the needs of their members.

In 1904, the New York State legislature established the State College of Agriculture at Cornell, with Bailey as its director. The home economics department was headed by Martha as the organizer and politician and Flora Rose as the teacher and professional expert. They became lifelong friends and companions, sharing a home for thirty years. When Martha began her work in 1900, her "office" was in the basement of Morrill Hall—water and steam pipes ran through it. She had a kitchen table with one drawer, two wooden chairs and a letter file. In 1904, her "office" also contained a classroom, a large laboratory, a tiny kitchen and a dining room. From these quarters, they often fed visiting VIPs with little notice.

Martha was successful in acquiring a separate building for home economics, Comstock Hall, which opened on February 10, 1913. By

1917, student enrollment had doubled, and the course bulletins were being sent to seventy-five thousand readers. She believed that these programs should coordinate with programs for agriculture, and she was later acknowledged as "the greatest leader in extension work."

The federal government called on Martha during World War I and also the depression for help with food and clothing conservation. In 1923, she and Flora spent five months in Belgium, studying the educational and nutritional needs of women and children. Both were awarded the Chevalier of the Order of the Crown by the Belgian king.

In 1925, the department was renamed the New York State College of Home Economics. Martha and Flora had greatly expanded the scope of the program to include all aspects of the home and family, including child training. They had outgrown their building. The cornerstone for a new building was laid on June 8, 1932, and dedicated on February 15, 1934, as the Martha Van Rensselaer Hall.

In 1930, President Herbert Hoover asked Martha to serve as assistant director of his White House Conference on Child Health and Protection. On one of her many trips to New York City, she had a physical exam and was diagnosed with lymphoidal sarcoma. She underwent heavy X-ray treatments and was able to continue her work and complete arrangements for the new building. She died on May 23, 1932, and is buried in the family plot in Randolph.

The Founders Dinner, College of Ecology. Program, September 1, 1992.

New York Herald Tribune. February 18, 1934.

Randolph Register. January 31, 1958.

Thompson, B. Dolores. "Martha Van Renesselaer." *Jamestown Post-Journal*, March 1999. Revised from original newspaper article.

Wolf, Eva Nagel. "The Delineator's New Homemakers Editor." January 1921. Private collection.

Researcher and author: B. Dolores Thompson, Jamestown Branch

GEORGIA VERDIER

19??–
COMMUNITY AND CHURCH ACTIVIST

Georgia Verdier came to New York from Fort Wayne, Indiana, where she attended Central High School. She now resides in Corning, New York. Georgia holds a master's degree in education from Elmira College and a master's in public service administration from Alfred University, and she is a certified diversity trainer.

She views herself as an activist, both in the church and the community. Georgia serves on numerous community boards and committees, such as the Economic Opportunity Program Inc., the VIBES—HIV/AIDS Task Force, the Guthrie Health Women's Advisory Group, the Corning Poverty Collaborative and more. Additionally, she works with the Elmira City School District and the criminal justice system. She is the president of the Elmira/Corning Branch of the NAACP and is a member of its state board of directors. She is a member of Delta Sigma Theta Sorority Inc. and other organizations.

However, her first love is serving and working for God, and she boldly declares that Jesus is the center of her joy. She currently serves as chairman of the deacon board, greeter and member of the women's ministry. Georgia believes individuals must lead by example. One of her mottos is "Footprints in the sands of time were not made while sitting down."

Information obtained from Georgia Verdier.

Researcher and author: Mary Hungerford, Elmira-Corning Branch

CHRISTINE VOLKMAR

19??–2008
ENGINEER/VOLUNTEER

Beloved by all, Christine was a brilliant engineer, a faultless leader, a fun companion, a consummate democratic organizer, a playwright, an amateur thespian who did a lot of radio work for college, a "strong advocate of higher education for Women and AAUW goals" and a tireless volunteer who put her heart into whatever she was doing. Born in Manhattan of a French/German (and touch of Irish) mother and a Swedish father, she was elected by special invitation to the New York Academy of Sciences and the American Association for the Advancement of Science. She attended Hunter College at night on a scholarship while working full time for the telephone company. She also received departmental honors when she graduated.

I first met Christine after a Founder's Day luncheon at the National Arts Club. Olga Henkel introduced us, and we went out for coffee afterward at the Gramercy Park Hotel with Olga and her husband, Henry. Olga said at the time that Christine was someone I needed to meet. We laughed a lot.

One of my requests upon my accepting the presidency of our branch was that she be my executive vice-president. When there was a crisis, she was ever present.

Along with several of us, she came to the New York State AAUW Leadership Conference at Delta Lake in the summer of 2007, and Barbara Geren was her roommate. Barbara arranged for several of us to take a fast boat ride across the lake. Christine loved it! We all did. When it was time to leave her room, Christine asked Barbara how much she should tip the maid (who had made her bed and folded her nightie so prettily). To Christine's amazement, Barbara said, "Nothing. You're looking at the maid!"

Christine had many talents. She was a Phi Beta Kappa and the youngest and only woman, just twenty-one, serving as head inspector of dangerous engineering materials for the United States Navy during World War II. A petite blond woman, her older, all-male subordinates trusted her in this most dangerous operation. They all volunteered to work for her. In 2001, she was invited by the Women of Science to go on a goodwill tour of Cuba.

Christine had a great heart. After Joyce Arkhurst initiated the Steps to End Family Violence project, Christine took on the responsibility of providing clothes to women in this battered women's shelter. Barbara Geren, her partner in this, carried on with the project. Christine's thoughtfulness had no bounds. She was always bringing me little gifts of all sorts, particularly two beautiful plants when I was so very ill in 2001–2. She was proud of her faultless seamstress skills and fashion sense.

Christine and I wrote the first Seven Star Award (a New York State AAUW program) together. Our branch (New York City) was the only one in the entire state to win that award that year. She was always writing up diversity bits, programs that we had during the year that won us the Peacock Award for Diversity. She wrote well. Following her lead the next year, I wrote up nineteen diversity projects/programs. The next year, there was a directive from the New York State diversity chair noting that you may submit only one diversity project/program for the Peacock Award!

Aside from these wonders, she ably chaired the Great Decisions Group, the Bylaws Committee, co-chaired the Literature Group and was ever a gracious hostess. Never was there a more successful vice-president of membership; she was twice selected for New York State AAUW's nominating committee.

Christine Volkmar is beloved and sorely missed by all who knew her. Au revoir, dear friend.

Information obtained from Christine Volkmar.
New York Times. Obituary. January 18, 2008. www.legacy.com/obituaries/ nytimes/obituary.aspx?n=Christine-M-Volkmar&pid=101384369#fbLo ggedOut.

Researcher and author: Julie Harrrison Kleszczewski, New York City Branch

SALLY ROESCH WAGNER

1942–
EXECUTIVE DIRECTOR, MATILDA JOSLYN GAGE
FOUNDATION/WRITER

Sally Roesch Wagner, founder and executive director of the Matilda Joslyn Gage Foundation in Fayetteville, New York, is a nationally recognized lecturer, author and performance interpreter of women's rights history. One of the first women to receive a doctorate in the United

States for work in women's studies (University of California–Santa Cruz) and a founder of one of the country's first college women's studies programs (California State University–Sacramento), Dr. Wagner is a pioneering feminist and social justice advocate in her own right.

Dr. Wagner said, "I have stalked a dead suffragist, Matilda Joslyn Gage, following her every move and word, determined to bring her to her rightful place in history." Wagner moved to Fayetteville and took on the task of saving from ruin Gage's run-down home and forming the Matilda Joslyn Gage Museum and Library of Feminism. She works passionately to fulfill the foundation's mission of spreading the story of Gage.

Dr. Wagner grew up in South Dakota, where the descendants of Matilda Joslyn Gage and L. Frank Baum lived. In 1978, she wrote her doctoral dissertation, "That Word Is Liberty: A Biography of Matilda Joslyn Gage," at the University of California–Santa Cruz.

Wagner appeared as a "talking head" in the Ken Burns Public Broadcasting System (PBS) documentary *Not for Ourselves Alone: The Story of Elizabeth Cady Stanton and Susan B. Anthony*, for which she wrote the accompanying faculty guide for PBS. She was also a historian in the PBS special *One Woman, One Vote* and has been interviewed numerous times on National Public Radio's *All Things Considered* and *Democracy Now*.

The theme of her work has been telling the untold stories. Her monograph *She Who Holds the Sky: Matilda Joslyn Gage* (Sky Carrier Press, 2003) reveals a suffragist written out of history because of her stand against the religious right one hundred years ago. *Sisters in Spirit: Haudenosaunee (Iroquois) Influence on Early American Feminists* (Native Voices, 2001) documents the influence of Haudenosaunee women on early women's rights activists. *The Wonderful Mother of Oz* focuses on the relationships between L. Frank Baum; his wife, Maud; and mother-in-law, Matilda, at the Gage home, where the seeds of Oz were born. L. Frank Baum went on to write about a feminist utopia in *The Wonderful Wizard of Oz*. Wagner also wrote the introduction in the reprint of Matilda Joslyn Gage's 1893 classic *Woman, Church and State* (Humanity Books, 2002).

Becoming the Jeanette K. Watson Women's Studies Distinguished Visiting Professor in the Humanities at Syracuse University in 1997, Wagner is presently an adjunct faculty member in the honors program at Syracuse University. She has been a research affiliate of the Women's Resources and Research Center at the University of California–Davis and a consultant to the National Women's History Project.

Wagner, a prolific writer, has written and published many essays and has been a well-received speaker across the United States. She is a member of the Syracuse Branch of the American Association of University Women.

Information from Sally Roesch Wagner, recorded by Nancy Clausen, 2009.

Researcher and author: Nancy E. Clausen, Syracuse Branch

MARY EDWARDS WALKER

1832–1919
PHYSICIAN/WOMEN'S RIGHTS ACTIVIST

Dr. Mary Walker is known for being one of the earliest women in the United States to graduate from medical school; for being the sole female doctor to help provide medical service to Union soldiers during the Civil War; for vociferously fighting for women's suffrage; for refusing to wear constrictive, unhealthy clothing, even donning male clothing; for insisting on women's right to wear what they chose; and for advocating temperance and women's causes of other kinds. Outspoken, she had a quick wit and defended herself vigorously when attacked. Her medical practice supported her only meagerly. This was supplemented with income from public speeches on her experiences, on dress reform and on other women's rights issues.

Mary Walker was born to Alvah and Vesta Walker on November 26, 1832, on the family farm on Bunker Hill Road in the town of Oswego, New York. Her parents thought that their daughters should be educated for professional careers. Mary's primary schooling was in a one-room school built by her father on the family farm; at eighteen, she attended the Failey Seminary in Fulton, New York. She taught for about two years in Minetto, New York, not far from home. Perhaps as a result of being influenced by her father's interest in medicine (in attempts to cure himself) and by Elizabeth

Blackwell's work for an MD degree from the medical college in Geneva, New York, in 1849, Mary applied in 1853 to the Syracuse Medical College.

She graduated from medical school in 1855, was the only woman in her graduating class and was one of very few female MDs in the United States. The school was a so-called "eclectic" school, including in its coursework the "standard" classes relating to medicine (physiology, anatomy, surgery, diseases of women and children, pharmacy and chemistry) but also classes in botany, herbalism and homeopathy. Eclecticism was not well looked upon by many of the doctors at that time. Mary ended up with a rather nontraditional degree—in today's terms a very abbreviated but intensive medical training that was somewhat disparaged by other doctors. After graduating with her MD, Mary moved to Columbus, Ohio, where she had relatives, to begin her medical practice. Her attempts to establish a practice met with serious problems, however, due in part to the extreme rarity of female practitioners.

She returned to Oswego after a short time and married a medical school classmate, Dr. Albert E. Miller, in November 1855. It was an unconventional wedding: she refused to include the word "obey" in her wedding vows and wore the so-called bloomer costume—a short, comfortable coat-dress of knee length over long pants. She didn't use her husband's name much, but used "Dr. Miller Walker" or left out the "Miller" entirely. Mary and Albert set up joint practices in Rome, New York, but again Mary had difficulty getting established. As before, this difficulty was due in part to the rarity of women in the medical field (people were unaccustomed to the idea of a female doctor and thought that women should stay "in their place in society"). Also contributing to Mary's difficulty in gaining patients was her habit of wearing the bloomer costume. Mary's refusal to wear the standard women's attire was also a fight for women to be able to wear nontraditional clothing if they so chose; she was harassed many times for wearing bloomers and, later, more pointedly male clothing in public. This habit derived apparently from her father's refusal to allow his daughters to wear traditional female clothing, as they had to help work the family farm. He also believed wearing corsets to be unhealthy.

After a few years, Mary's husband proved unfaithful. She eventually divorced, and this experience presumably led to her becoming quite distrustful of men and outspoken in favor of good marriage relations and divorce.

When the Civil War started in 1861, she went to Washington to offer her services as a medical doctor. Her efforts here were frustrated. She was discriminated against for being a woman—she could be a nurse but not a doctor—and her medical training was nontraditional as well; of course, her bloomer costume was totally outside the pale, too. The army medical establishment could not see beyond these things, even though doctors were sorely needed.

She stayed in Washington and worked as a volunteer in a temporary army hospital set up in the United States Patent Office. In 1862, she attended the Hygeia Therapeutic College in New York City for a few months, where she obtained a second (nontraditional) medical degree. She also assisted women who had come to Washington looking for their husbands and sons. Women alone were suspected of being prostitutes and had difficulty obtaining lodging. She established a boardinghouse for such women and helped found the Women's Relief Association for them.

She had supporters among the doctors she'd worked with as a volunteer, and in 1864, she got an official position that sent her to Chattanooga, Tennessee. There was not much for her to do there, so she went around the countryside helping civilians as well as soldiers. During this activity, she got captured and put in a Confederate prison for four months. She complained about the poor diet and was able to obtain fresh vegetables for the prisoners. Mary was released as part of a prisoner exchange. There is some evidence that she served as a spy for the Union army during this period. Other efforts she made for soldiers during the war included insisting on cleanliness and good hygiene and foraging for bandages, food, kettles and pails for boiling water to help improve conditions. She also objected to what she felt were unnecessary amputations of wounded limbs. Not wanting to make things worse by objecting aloud to the other doctors, she encouraged wounded soldiers not to allow removal of their limbs. Her efforts presumably helped save the lives of many soldiers with whom she had contact.

She was given a Congressional Medal of Honor for "Meritorious Service" during the war. She was very proud of this. She was the first woman to receive one, and she wore it all the time. Unfortunately, her medal and those of about nine hundred other Civil War veterans were rescinded in 1917, but she refused to give hers back. Many years later, her grandniece and others in Oswego petitioned to have the medal restored, and in 1977 it was.

After the war, she went back to her medical practice and to the dress reform and suffrage movements. She was invited to a conference in England in 1866 and spent about a year in Europe, observing at hospitals and supporting herself by speaking on her experiences.

Back at home, she petitioned the government for a pension; it balked at giving her much. She obtained a job as a clerk in the Pension Office in Washington. That did not last long. She continued her speaking engagements, but eventually this income source dried up, too. Mary inherited the family farm when her father died, but he left it with a mortgage that she had difficulty paying.

She spent time working with the women's suffrage movement, continued wearing bloomers and continued to be harassed for it. She spent a lot of time going to Washington to lobby for various causes. She wrote for the magazine *Sibyl: A Review of the Tastes* and *Errors and Fashions of Society*, and she published two books—*Hit: Essays on Women's Rights* (1871) and *Unmasked, or the Science of Immorality, to Gentlemen by a Woman Physician and Surgeon* (1878). Her writings and speeches discussed a variety of issues important to women, as well as society as a whole: love, marriage, divorce, problems caused by alcohol and tobacco, dress reform, women's suffrage, religion, social diseases, various aspects of health and women's physiology, labor laws, immorality, diet, war, inhumane prison conditions, the need for social and political equality for all and the idea that women should become able to support themselves and receive equal pay for equal work.

Among other things, she kept repeating that the traditional heavy women's clothing, with very constrictive corsets, was unhealthy—and it was. Because bones change shape when continual pressure is put on them, the rib cage becomes misshapen permanently. There is a woman's skeleton in the Women's Rights National Historical Park Museum in Seneca Falls that shows how serious the damage was that constriction could cause.

Mary eventually broke with the women's suffrage movement. Other suffragists had given up trying to get the vote by butting heads with the establishment and were trying for a constitutional amendment. Mary was adamant that because the United States Constitution said that all men were created equal—and that included women—women should just demand the right to vote. Mary wouldn't give up and even spoke against the idea of an amendment. She continued actively working for dress reform and even took to wearing men's clothing in the 1880s—long pants, tailcoat and top hat. She continued to insist on women's rights and for freedom in dress, marriage and voting.

She was apparently a bit difficult to get along with. She had trouble with her tenant farmers and ended up with little money and few friends. In 1917, while in Washington, D.C., to lobby, she fell on the steps of the Capitol and never recovered. She died in Oswego on February 21, 1919, at the age of eighty-six.

She is remembered today by the State University of New York College–Oswego, which named the campus health center for her. There was a commemorative United States postage stamp with her picture in 1982. She was inducted in 2001 into the National Women's Hall of Fame in Seneca Falls. The town of Oswego has a statue of her at the town hall, and a number of articles and books have been written about her.

Arden-Sebold, Lorrie. "Dr. Mary E. Walker: Civil War Doctor and Congressional Medal of Honor." *Oswego: Its People and Events.* Edited by Anthony M. Slosek. Interlaken, NY: Heart of the Lakes Publishing, 1985.

Snyder, Charles M. "Dr. Mary Walker, Stormy Petrel of the Woman's Rights Movement." Chap. 16 in *Oswego: From Buckskin to Bustles.* Empire State Historical Publications Series 56. Port Washington, NY: Ira J. Friedman Inc., 1968.

———. *Dr. Mary Walker: The Little Lady in Pants.* New York: Arno Press, 1974. Originally published by Vantage Press, 1962.

Walker, Dale L. *Marv Edwards Walker: Above and Beyond.* New York: Tom Doherty Associates, LLC, 2005.

White, Justin D. "Dr. Mary Walker: A Missionary Spirit." *Three 19th-Century Women Doctors.* Edited by Mary K. LeClair, Justin D. White and Susan Keeter. Syracuse, NY: Hofmann Press, 2007.

Photograph courtesy of the State University of New York–Oswego, Penfield Library Archives.

Researcher and author: Emily Oaks, Oswego Branch

JEAN WEBSTER

1876–1916
AUTHOR

Alice Jane Chandler Webster, better known as Jean Webster, was born in Fredonia, New York, in July 1876. Her parents were Annie Moffet Webster and Charles Webster. Her father was a publisher and an author, as was her mother's uncle, Samuel Clemens (Mark Twain). As one might imagine, Webster grew up surrounded by books and people who valued them.

In 1897, she entered Vassar College (which now has a collection of her papers, letters and manuscripts) as a member of the class of 1901; she majored in economics and English as she prepared for a literary career. While at Vassar, she wrote a weekly column for the *Poughkeepsie Sunday Courier* and several stories for the *Vassar Miscellany*. She also visited homes for delinquent and destitute children. She would use what she learned during these visits as background information for future books, including *Daddy-Long-Legs* and its sequel, *Dear Enemy*.

After graduating from Vassar, she moved to New York City to pursue a career in writing. It only took two years for her first novel, *When Patty Went to College*, to be published. Her great uncle, Mark Twain, advised her to write about what she knew, so her first book was about life at a women's college. She had actually written many of the stories in the book while still a student.

A hardworking, observant person, Webster gleaned information that she might use from any situation. She found material during a trip to Italy that she included in her books *Jerry Junior* and *The Wheat Princess*. For articles and books, she wrote reams of text and then would work tirelessly to edit and pare it down to her final product.

In 1912, she published what was probably her most famous novel, *Daddy-Long-Legs*. It was a popular book that was well received by the critics. Due to its popularity, it was adapted as a play. This, too, was a success, with profits being used for charitable works and to promote reform. The proceeds from the *Daddy-Long-Leg* dolls that were sold went to support the adoption of orphans.

Webster was concerned for the plight of orphans and in orphan asylum reform, as well as prison reform. She was also a staunch suffragist. One story tells of Webster being thrilled when she was called to serve on jury duty. She was upset, however, when she found out she had been asked to serve because they thought she was a man. When they found out that she was a woman, she was not allowed to serve.

Webster married Glenn Ford McKinney, a wealthy lawyer, in September 1915. This was after a lengthy (seven years) secret engagement. McKinney was married when Webster met him, and his divorce was not final until June 1915.

On June 10, 1916, Webster entered Sloan Hospital in New York City to give birth to her daughter, Jean Webster McKinney. The next morning, on June 11, Jean Webster died at the age of thirty-nine of complications from childbirth.

Throughout her life, Webster was a world traveler and an advocate for orphan and prison reform and women's rights. She is probably best remembered, however, for her novels. Two of the novels, *Daddy-Long-Legs* and *Dear Enemy*, are still in print. *Daddy-Long-Legs* has been translated into at least eighteen languages, performed on the stage and made into a movie at least four times. Jean Webster left quite a legacy.

Cover of *Jerry Junior* by Jean Webster. www.digital.library.upenn.edu/women/webster/jerry/jerry.html.

Encyclopedia Americana. "Webster, Jean." Grolier. http://ea.grolier.com/cgi-bin/article?assetid=0413100-00.

Howard, Melissa. "Alice Jane Chandler McKinney (Webster)." Geni. http://www.geni.com/people/Jean-Webster/6000000007302870301.

Simpson, Alan, and Mary Simpson, with Ralph Connor. *Jean Webster: Storyteller*. Poughkeepsie, NY: Tymor Associates, 1984.

Vassar College Library. Jean Webster Papers. http://specialcollections.vassar.edu/findingaids/mckinney_webster.html.

Photograph from the Library of Congress.
Researcher and author: Susan Pepe, Dunkirk Fredonia Branch

JOAN WELCH

1932–
EDUCATOR/COMMUNITY SERVICE

Joan Welch, a native Corinth, earned a BS at the State University of New York–Plattsburgh and did further graduate work at the College of Saint Rose and Russell Sage. She taught family and consumer science for two years in Shenendehowa and twenty-six years in Corinth.

Joan served on several New York State curriculum writing teams, including one for the development of the Regents Action Plan. She was chosen Saratoga County and New York State Teacher of the Year by both the Family and Consumer Science Association and New York State Occupational Education Teacher's Association.

Besides teaching, Joan chaired the consumer science department, served on the Awards and Graduation Committees and advised both the Junior and Senior High Honor Societies, as well as three senior classes. During her career, she supervised more than twenty student-teachers.

Joan is the cofounder of Operation Joy, a community-wide adult/student effort that helps meet emergency needs of deserving families. She is a board member of Dollars for Scholars and serves on the Young Men's Christian Association Program Committee.

In 1968, Joan was initiated to Delta Kappa Gamma International and was one of the original founders of the Beta Omega Chapter. Welch was named to the list of Women of Distinction by the Girl Scouts of the Adirondack Council in 2005. She is a two-time recipient of the Corinth Mayor's Award and was honored with the DeWitt Clinton Masonic Award. In 2006, Joan was appointed to the Saratoga National Bank and Trust Company's Community Advisory Board.

Joan Welch's life has been one of service and commitment to others. Joan has made a positive difference in thousands of lives. She is an honored member of Beta Omega and is truly a woman of distinction. Joan currently resides in Corinth, New York.

Letters of reference from Louise Carney (school secretary); Kathy Black and Kathy Hoeltzel (teachers); Nick Matino and Ron White (school counselors); Reverend Parti Gerard; and Mayor Dick Lucia. Letters in the personal collection of Kathleen Hoeltzel.

Post Star. Various articles.

Saratogian. Various articles.

Welch, Joan. "A Personal Interview." Recorded by Kathy Hoeltzel, October 19, 2006.

Researcher and author: Kathleen Hoeltzel, Adirondack Branch

NARCISSA PRENTISS WHITMAN

1808–1847
EDUCATOR

Narcissa Prentiss was born on March 14, 1808, to Stephen and Clarissa Prentiss in Prattsburgh, Steuben County, New York, twenty-five miles from Rushville, where Marcus Whitman, her future husband, was born. Her first ancestor in America emigrated from England to Massachusetts in the 1600s. Narcissa's family moved to this wilderness area in 1805, and Stephen Prentiss began farming. He was a carpenter and joiner and began operating a sawmill that produced lumber to build houses in the growing community.

Narcissa, the eldest daughter in a family of nine children, helped with the younger children and enjoyed church and social activities. When she was eleven, she had a conversion experience and joined the Congregational Church. As she matured, she yearned to become a missionary. Both she and her future husband were inspired by the religious revival that swept the nation in the 1800s.

After attending several terms at the local Franklin Academy and at a female seminary (normal school) in Troy, Narcissa taught in a district school in Prattsburgh and in nearby Bath. In 1834, she moved with her family to Amity (now Belmont).

In Amity, she heard a clergyman speak of the need for missionaries, and she answered the call. In the meantime, Dr. Marcus Whitman, who had a medical practice in the area, also offered himself as a missionary. He proposed to Narcissa, and she accepted. While he went on a long trip of exploration to Oregon, Narcissa formally applied and was accepted as a missionary. Marcus returned with the conviction that they could travel by wagon over the Rockies, and they invited another local missionary couple, the Spauldings, to travel with them. They were married on February 18, 1836, and the next day began their long and difficult journey west.

Narcissa and Elizabeth Spaulding were the first white women to cross the Continental Divide on foot, pioneering the way for women and children to follow the trail. In Oregon territory, the families separated, and the Whitmans ministered to the Cayuse Indians at Waiilatpu. They introduced new farming methods and built a sawmill. Narcissa taught school for the Indians and wrote long letters to her family and friends. For several years, the Whitman mission was a resting place for weary travelers over what became known as the Oregon Trail.

The Whitmans' daughter, Alice, born in 1837 and the first child of American parents born in Oregon, tragically drowned in the river when she was two. Narcissa became depressed with no family to comfort her. Eventually, she became mother to seven orphan children and several half-Indian foster children. They told of her love of nature, her sense of humor and her beautiful singing voice.

Narcissa and Marcus Whitman died in an Indian massacre that claimed the lives of fourteen people on November 29, 1847. Soon after this dreadful event, Congress passed legislation making Oregon a United States territory. Narcissa is remembered at her last home in Walla Walla, Washington, and at her childhood home in Prattsburgh, New York. She was inducted into the Steuben County Hall of Fame in 1976.

Allen, Opal Sweazea. *Narcissa Whitman, an Historical Biography.* Portland, OR: Metropolitan Press, 1959.
Drury, Clifford. *Marcus and Narcissa Whitman and the Opening of Old Oregon.* Seattle, WA, 1897. Reprint Washington: Pacific Northwest National Park and Forest Association, 1986.

Researcher and author: Mary E. (Betty) Langendorfer, Bath Branch

JEMIMA WILKINSON

1752–1819
RELIGIOUS LEADER

There was, and still is, considerable mystery about the woman named Jemima Wilkinson. She was born on November 29, 1752, in Cumberland, Rhode Island, and died on July 1, 1819, in Jerusalem, New York, in a lovely house on a hilltop overlooking Keuka Lake.

Many stories and myths have been created about this woman, who was one of twelve children and whose mother passed away when Jemima was only twelve years old. Apparently, when Jemima was eighteen, she became ill with the plague, which had been carried to Rhode Island by British prisoners. She was pronounced dead, but soon her body warmed again, and her voice said, "Jemima Wilkinson has left the world of time's reckoning, but her earthly form is chosen to serve as the Spirit of Life from God and should be known as the Public Universal Friend."

A religious cult developed under her leadership. They were known as the Jemimakins, and although there were many believers, there were also many people who spoke against her. Because of this, she wanted to leave Rhode Island. A group of followers was sent to find a place where they could live in peace and harmony, a new Jerusalem. The Finger Lakes area was selected, even though it was Indian territory. They built a house on the shore of Seneca Lake, and Jemima joined them. Later, they built a large, beautiful home for the Friend in what was called Jerusalem (still known as that today). Keuka Lake could be seen from the upper windows.

The Friend traveled on horseback, wearing her beaver hat and carrying her saddlebags of medicines. She cared for the followers who were ill or needed comforting and preached the word of God to all. She was also admired and respected by the Indians. Red Jacket and the members of his tribe apparently welcomed the white people because of their desire for peace, honesty and communal living.

The Universal Friend made a difference not only with her powerful sermons and her ability to inspire her followers but also because she opened up a portion of the wilderness without violence and treated the Indians as equals.

Carmer, Carl. *Listen for a Lonesome Drum*. Rahway, NJ: Quinn & Boden Company, 1936.
Yates County Historical Society at the Oliver House Historical Museum, Penn Yan, New York.

Researcher and author: Barbara Welles, Bath Branch

ROSEMARY WILSON

1927–2003
EXECUTIVE DIRECTOR, FAMILY AND CHILDREN'S SOCIETY

Miss Rosemary Wilson was born in 1927 and raised in Binghamton, New York, in Broome County. She dedicated her life to the residents of that area. Rosemary was a certified social worker who envisioned a better life for the children and families of this Southern Tier area, and she implemented creative programs to attain that goal.

Rosemary was raised on Binghamton's west side. She graduated from Fordham University, School of Social Work, in 1953 and returned to Binghamton after graduation. She was employed by the City of Binghamton's Department of Social Services and was quickly recognized as a leader in her profession. In 1957, Rosemary was selected to be the first woman in the state of New York to hold the position of commissioner of social services. She was also the youngest person to hold that office. Rosemary served in that capacity until 1970, creating many unique programs, developing statewide affiliations and garnering the respect of many professionals during her tenure.

In 1970, Rosemary became the executive director of the Family and Children's Society of Broome County, a nonprofit agency that was founded in 1941 by Esther W. Couper and other philanthropists in this area in the Southern Tier of New York. Rosemary utilized her knowledge of the local community and her affiliations with individuals throughout New York State to secure funding and develop creative human service program to address unmet needs of children and families. Under her leadership, the Family and Children's Society was an outstanding United Way agency. Although accomplishments were numerous, some of the society's unique efforts include significant expansion of the Home Care Program (starting with eight home health aides and eventually reaching an impressive two hundred aides), creation of a program to prevent child abuse and neglect, creation of the Parent Aide Program to provide modeling and support for families at risk, the institution of a sexual abuse treatment program, collaboration with the local Department of Social Services to provide training for its staff and the creation of the Family Homes for the Elderly program.

In addition to her contributions to Family and Children's Society, Rosemary was known for her dedication to the profession of social work and for contributions to her community. She provided internship opportunities and facilitated the social work education and career development of more than twenty social workers practicing in the Broome County area. As an individual concerned with unmet community needs, Rosemary initiated collaboration among leaders of community agencies to dialogue about home healthcare voids. After many months of planning and navigating the New York State process, a new, community-based agency, Twin Tier Home Health Care Agency, was formed and began serving residents in need as a Certified Home Health Agency.

In 1994, Rosemary retired from the Family and Children's Society after twenty-four years of dedicated service. Not surprisingly, many honors were bestowed on Rosemary during her career: Distinguished Social

Worker Award, Spring 1994, Southern Tier Division of NYS Chapter, National Association of Social Workers; honored as the first recipient of the Esther W. Couper Memorial Award, named for the founder of Family and Children's Society of Broome County (1941); and honored with a proclamation by Senator Thomas Libous, declaring March 31, 2002, as Rosemary Wilson Day in the Fifty-first New York State Senate District.

The Broome County community lost a treasure when Rosemary Wilson died on November 11, 2003. It was said that a fitting epitaph for her was a letter from Paul to son Timothy, describing himself from a Roman prison: "I have fought a good fight, I have finished my course, I have kept the faith." And so did Rosemary.

Interviews with staff of Family and Children's Society of Broome County, New York.

National Association of Social Workers. *NASW—Southern Tier Division—New York State Chapter.* (Spring 1994). Newsletter.

Rossie, David. *Press and Sun Bulletin.* Commentary, November 28, 2003.

Researcher and author: Catherine McGowan, Southern New York Branch

HARRIET NEWALL WALTON WING

1815–1887
COMMUNITY SERVICE

Harriet Newall Walton was born in Montpelier, Vermont, in 1815. Her father, General E.P. Walton, a Revolutionary soldier, was editor and owner of the *Vermont Watchman and Journal* and founder of *Walton's Almanac*. Harriet attended schools in Montpelier and finished her education at Emma Willard School in Troy, New York, one of the leading schools for girls in the country at that time.

She came from a strong Whig (Republican) family. On August 31, 1835, she married Halsey Rogers Wing, the great-grandson of Abraham Wing, and came to support his Democratic political persuasion. Halsey served on the Civil War Committee in Queensbury during the war. He and Harriet came to Glens Falls in 1841, where she and Halsey raised six children:

Walton S., Halsey McKie, Edgar Murray, George Henry, Daniel W. and Angeline. Mrs. Wing gave two sons to the Civil War. Lieutenant Edgar Wing was mortally wounded at the Battle of Drewry's Bluff. His name is on the Soldiers' Monument. Her second son, George Henry Wing, died shortly after the war from his sufferings in Andersonville Prison.

When 644 volunteers left Queensbury for the Civil War, there was a strong civilian commitment to support the war and to aid the cause. Local efforts supported soldiers through contributions of clothing, foodstuffs and letters of support. These were organized nationally by the United States Sanitary Commission, founded in July 1861.

In Warren County, Harriet Wing became the president of the Women's Sanitary Commission. She devoted her time and energies to the work on the homefront, often at a cost to her own personal health, according to her son Halsey McKie in his *Reminiscences*. Mrs. Wing organized the Ladies Patriotic Association in Glens Falls and later promoted the formation of the Ladies Alert Club, an active fundraising group of young women in the community. As the secretary and later the treasurer of the Patriotic Association, she reported frequently to the press, keeping the public informed while appealing for garments and edibles for the soldiers. The groups met on a regular basis to sew garments of flannel, to create comfort bags, to receive foodstuffs and to collect reading materials for convalescent soldiers.

Mrs. Wing was an active, community-minded woman. She became interested in the national women's effort to purchase Mount Vernon, the home of George Washington, and raised several hundred dollars locally for this cause. She was an active member of the Presbyterian Church and participant in its mission work.

Harriet Wing died on June 21, 1887, at age seventy-two. She is buried at Bay Street Cemetery with her husband and family members.

Van Dyke, Marilyn. "Adirondack Civil War Round Table." *The Torchlight*. (2nd Quarter, June 1998). Article located at Chapman Historical Museum, 348 Glen Street, Glens Falls, New York.

Researcher and author: Kathleen Hoeltzel, Adirondack Branch

LUCY WING

?–1974
EDUCATOR/PSYCHOLOGY/COLLEGE ADMINISTRATOR

The newsletter of the counseling and psychological services department of Oswego State University, published in the spring of 1979, nearly thirty years ago, speaks of "one woman's personal vision." It is referring to Dr. Wing as the guiding force and visionary behind the establishment of the department at Oswego State.

Dr. Wing joined the psychology department of Oswego State (a teachers' education college) in 1958 after twenty years in public school education. She received her Bachelor of Arts degree at Albany State and master's degrees from both Albany State and Columbia University. She completed her doctoral requirements at Syracuse University when she joined the Oswego faculty.

Dr. Wing envisioned a graduate program that would credential practitioners in guidance counseling and school psychology. Initially interested in the education of school counselors, she developed the graduate counseling program, a thirty-two-hour program in counselor education yielding permanent certification for guidance counselors. Organizational administration and most of the teaching practicums were handled by Dr. Wing personally.

In the mid-1960s, the program experienced considerable expansion, with school psychology developed as a parallel program. In 1968, Dr. Wing chaired the Adhoc Committee of the Admissions Council, planning for higher education for disadvantaged students; she was a presenter at the New York State Personnel and Guidance Association annual conferences, and in 1969, she introduced new courses including Analysis of Individual Learning and Personality Assessment, taught by Dr. Eugene Perticone. By 1970, no longer under the psychology department, Dr. Wing's program became recognized formally as the Department of School Psychology, with herself as chair.

In the spring of 1974, Dr. Wing became ill and succumbed to cancer within four months. A memorial service was held for her on September

15, 1974. When Dr. Wing died, she had been head of the department for sixteen years. Upon her death, Dr. Eugene X. Perticone assumed the post of department chair. He was succeeded after three years by Dr. Bruce Lester. By 1978, the Department of School Psychology and Counseling was formally established with two sixty-hour programs (School Psychology, Counseling).

Dorothy Rogers cited Provost Spencer in referring to the Department of Counseling and Psychological Services in 1981 as one of two departments on campus possessed of special excellence—having consistently placed all graduates. Colleagues brought into the department by Dr. Wing included Dr. Fred Ratzeburg, Dr. Fran Koenigsburg, Dr. Owen Pittenger, Dr. Perticone and Dr. Bruce Lester.

Dr. Wing is cited in Dorothy Rogers's *Oswego: Fountainhead of Teacher Education* as being honored through an International Delta Kappa Gamma Society Scholarship and the Syracuse Tuition Scholarship. Dr. Wing was a member of Pi Lambda Theta and Delta Kappa Gamma. She was coauthor of *Developmental Trends in Preferences for Goals that Are Difficult to Attain* and had interest in photography, growing gladioli and stamp and antique button collecting. She was a contributor along with Barbara Gerber, Judith Wellman, Blanche Judd and Fran Koenigsburg to the launching of the Women's Studies Program at Oswego State.

Newsletter of the Department of Counseling and Psychological Services, Spring 1979.

Oswego State University Special Collections, Penfield Library, Oswego, New York.

Rogers, Dorothy. *Oswego: Fountainhead of Teacher Education.* New York: Appleton-Century-Crofts, 1961.

Photograph courtesy of the State University of New York–Oswego, Penfield Library Archives. Researcher and author: James C. Tschudy, Oswego Branch

Lucile M. Wright

1900–1990
Pilot/Volunteer

Lucile M. Wright believed that Jamestown and Chautauqua County deserved a proper airport. She also believed in girls and knew that they deserved to have a place to go after school and on school vacations. She made both happen.

Lucile Miller Wright was born on August 26, 1900, in Beatrice, Nebraska, and grew up in Montana. Following high school, she earned bachelor's degrees in languages and science, attended law school and audited medical courses. She worked with her first husband, a doctor, in various capacities until their divorce.

As a child, Lucile vowed, "If humans are going to be up in the air, I'm going to be one of them." As an adult, getting her pilot's license was a difficult and frustrating task, but she ultimately accomplished it despite the resistance of the men who had to train her. She was the first female courier for the Civil Air Patrol and flew search and rescue missions. She joined an international association of female pilots in 1935 and became a good friend of its founder, Amelia Earhart. Lucile owned a total of seven airplanes in her life, logged thousands of flying hours and received countless awards and honors from the aviation industry. Her second husband, John H. Wright, owned an airplane but did not fly. She became his pilot and then his wife, moving in 1947 to Jamestown, where he owned the telephone company. Lucile was appointed the chairwoman of the Jamestown Airport Commission in 1951. She was convinced that airplanes were the mode of transportation of the future. City council members were not convinced and refused to authorize funding for any airport expansion or expenditures, claiming that she presented no formal plans or budget. Eventually, a more modern airport was built, with Lucile claiming that she had built it singlehandedly. It is now the Chautauqua County Airport. Lucile was the first (and, for forty years, the only) female member of the American Association of Airport Executives.

Lucile was an equally ardent supporter of the Jamestown Girls Club (now incorporated with the Boys Club). She served on the board from its beginning in 1947 and served as president from 1949 until 1975. Under her leadership, the Girls Club purchased its own building in 1949 and established Camp Hiak Tilikum, for which she donated funding. The camp's name was the name she was given by the Northwest Indians on the Crow Reservation in Montana. She served on the Girls Clubs of America Board of Directors for forty years. She initiated the Lucile M. Wright Citizenship Award, presented annually to a young lady nominated by her local Girls Club, and personally presenting the award until 1981.

Lucile moved to Cody, Wyoming, in 1976 and continued her aviation involvement, flying at least twenty inaugural airline flights and serving as a consultant for airlines and airports. She died in Cody on June 12, 1990.

Blossom, David R. Personal files, unpublished.
Jamestown Girls Club record books.
Thompson, B. Dolores. "Lucile M. Wright." *Jamestown Post-Journal*, March 1992.

Researcher and author: B. Dolores Thompson, Jamestown Branch

RITA WRIGHT

1953–
SOCIAL WORKER

The women who meet Rita Wright in Cortland, New York, are struck by her confidence and her ability to search for a solution. When there seems to be no other path than the one the victim is presently on, Rita will remind her that a passion for living and her will to change dominate over training or education. She reminds her to never forget her dreams, that there is still time to learn something new and that nothing is too hard to learn. She tells her that developing her character allows an individual to mold herself into the person she wants to be. At the Young Women's Christian Association in Cortland, the Aid to Victims of Violence program begins the guiding process that results in creating a new life for a woman in need.

"Search for a solution; there is one," is Rita Wright's motto. After the pep talks come a complimentary hairstyle, makeup, a new set of clothes and professional photographs. The victim may not feel ready to begin a new lifestyle, but she does look the part and has the photographs to remind her of how things can be in the future. Steady and permanent changes begin to influence the woman's character, as guided by Rita Wright. "You must give and not take advantage of others. You cannot do the minimum; you must do above and beyond." The seed of change, buried deep in the program and in the woman, is powerful: "Believe in yourself." The woman begins to acquire skills that will allow her to make a living and no longer be a victim.

This woman is not alone in Cortland, New York. She has joined about three hundred others in one year that have been helped by the Aid to Victims of Violence in Cortland County led by Rita Wright. If the change that is needed seems to be too much for the woman, she often says, "You do not know what it is like. I cannot do this. It is too much. You do not know what you are asking of me." Rita, in her firm but calm voice, will say, "Come, let us sit down. Let me tell you my story. Yes, I do know about this."

Rita Wright was born in Skibo, Portland Parish, Jamaica, on July 5, 1953. She was the tenth child of twelve children. Since the two previous babies had died in infancy, Rita was not given either a name or clothes. Rather, she was "toweled" until the family saw whether she would live or die.

Her mother, who had started having babies at the age of fifteen, saw her daughter as one of many, outstanding mainly by her active character. Rita's father had gone to the United States to get construction work. During his stay there, he saw a film with Rita Hayworth in it and decided that this new girl baby would be given the name Rita. The family saw that the baby would indeed live and gave her a set of clothes.

Rita's grandmother, the matriarch of the family, received Rita along with any other children between the ages of nine months and eleven years to raise up. Aunt Sybil Clarke was also an influential adult during those years. Rita was told by others that she would never amount to anything when she grew up. However, Aunt Sybil would keep working on developing values, aiming for the future, instilling an inner compass that tells right from wrong and keeping her confidence alive in a good future.

Rita said that she was a challenging child—outspoken to the level of trouble and the black sheep of the family. She was wild, able and individualistic. Even though the regular school path was not made for Rita, the family searched for a solution. It came by having Rita work along with her father in construction from the ages of twelve to fifteen. There she learned the work culture, gained organizational skills and learned how to get along with various types of personalities. Those early teen years were good for Rita in Jamaica.

Later, Rita became a police officer in Jamaica. The training was rigorous—running up the tilted walls daily, for instance—and the work was dangerous; police officers were targeted for death by the gangs. Along the way, Rita married and had a little girl. It became so life threatening that Rita had to create an escape solution. She saved vacation time, went to Canada with her daughter and then joined her husband in Cortland in 1980.

Rita's arrival as a wife, unannounced, was not welcome. Although they had been married for seven years, Rita's relationship was tense and unpleasant. Her husband was controlling and abusive. Rita, however, had no education and no skills. She did find a job dyeing fish lines at the Cortland Fish Line Company. The work was hard, and the pay was low. She began to get a college degree at Tompkins Cortland Community College (TC3) in 1982. To pay for her tuition, she cleaned homes on the market for the Yaman Real Estate Company. She also got a scholarship from Hugh Bakar, the president of TC3. As a result, Rita Wright graduated TC3 with an associate's degree and twenty-two credits.

Going forward, Rita then worked at the Lansing School for Girls as a youth division aid counselor, beginning in 1984. The girls sent there were not only abused but also neglected. Along the way, they had never had regular childhood experiences. Rita saw herself progress professionally. At home, however, the situation got worse. While Rita was using her income to purchase the family home in Cortland, she was having major problems with her husband's continuing abuse. After a particularly bad interaction, Rita called the police, who responded by removing Rita from her home, citing her as the cause of the family squabble.

A victim of domestic violence, Rita connected with Cortland County Community Action Program (CAPCO) to get some help. The members, in turn, sent her to Aid to Women Victims of Violence. She got guidance and support. The group helped her search for a solution. After several years, Rita was selected to head the unit, which she did until her retirement in 2011.

There was also a joint project that dovetails into abuse cases in Cortland County. From July to December 2008, there were 540 child abuse cases reported in the county. This overwhelmed the resources of the county Child Protective Services. Up until then, a client's family had to go all over for one service or another.

The Child Advocacy Center, opened in 2008–9, was in the planning stages for about a decade. Now there is one location a family goes to with their abused child or teen for all the services. Medical services, counseling services, police interviews and supportive services are all given in the same room, and records are kept by the same personnel. Men who are repeat offenders are easily tracked and identified. One-stop help, then, is possible for the client, and in addition, communication is easier for the team of professionals that offers the services. Rita Wright is elated that this component is now in place and that she is a part of it.

And what about the abusive husband? Well, as Rita says, the young woman changed spouses and now lives with someone who loves her and her family. Rita has had five children of her own and has brought up eight more in her home. Today, she is a minister with a strong faith in God and finds that music is a balm to her soul.

In the far future, Rita Wright would like to return to her home country of Jamaica and rejoin her brothers and sisters. There is work to be done to begin a Jamaican Aid to Women Victims of Violence group, to begin a teen program, to begin a Child Advocacy Center and to institute a safe house for abused women and children. She believes in searching for solutions and is sure that they are available.

Wright, Rita. Interview by Dorothy Hopkins, April 16, 2009, at the YWCA, Cortland, New York.

Author: Dorothy Hopkins, Cortland Branch

Appendix I

LIST BY AUTHOR

AUTHOR	BIOGRAPHIES/ AUTOBIOGRAPHIES	BRANCH
Anderson, Phyllis	Hall	Smithtown
Beall, Sheila	Flood	Kingston
Beardsley, Kathleen	Bloomer	Cortland
Bernal-Lederer, Dayra	Bernal-Lederer, Stewart	Member at Large
Biviano, Julie	Collins, Hallock	Elmira-Corning
Bolton, Arlene	Tubman	Syracuse
Brill, Joan	Brill	East Hampton
Burgess, Julie	Blodgett, Quirini	Schenectady
Burns, Eleanor	Beck	Islip Area
Chapin, Mary	Chapin	Greater Rochester, Mohawk Valley
Charwat, Eleanor	Roosevelt	Poughkeepsie
Clausen, Nancy E.	Colvin, Gage, Wagner	Syracuse
Clinton, Ann M.	Sansone	Staten Island
Coe, Margaret	Common, Johnson	Jefferson County
Cummings, Jan	King	Elmira-Corning
Cvetkovic, Marlene	DiSomma	Islip Area
Davis, Mary Lou	Mitchell, Peale	Poughkeepsie
Eckers, Susan	Eckers	
Ellis, Maria L.	Ellis	New York City
Engel, Helen Butterfield	Lockwood, Parker	Oswego

AUTHOR	BIOGRAPHIES/ AUTOBIOGRAPHIES	BRANCH
Fish, Caroline	Fish	Rockland County
Ford, June	Eastman	Elmira-Corning
French, Ann Marie	Penfield	Oswego
Gilliam, Marlene	M. Brown, Hancock, Hogeboom, Mizzi, J. Rogers	Islip Area
Goffe-McNish, Jacqueline	Truth	Poughkeepsie
Goldson, Lillian	Cohn	Islip Area
Haller, Pam, and Pinkerton, Gerri	Currie	Schenectady
Hallett, Marjorie, and Silberman, Myrna	Tonetti	Rockland County
Haney, Diane	Hoffman	North Shore
Hegarty, Ellen	Talman	Yates County
Hoeltzel, Kathleen	Barber, Welch, H. Wing	Adirondack
Hopkins, Dorothy	Wright, R.	Cortland
Hungerford, Mary	Verdier	Elmira-Corning
Kleszczewski, Julie Harrison	D'Ambrosio, Kleszczewski, Tsien, Volkmar	New York City
Knitter, Jacqueline C.	Huddle	Elmira-Corning
Kohli, Virginia	Bhitiyakul, Johnson	Kingston
Langendorfer, Mary E. (Betty)	Davenport, Hille, Whitman	Bath
Levitt, Barbara	Popp	Staten Island
Levy, Elizabeth Ann	Levy	New York City
Linville, Judith	Pattison	Poughkeepsie
Mahoney, Marion	Elion, McClintock, Mead, Mion, Plain	Islip Area
Marten, Antoinette (Annette)	Marten	Staten Island

Author	Biographies/ Autobiographies	Branch
Mazur, Virginia (Ginni)	Knox, Stanton	Amsterdam-Gloversville-Johnstown
McCormack-Raso, Tess	McCormack-Raso	Rockland County
McGowan, Catherine	Wilson	Southern New York
Mills, Franca Lippi	Mills	Farmingdale
Mindel, Barbara	Buchholz	Poughkeepsie
Mion, Nancy	Erwoo, Fields	Islip Area
Mitchell, Lynne M.	Anthony	Greater Rochester Area
Nakazawa, Maria	Nakazawa	Rockland County
Nixon, Onalee	Maltby	Bath
Norton, M. Edwina	Clark, DeCrow, Towner	Syracuse
Oaks, Emily	Walker	Oswego
Pepe, Susan	Barker, McNeil, Richmond, Saulitis, Staub, Webster	Dunkirk Fredonia
Pinkerton, Gerri, and Haller, Pam	Currie	Schenectady
Rajchel, Joan	Miga, Moses, Shuck	Mohawk Valley
Ramirez, Beatrice	Connelly	Staten Island
Regan, Marjorie	Perkins	Kingston
Reiter, Elizabeth	Spaulding	Elmira-Corning
Rivette, Barbara S.	Rivette	Syracuse
Robertson, Lillian	Ingraham	Manhattan
Ruchman, Trudy	Donovan	North Shore
Russen, Joan	Locke	Elmira-Corning
Russo, Elizabeth	Bloomer	Amsterdam-Gloversville-Johnstown
Schlefstein, Muriel	O'Callaghan	Staten Island
Silberman, Myrna, and Hallett, Marjorie	Tonetti	Rockland County

AUTHOR	BIOGRAPHIES/ AUTOBIOGRAPHIES	BRANCH
Smiley, Marilynn	Allerton, Barnes, F. Brown, Dean, Faletta, Numann, Radley, Robineau, D. Rogers, Sills	Oswego
Snell, C. Jane	Bentley	Cortland
Spearman, Donna	Oldwine	Southern New York
Stafford, Joan	Harley	Garden City
Stedge, Patricia	Green, Pfeiffer, Pickhardt	Kingston
Stern, Inger	Allen	Oswego
Taylor, Wendy Maragh	Bolin	Poughkeepsie
Thompson, B. Dolores	Ball, Burchard, Fuller, Hare, Harris, Jones, Prendergast, Stitt, B. Stoneman, K. Stoneman, Van Rensselaer, Wright L.	Jamestown
Tomko, Margarita Duncan	Tomko	Farmingdale
Treicher, Martha	Barton, Comstock	Bath
Tschudy, James C.	Nesbitt, L. Wing	Oswego
Tschudy, Juanita	Rudolph, Simkiewicz	Oswego
Vallone, Elizabeth P.	Colden, Hayes, Sneden	Rockland County
Van der Linde, Gail	Connor	Skaneateles
Weber, Bonnie	Tears	Bath
Weidemann, Julia (Judy)	Bozer	Buffalo
Welles, Barbara B.	Tetor, Wilkinson	Bath
Wilman, Barbara	Brett	Poughkeepsie
Zekauskas, Phyllis	Gitchel	Westchester

LIST BY AMERICAN ASSOCIATION OF
UNIVERSITY WOMEN NEW YORK BRANCHES

BRANCH	AUTHOR	BIOGRAPHIES/ AUTOBIOGRAPHIES
Adirondack	Hoeltzel, Kathleen	Barber, Welch, H. Wing
Amsterdam-Gloversville-Johnstown	Mazur, Virginia (Ginni)	Knox, Stanton
	Russo, Elizabeth	Bloomer
Bath	Langendorfer, Mary E. (Betty)	Davenport, Hille, Whitman
	Nixon, Onalee	Maltby
	Treicher, Martha	Barton, Comstock
	Weber, Bonnie	Tears
	Welles, Barbara B.	Tetor, Wilkinson
Buffalo	Weidemann, Julia (Judy)	Bozer
Cortland	Beardsley, Kathleen	Bloomer
	Hopkins, Dorothy	Wright
	Snell, C. Jane	Bentley
Dunkirk Fredonia	Pepe, Susan	Barker, McNeil, Richmond, Saulitis, Staub, Webster
East Hampton	Brill, Joan	Brill
Elmira-Corning	Cummings, Jan	King
	Ford, June	Eastman
	Hungerford, Mary	Verdier
	Biviano, Julie	Collins, Hallock
	Knitter, Jacqueline C.	Huddle
	Reiter, Elizabeth	Spaulding
	Russen, Joan	Locke

Branch	Author	Biographies/ Autobiographies
Farmingdale	Mills, Franca Lippi	Mills
	Tomko, Margarita Duncan	Tomko
Garden City	Stafford, Joan	Harley
Greater Rochester Area	Mitchell, Lynne M.	Anthony
Greater Rochester, Mohawk Valley	Chapin, Mary	Chapin
Islip Area	Burns, Eleanor	Beck
	Cvetkovic, Marlene	DiSomma
	Gilliam, Marlene	M. Brown, Hancock, Hogeboom, Mizzi, J. Rogers
	Goldson, Lillian	Cohn
	Mahoney, Marion	Elion, McClintock, Mead, Mion, Plain
	Mion, Nancy	Erwoo, Fields
Jamestown	Thompson, B. Dolores	Ball, Burchard, Fuller, Hare, Harris, Jones, Prendergast, Stitt, B. Stoneman, K. Stoneman, Van Rensselaer, L. Wright
Jefferson County	Coe, Margaret	Common, Johnson
Kingston	Beall, Sheila	Flood
	Kohli, Virginia	Bhitiyakul, Johnson
	Regan, Marjorie	Perkins
	Stedge, Patricia	Greene, Pfeiffer, Pickhardt
Manhattan	Robertson, Lillian	Ingraham
Member at Large	Bernal-Lederer, Dayra	Bernal-Lederer, Stewart
Mohawk Valley	Rajchel, Joan	Miga, Moses, Shuck

BRANCH	AUTHOR	BIOGRAPHIES/ AUTOBIOGRAPHIES
New York City	Ellis, Maria L.	Ellis
	Kleszczewski, Julie Harison	D'Ambrosio, Tsien, Volkmar, Kleszczewski
	Levy, Elizabeth Ann	Levy
North Shore	Haney, Diane	Hoffman
	Ruchman, Trudy	Donovan
Oswego	Engel, Helen Butterfield	Lockwood, Parker
	French, Ann Marie	Penfield
	Oaks, Emily	Walker
	Smiley, Marilynn	Allerton, Barnes, F. Brown, Dean, Faletta, Numann, Robineau, Radley, D. Rogers, Sills
	Stern, Inger	Allen
	Tschudy, James C.	Nesbitt, L. Wing
	Tschudy, Juanita	Rudolph, Simkiewicz
Poughkeepsie	Charwat, Eleanor	Roosevelt
	Davis, Mary Lou	Mitchell, Peale
	Goffe-McNish, Jacqueline	Truth
	Linville, Judith	Pattison, Lucille
	Mindel, Barbara	Buchholz
	Taylor, Wendy Maragh	Bolin
	Wilman, Barbara	Brett
Rockland County	Fish, Caroline	Fish
	Hallett, Marjorie	Tonetti
	McCormack-Raso, Tess	McCormack-Raso
	Nakazawa, Maria	Nakazawa
	Silberman, Myrna	Tonetti
	Vallone, Elizabeth Palombella	Colden, Hayes, Sneden

BRANCH	AUTHOR	BIOGRAPHIES/ AUTOBIOGRAPHIES
Schenectady	Burgess, Julie	Blodgett, Quirini
	Pinkerton, Gerri, and Haller, Pam	Currie
Skaneateles	Van der Linde, Gail	Connor
Smithtown	Anderson, Phyllis	Hall
Southern New York	McGowan, Catherine	Wilson
	Spearman, Donna	Oldwine
Staten Island	Clinton, Ann M.	Sansone
	Levitt, Barbara	Popp
	Marten, Antoinette (Annette)	Marten
	Ramirez, Beatrice	Connelly
	Schlefstein, Muriel	O'Callaghan
Syracuse	Bolton, Arlene	Tubman
	Clausen, Nancy E.	Colvin, Gage, Wagner
	Norton, M. Edwina	Clark, DeCrow, Towner
	Rivette, Barbara S.	Rivette
Westchester	Zekauskas, Phyllis	Gitchel
Yates County	Hegarty, Ellen	Talman

ABOUT THE EDITORS

Helen Butterfield Engel is a graduate of the Ohio State University with BS and MS degrees. She retired as laboratory supervisor for the City of Oswego, New York Water Department, and has taught in the biology departments of the State University of New York–Oswego and Onondaga Community College in Syracuse. For the American Association of University Women, she has served in many capacities in the Oswego branch, as a New York state officer and on the board of directors, where she is currently historian. She is a life member of the Sterling, New York Historical Society and a member of the Oswego County Historical Society. She is also a member of the National Milk Glass Collectors Society and Snobelt Quilters. She and her husband, Ronald, have two children, several grandchildren and a great-grandchild.

Marilynn J. Smiley is a Distinguished Teaching Professor at the State University of New York–Oswego, where she teaches courses in music history and literature. She earned a BS from Ball State University, an MM from Northwestern University and a PhD in musicology from the University of Illinois. Areas of research are Renaissance music and American music. An active member of the American Musicological Society and the Society for American Music, she has served on many committees and is currently a member of the Early American Music Interest Group in the latter organization. Locally, she directs and plays in the Oswego Recorder Consort. With the AAUW, she has had many roles at both the local and state levels, but the most recent one was as co-historian for New York State.

www.ingramcontent.com/pod-product-compliance
Lightning Source LLC
Chambersburg PA
CBHW071151160426
42812CB00079B/1598